T0350499

A Tale of Two Systems

Lean and Agile
Software Development
for Business Leaders

A Tale of Two Systems

Lean and Agile
Software Development
for Business Leaders

Michael K. Levine

CRC Press
Taylor & Francis Group
Boca Raton London New York

CRC Press is an imprint of the
Taylor & Francis Group, an **informa** business

A PRODUCTIVITY PRESS BOOK

CRC Press
Taylor & Francis Group
6000 Broken Sound Parkway NW, Suite 300
Boca Raton, FL 33487-2742

First issued in hardback 2019

ISBN-13: 978-1-4398-0389-9 (hbk)

This book contains information obtained from authentic and highly regarded sources. Reasonable efforts have been made to publish reliable data and information, but the author and publisher cannot assume responsibility for the validity of all materials or the consequences of their use. The authors and publishers have attempted to trace the copyright holders of all material reproduced in this publication and apologize to copyright holders if permission to publish in this form has not been obtained. If any copyright material has not been acknowledged please write and let us know so we may rectify in any future reprint.

Library of Congress Cataloging-in-Publication Data

Levine, Michael K.
   A tale of two systems : lean and agile software development for business leaders / Michael K. Levine.
      p. cm.
   Includes bibliographical references and index.
   ISBN 978-1-4398-0389-9 (hbk. : alk. paper)
   1. Information technology--Management--Case studies. 2. Information technology projects--Management--Case studies. 3. Computer software--Development--Case studies. 4. Management information systems--Case studies. I. Title.

HD30.2.L476 2010
005.068'4--dc22   2009017444

Visit the Taylor & Francis Web site at
http://www.taylorandfrancis.com

and the CRC Press Web site at
http://www.crcpress.com

Contents

SECTION I The First 6 Months:
September 2005–February 2006

SECTION II The Second 6 Months:
March 2006–August 2006

SECTION III Year 2: September 2006–February 2007

SECTION IV The Beginning of the End: The Last 6 Months of 2 Years of Work

SECTION V Final Lessons for Leaders

Acknowledgments

There are very few original ideas in this book; it is merely a popularization of many great ideas that I have been taught, integrated through the lens of my own experience and approach. To those who taught me, a great note of thanks. These include friends and colleagues: Bob King, who has taught me more, and exposed me to more, about software development than anyone else; Chris and Chad Vogel, who introduced me to Lean; Meeghan McGahan, who gave her team the freedom to experiment with Agile and thereby introduced me to it as well; and Lucy Buckley, who crystallized for me an approach to facilitative leadership.

I also owe debts to the students of Lean who have made it accessible to me via books, training, and consulting, most of whom I know only through their writings: Jeff Liker and James Morgan, Michael Kennedy, Mary and Tom Poppendieck, and Allen Ward. A special note of thanks to the Lean Enterprise Institute and its group of experts, including Beau Kyte, Freddy and Michael Balle, and John Shook, some of whom I've had the good fortune to see directly at work helping an operation make a Lean transformation. Similarly, I admire and thank the Agile Alliance, which broke the movement toward overspecified and rigid software development processes and made it respectable for software to be fun again. Thanks go also to writers such as Mike Cohn, Ken Schwaber, and Mike Beedle, who have codified what most of us knew: The best software comes from expert teams of people working together in the ways that work for them.

No book on Lean can fail to acknowledge and thank Toyota. Many of the idea formulations stem from work inside Toyota, which the company has been generous enough to share with others. Toyota doesn't provide a silver bullet for all of us to emulate but it does give us some great ideas and techniques to absorb and make our own.

Ruth Mills, my editor, greatly improved this book, and my readers and I owe her a debt of gratitude.

Finally, thanks to my wife, Holly Lindsay. In my first book, published over 20 years ago, I thanked her for patience and support of my work and noted that, during the events of that book, she had to find me at work after midnight because she had begun labor with our first child. Now, that child is a budding young software engineer, and I'm a middle-aged maven writing in the basement instead of raking the leaves. Holly continues to be my friend and partner through it all, listening to my stories and supporting me in pursuing my interests. Aloha!

Introduction

This is the tale of two systems development projects: Troubled-Real-Estate Information Management (TRIM) and Cremins United (CU). Both were done at Cremins Corporation, a venerable printing company trying to transform itself to survive in the Internet age. The Cremins United project was an abject, expensive failure, while TRIM succeeded in creating a major new revenue stream, bringing in new customers, and helping the country, in a small way, deal with the accelerating housing-centered financial crisis. Reading the tale of these two systems will help you make your projects succeed like TRIM, instead of failing like CU.

Cremins Corporation was founded in the late 1800s by the Cremins family in St. Paul, Minnesota, and had been led by a Cremins ever since, most recently by "the old man," Pete Cremins. It had thrived by providing preprinted and custom forms and labels of all kinds, and it had tentatively stepped into the information age by linking its printers to customers' systems to print invoices and reports on their behalf. By 1990 it had grown to over $2 billion in revenue and $200 million of profits. Unfortunately, that was Cremins Corporation's peak.

As information technology invaded its space and more nimble competitors ate into its base, Cremins moved too slowly to maintain its growth. Its first reaction was to merge with similarly threatened competitors, including commercial printers of items such as magazines. Although this grew revenue and transformed Cremins from a Midwestern regional printer to a national player, it was not sufficient to return Cremins to profitable growth. Instead of solving Cremins's problems, this merely exacerbated its problems of managing capacity downward. Then, with help from a consulting firm, it began using its still strong but slowly decaying balance sheet and cash flow to buy companies that delivered and managed information electronically. The hope was to provide new sources of growth, to infuse a technology capability into its printing operations, and to provide new outlets for print sales. With a new strategy in place, Pete Cremins handed off the reins to Evan Nogelmeyer, the consultant who had driven the new strategy.

Cremins United was Nogelmeyer's transformative project. Its goal was to enable the delivery of all of Cremins's capabilities, venerable as well as newly acquired, through its several sales forces, also venerable and newly acquired. Evan Nogelmeyer was rolling the dice with his remaining resources to implement the vision he'd sold Pete and that had brought him into his position as CEO of a major U.S. company. He put his best people on the project, gave them essentially unlimited budgets and access, and was patient with stumbles and missteps—ultimately, to no avail.

At the same time, Cremins's newly acquired Real Estate Division saw an opportunity in the early hints of the real estate crisis. It had a solid base in the industry serving multiple listing services, realtors, and real estate brokers, and it saw the need to bring together real estate sales, mortgage servicing, and real estate tax data in a new way to meet a new set of needs. The Real Estate Division foresaw that local governments, banks, journalists, and others would need a reliable source of data on mortgage delinquencies, home foreclosures, tax payment delinquencies, and home sales, and that it could get those future customers to cooperate in a new system's development and pay for its delivery. Evan and his team gave this project support as well, as part of the strategy of growing his electronic information management businesses. This project was a spectacular success.

How did these projects differ, and why should you care? The Cremins United project followed many accepted software project development methods. It had clearly defined governance, strong architecture controls, clearly articulated roles, and highly detailed and monitored project plans. Gathering of requirements was rigorous, consistent, and well supported by documentation tools. The resulting requirements were handed off formally to design and development teams, and issues were faithfully logged and tracked. Costs and time were estimated using models, and scope management was well understood and tightly enforced. An independent testing team enforced stage-gate entrance and exit criteria, tested directly from the requirements documents, and reported results factually. These are many of the things that an auditor would look for in a project; indeed, early in the CU project, an auditor would find much to admire. Yet, Cremins United's failure was complete.

The TRIM project, in sharp contrast, had no detailed centralized project plan. It did requirements as it went along instead of all up front. It never had a detailed estimate to completion based on a comprehensive understanding of requirements. Architecture was done by the development teams themselves, in tight collaboration with the product owners and business partners, instead of by architects with special skills. Team member roles overlapped in a variety of ways, with some developers doing testing, some analysts doing project management, and no one checking up on specific tasks to be sure they were getting done. There were no formal stage gates between "inception," "requirements," "design," "development," and "testing." Scope was allowed to change continually, as did delivery priorities from month to month. Testing was far from independent of development and was not based directly on requirements documents. Yet, TRIM's success was complete.

How can we explain this seeming contradiction of some of the most cherished concepts of software project development? Conventional wisdom would likely predict success for the CU project and failure for TRIM. The answer is an evolving body of ideas and practices based on the experience of some of the most successful companies and practitioners in the world, loosely grouped under two terms: Lean product development and Agile software development.

Lean product development (LPD) is most prominently associated with Toyota Manufacturing Company and has been popularized in a series of recent publications to which I will refer in the book. Toyota's approach drew from its experience in Lean manufacturing, adapted to the demands of new knowledge creation inherent in product development. Agile software development independently grew out of a group of prominent U.S. software developers who rebelled against the "conventional wisdom" and articulated a better way. The two approaches, taken together, provide a compelling framework for business leaders anxious to improve their critical software development projects. Although neither approach intended to do so, Agile provides a specific implementation of LPD for software, and LPD provides the broader framework that can enable Agile to thrive.

The tales of these two systems illustrate the competing approaches. Through the telling of the interlocking tales, you will see how the approaches flow in practice: how business leaders start and control the projects, what teams look like, how teams interact, what kinds of people and roles are required, how uncertainty is (or is not) dealt with. You will also see that technical decisions are often, at their roots, poorly understood business choices, as well as how they are made, including the setting of architectures and the making of buy or build decisions. Technology partner management, akin to Toyota's supplier chain management, will be illustrated in successful and less successful ways. Lean and Agile ideas will come to life as the projects wind forward, or spin backward, with just enough pausing to explain the concepts for you; footnotes guide you to more detail provided by other leading authors if you wish to further explore.

My goal in writing this book is to make the usually arcane topics of software development and project management methodologies tangible and accessible for business leaders. As our imaginary CEO Evan Nogelmeyer finds to his eventual dismay, technology is not just for technologists today. Our companies are increasingly dependent on the success of our software, but gaining the knowledge and judgment needed to manage this area is difficult for business leaders, most of whom come out of sales, marketing, finance, and operations areas.

Evan and his team were all smart, well-intentioned, successful business leaders driving their project in the best way that they knew; yet their failure risked ending their careers at Cremins and driving a final stake in Cremins's heart. By reading an engaging story told through the eyes of two business leaders who are not expert in technology or project management, you will gain an appreciation for what is required to enable your technology initiatives to succeed. Along the way, signposts and guides will be planted to help you keep track of the systems development projects and to point out learning that you should take from the tales.

The story will be told by two narrators, Beth Dumas and Jim "Wes" Wesleyan. Beth is the director of Human Resources supporting the Real Estate Division, with a part-time role supporting organizational change for the Cremins United project; she will tell most of the TRIM tale. Wes is a lawyer who has spent most of his career as a strategy consultant, now providing staff support to the Cremins United project's governing body; he will tell most of the CU tale. Because the projects are in the same company, they will overlap to some extent, providing rich opportunities to compare and contrast.

To help you navigate the key players in this story, Figures 1 through 5 provide some background information: a "cast of characters"; an organization chart for the fictional Cremins Corporation; a partial view of each of the two projects, TRIM and Cremins United; and a list of abbreviations and acronyms that some of the characters use in their conversations with each other. I've included all these figures here, rather than at the end of the book, so that you can refer back to them as you read on.

At the end of the tales, I will articulate a series of conclusions and principles based on LPD, Agile, and my 25 years of experience in business systems development. The principles will be illustrated with examples from the tales, giving you a final chance to consolidate your thinking and providing guidance on how to manage business software technology in a more successful, rewarding manner.

The events and people in the story are all fictional. This is not a story of any single project, any specific person, or any real company; rather, it's a universe I constructed for the sole purpose of instruction and entertainment. Neither is it about the specific technical debates, the nature of the systems being built, or the businesses in which Cremins Corporation competes; I created all of these merely as a foil to illustrate the principles. The goal of the book is not to examine these two projects and "prove" that one approach, i.e., Lean/Agile, is superior to others; instead, the projects, people, and technical situations were created as idealized, even caricatured illustrations of valuable general principles. I caution readers against drawing conclusions from this fiction about people, events, or technologies in real life.

Furthermore, all the opinions, perspectives, and conclusions are mine and mine alone. While I have learned much from my associates and experiences, all of the opinions expressed are personal and do not reflect any company's policies or perspectives in any way.

Michael K. Levine

Note: Use this cast of characters with organization charts on the following pages.

Cremins corporate management:
1. Evan Nogelmeyer, chief executive officer
2. Gina Sebastian, president, Specialty Communications Group

Cremins United project team:
1. Tom Stillman, project lead, director of Project Control Authority (PCA)
2. Jim "Wes" Wesleyan, chief of staff for PCA
3. Frankie Alexander, technology lead, PCA member
4. Neil Gottschalk, Project Management and Finance, PCA member
5. Jamie Kawolski, business liaison lead, PCA member
6. Mary O'Connell, Sales Group technology lead
7. Jennifer Phillips, account manager, CSMPro (vendor to CU Sales Group)
8. Deb Dillingham, testing manager for Sales
9. Amit Banerjee, Management Information Reporting technology lead
10. Joe Karras, Production Management technology lead
11. Tammy Sills, Production Management design engineer
12. Steve Tolbert, Production Management design engineer
13. Janice Neustal, Architecture Department manager
14. Scott Diggs, architect assigned to Sales
15. Tabitha Albertson, architect assigned to Production Management
16. Dillon Flaherty, data architect assigned to Sales
17. Dave Prentiss, Technology Group testing lead
18. Trevor McDonald, overall project management lead, on extended assignment from information technology outsourcing and consulting firm Global Resources, Inc. (GRI)
19. George (GG) Giordano, project manager for Sales
20. Sam Baker, business lead for Sales
21. Ken Fong, business lead for Production Management, on assignment from Commercial Printing Division

FIGURE I
Cast of characters.

22. Phyllis Gould, business analyst for Production Management, on assignment from Business Communications Group
23. Angela Lockhart, business lead for Testing

TRIM project team:
1. Neville Roberts, chief engineer of TRIM project
2. Walt Jones, CFO of Real Estate Division, financial manager of TRIM project
3. Beth Dumas, director of Human Resources for Real Estate Division, and part-time member of Cremins United project organizational change team
4. Brian Bannion, Information Management lead, overall TRIM development manager
5. Kamau Kahero, software engineer, lead for data matching development
6. Qin Tsen, scrum master for Information Management team
7. James Pasternak, software engineer, lead for file transfer development
8. Sybil Gutierrez, technology manager, San Diego Multiple Listing Service, and property management lead for TRIM project
9. Basim Chandrasekharan, mapping technology lead, representing Mapomatic Corporation
10. Melissa Brown, public records lead, representing Public Records Aggregators
11. Martin Fowler, National Servicing Corporation, lead mortgage servicing participant on TRIM
12. Jeff Zambrow, Universal National Bank, mortgage servicing participant
13. Alex Fuegos, lead project manager for TRIM
14. Judy Hollendar, systems analyst
15. Jack Spence, regional manager, Home Renovators for Resale, a buyer, renovator, and reseller of distressed properties, representing the needs of property buyers on the TRIM project
16. Janani Mugombe, test manager for TRIM
17. Nancy Mills, national TRIM sales manager

FIGURE I (continued)
Cast of characters.

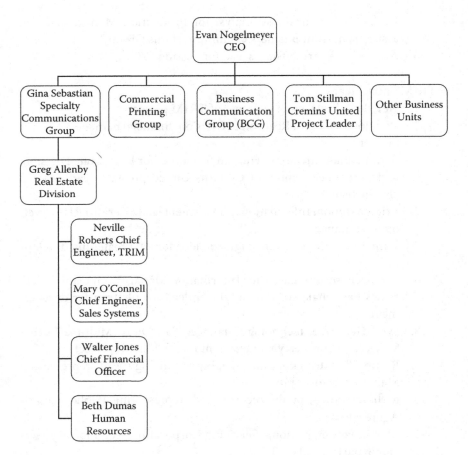

FIGURE 2
Cremins Corporation, partial organization chart.

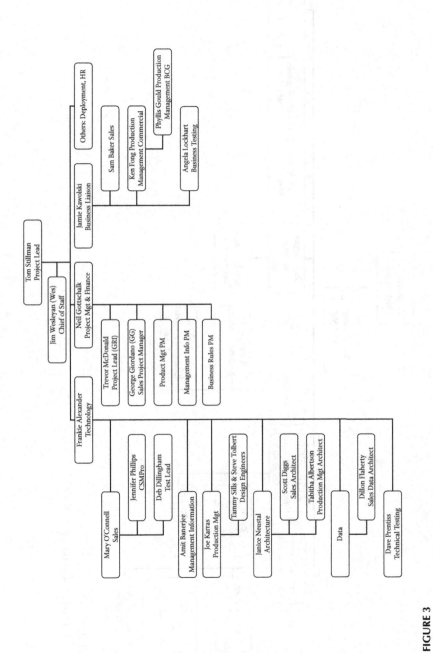

FIGURE 3

Cremins United project structure, partial view.

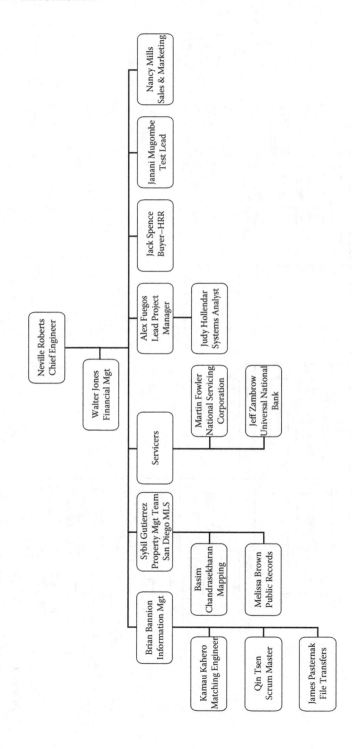

FIGURE 4

TRIM project structure, partial view.

AC: Architectural Council
BCG: Business Communications Group
BRD: Business Requirements Document
CAS: Cremins Architecture Specification
CDM: Common Data Model
CIO: Chief Information Officer
CR: Change Request
CSF: Common Service Facility
CU: Cremins United
FTP: File Transfer Protocol
GRI: Global Resources Incorporated
LOB: Line of Business
LPD: Lean Product Development
PCA: Project Control Authority
PM: Production Management
PMO: Project Management Office
SMEs: Subject Matter Experts
SOA: Service-Oriented Architecture
SOW: Statement of Work
TRIM: Troubled-Real-Estate Information Management

FIGURE 5
Table of acronyms and abbreviations.

Prologue

JANUARY 2008

Beth:

It was a dark and bitterly cold late afternoon in St. Paul, and my mood was as dark and cold as the weather. The strange calm of the holiday season had just come to an end, and the hallways at Cremins Corporation, normally a staid and placid place, were buzzing with nervous energy. Was the Cremins United (CU) project really cancelled? Who were losing their jobs, and who were still left? What was going to happen? As the Human Resources generalist for the Real Estate Division, I had the unfortunate privilege of knowing before most of the others and the duty to tell them about their fates, which I had done today.

The hardest part for me was telling Mary O'Connell, who, over the course of the Cremins United project's 2+ years, had become one of my very best friends. Mary was formally a member of the Real Estate Division—in fact one of its rising stars, leading the development of some of its most successful products. In the spirit of providing the broader enterprise some of the systems development expertise of its newly acquired information technology groups, Mary had been lent to the CU effort as one of its development managers. In the harsh light of retrospect, this hadn't been such a good move for her because the news I'd delivered today wasn't good, for her or for her team.

The Failed Cremins United Project

The Cremins United project was the biggest project that Cremins Corporation had ever undertaken. It had begun with such hope and promise over 2 years ago: We were going to bring together all of Cremins's traditional and printing capabilities with its new information technology skills and enable the delivery of existing and new products through all of our sales channels. The plan was to boost printing sales through the newly acquired sales channels, better manage our expensive-to-maintain printing capacity, and develop new printing-oriented products by becoming more customer focused instead of product focused. It was a vision that would restore the shine to Cremins Corporation, which had been sadly tarnishing over the past decade or more as it uneasily grappled with the Internet age.

The project started with such enthusiasm and excitement. Evan Nogelmeyer, our then (and for now) CEO, had personally sponsored it, and he put some of his most trusted business leaders in charge. Money had been no object, and the Project Control Authority (PCA), the governance body, took great pains to establish methods, control scope and schedules, and identify and mitigate risks. Architectures were established and enforced, independent testing groups built to report status factually, and project phase gates and reviews rigorously applied. Despite all this—or perhaps because of all this, as I have learned and plan to tell you about—the project now appears to be a complete and spectacular failure.

The CU project ended first with a whimper, then with this bang. It had gone "live" 2 months ago, in November 2007, officially 1 year late. Its debut had been quietly downgraded from a triumphant rollout to a "beta test." Not even the people working on the project were by this time proud of it, with its hundreds of carefully documented "work-arounds" and painfully slow performance. Most were just hoping that it would work well enough to support a few sales transactions and show the company that the system had enough potential to justify continued investment. Optimism is a very powerful force; with enough time and money, anything can be fixed! After all, the vision upon which CU was based remained as compelling as ever, probably more so. The decline of the traditional printing businesses had accelerated over the intervening 2 years, so the new business model that CU would support was desperately needed.

Sadly, it rapidly became clear in production how far the system had to go. While the promise was evident, the incompleteness of the business processes, the slowness of the screens, and the astonishing number of bugs compelled the PCA to pull CU from production for "needed repairs" right after the teams worked through most of the Thanksgiving holiday. This was the "whimper"; a subdued victory was declared, the teams were thanked profusely, encouraging messages about the dozens of sales executed were distributed, and team members were given much needed time off. Behind the scenes, CU was being evaluated in light of the accelerating decline of the company's primary business, and the math just didn't work: Less investment capital was available, and the projected expense until it would produce value looked too high and too risky to be justified.

Therefore, the complete cancellation of the project had been decided, and I was now part of its execution (i.e., the "bang"). But the ripple effects were still unknown: Would Evan Nogelmeyer, the project's sponsor and the CEO of the company, survive? Would his strategy of integrating the Cremins business lines around merging printing capabilities and technology skills and focusing both on customer needs continue? Would the company be broken up or sold and Nogelmeyer and the PCA leaders be fired in disgrace? The full impact of the CU project failure remains to be seen. For now, we are eliminating the bulk of the team members who have been working on it and stopping the financial bleeding and management distraction.

My part, as a Human Resources staff member, came in eliminating the team members. This was a highly orchestrated and scripted process, carefully designed to reduce the risk of litigation. Professionally, I know this was the best approach for Cremins and for the affected employees, and the severance benefits provided to our team members are generous.

The Successful TRIM Project

Looking out my frosted window over the frozen suburban landscape of the freeway; dirty, semiwhite snow; and denuded trees, I think back over the years and consider the two projects and why one succeeded so dramatically while the other failed. I don't think it was that TRIM was simpler and smaller than CU; that's true to some degree, but it certainly wasn't simple and small!

TRIM was conceived largely by Greg Allenby, the head of the Real Estate Division that was recently acquired by Cremins. The Cremins acquisition and Nogelmeyer's desire for technology-driven growth had suddenly made investment capital available, and Greg had ideas on how to use it. Greg saw the early signs of a coming real estate collapse: galloping home prices, ubiquitous advertisements for home mortgages for people with "less than perfect credit," television shows about flipping homes and making a fortune, Super Bowl advertisements for subprime lenders. He worked with existing customers in the multiple listing and real estate brokerage businesses and recruited others he believed would be in need of and willing to pay for better information and technology services, including banks, investors, and government agencies. With Neville and his team's help, Greg assembled a group of business partners to come together to build a system to prepare for what these far-sighted people believed was coming— a system to deal with troubled real estate—TRIM.

TRIM had at its heart a set of integrated data about loans, property, homes for sale and sold, and geography that had never before been assembled. Its "brains" was a set of business relationships, privacy controls, and information security provisions that likewise were newly conceived. Its arms and legs were business functions such as information analytics, foreclosure sale management, and property management services. Customers would include, most importantly, all the development partners, plus others such as journalists, data aggregators, and resellers. The biggest opportunity would come from others in the categories represented by the initial set of partners (e.g., once the system was proven useful by National Servicing Group, other large loan servicers would be likely to sign on as well). Greg put this concept and coalition together, and then he assembled and led a group to build it quickly enough so that it would be ready when the crisis materialized and cheaply enough so that it wouldn't bankrupt the company if the crisis were to be averted. This was hardly a simple business or technical task.

How the Cremins United and TRIM Projects Differed

No, the reason TRIM succeeded while CU failed wasn't in the nature of system development projects themselves. It was in the way the projects were approached and led. Cremins United adopted a process-centric, document-centric, and project-management-heavy approach, as illustrated by the name of the governance team: the Project Control Authority. On the other hand, TRIM adopted a "Lean and Agile" approach. Lean and Agile emphasizes knowledge building over following processes, teamwork over control, working code over documentation, and business partnerships over vendor management. It abhors some of the practices that CU emphasized, such as detailed, centrally maintained and integrated project plans; highly defined and enforced document templates; cookbook-like methodologies; and architecture provided by noncoding, outside-the-team architects.

When I started my job as director of Human Resources for Cremins Real Estate Division several years ago, I knew very little about large-scale business software development projects. As I began to see the two projects unfold from that perch and as a part-time member of the Cremins United organizational change team, at first I couldn't tell which approach was superior. The activities of the CU project seemed to make great sense; only because Mary was trying to teach me about Lean and Agile while she fought to run her part of the CU project that way and because I was simultaneously observing the TRIM project did I have any perspective that something in CU might be amiss. This brings me to the reason we wrote this book and our approach to writing it.

Overview of "Tale of Two Systems"

By "we," I mean Wes and me. Wes led the support staff for Cremins United's Project Control Authority, and when he joined that project he was as green at large-scale software development as I was. Wes was trained as a lawyer, but he never practiced; instead, he joined a strategy consulting firm, eventually following a partner to Cremins Corporation. Wes had a ringside view of Cremins United, and he and I went through similar learning curves. Much of my connection to Cremins United had been through Mary's eyes and my loose connection through the organizational change team versus my firsthand connection to the TRIM project. Therefore, when I decided to write a book on the two projects to help others hooked into software development projects to do better than we did with CU and, frankly, as a sort of restorative therapy, I decided to recruit Wes to help describe the projects from his perspective and to share what he learned. He was very happy to join in the writing, especially because he has now left Cremins and is "between jobs."

Wes and I are going to describe the two projects, as best we can, chronologically as we saw them evolve. I will primarily tell the story of TRIM, while Wes tells the tale of Cremins United. We will mix this up a bit because Wes had the opportunity to see some of the TRIM project, mostly at Mary's prodding in a valiant attempt to improve CU, and I saw parts of the CU project as Mary's Human Resources support and as a member of the Real Estate Division's management team. At the beginning of each chapter or section, we'll make clear who is doing the writing. This will give you the opportunity to see the two system development efforts through the eyes of nontechnical professionals who are not project management experts. We'll describe what we saw and what we learned, as we learned it.

Large-scale software development projects are by their nature complex and involve a lot of people, so although we've tried to simplify as much as possible, there are limits to our ability to do so and still be faithful to the nature of the endeavors. Accordingly, we're going to provide some assistance for you as you peruse the tales. For ongoing reference, in the book's Introduction there are organization charts, a list of people with brief descriptions of their roles, and a table of acronyms. Then, at the end of each chapter, we have written brief summaries with three sections:

- "Signposts" will summarize the major events of the chapter with respect to each project.
- "Guides" will point out lessons as we see them now, at the ends of the projects. We both wish that we had known then what we think we know now!
- "Coming up next" will give you a preview of the next chapter, including who will be narrating and what the topic will be.

We know from the TRIM results that large-scale systems development projects can succeed and be fun and rewarding to participants. We also know from Cremins United that they can fail miserably. We think we now know some of the ideas that can help tilt projects one way or the other. So now, go back with us to the beginning of the two tales and observe and learn with us!

Beth Dumas, with James "Wes" Wesleyan, January 2008

Section I

The First 6 Months: September 2005– February 2006

1

Kicking Off Project 1—TRIM: The "Troubled-Real-Estate Information Management" Project

3 YEARS EARLIER: SEPTEMBER 2005

Beth:

I looked around the Cremins Real Estate Division's conference room and liked what I saw this early Tuesday morning as the management team was gathering for its regular weekly meeting. It was my first such gathering; I'd just joined this software company after 15 years in the computer hardware business. I'd worked hard to find this job—I didn't want to leave my native San Diego, where most of my family still lived and where, as the sun streaming in the large windows reminded me, the weather was usually spectacular. I'm one of those meticulous career planners, and a year ago I'd decided that I'd had enough of electrical engineers and assembly plants, so I'd decided to try my hand in the software business. I hoped to find a more dynamic, interpersonally intense environment, where I could add more value than trying to get engineers to talk to each other instead of stare at their shoes and trying to repair misunderstandings between U.S.-based designers and manufacturing managers in China and Taiwan.

The Real Estate Division attracted my attention because of its reputation in the local software technology community, which I'd infiltrated during my job search. I'd learned that it led the national field of real-estate management software from its office here in suburban Poway. During my interviews I'd learned of its innovative, people-oriented approach to software development, which the company called Lean and Agile development. I knew something about Lean manufacturing, but this seemed to be a horse of another color. I'd also learned of the challenges this group would be facing as it became part of Cremins Corporation, its new owner. I thought I could learn, and I thought I could help.

The conference room was like the rest of the Real Estate Division's quarters, modern and comfortable but unremarkable. A 12-seated table occupied the center of the room, surrounded by comfortable chairs; we wouldn't quite fill them for this meeting. Opposite the window on a credenza stood a couple of coffee pots, some pastries, and a tray of fruit. Mary O'Connell, one of the software development managers, had already kindly warned me not to take the chocolate-covered donut, telling me the story of an earlier newcomer who had gotten off on very much the wrong foot with the boss, Greg Allenby, by eating his regular repast.

I'd been chatting with Mary and Walter Jones, the chief financial officer, for several minutes, while the other team members, which included leads for Sales, Customer Service, Operations, a couple of Product Development groups, and Marketing, talked in small groups. About 10 minutes past 9:00, Greg Allenby walked into the room, waved a hearty "good morning," grabbed his chocolate donut and a cup of coffee, and sat down at the head of the table. The rest of the team followed suit and took their regular positions—after the donut warning, I'd waited until all of them were situated and took one of the remaining open chairs.

"Good morning, Cremins Real Estate Division leadership team," Greg opened. "Are we starting to get used to our new name?"

Neville Roberts, a tall, lanky, graying Brit sitting on Greg's left, responded on behalf of the group. "We should be by now, shouldn't we? I suppose you are referring to the new signs outside? It's been almost a year now, what next? Did they turn off our old e-mail addresses?"

Walter Jones, on Greg's right, laughed quietly. "Yes, indeed, Neville, that's coming as well. But on a more serious note, integration work is beginning really to pick up. Our budgeting for next year is now integrated, and a big new integration project called 'Cremins United' is about to kick off."

Greg took back control of the meeting. "Let's get started. I was actually on a call about Cremins United, talking through Mary's proposed new role and other ways we might be able to help. We'll touch on that later.

First, I'd like us all to welcome Beth Dumas to the team, as our new direc-tor of Human Resources. I think you've all met her, either in the interview process or at yesterday's welcome reception. Beth, anything to say yet?"

I'd prepared for this little speech this morning and kept it short and sweet. "Thanks, Greg, and thanks to all of you for the warm welcome. As Walt mentioned, there is going to be a lot more effort to finish our integra-tion work with Cremins's human resource policies and benefits, so that's going to be one of my key focuses. Managing the routine work of compen-sation, recruiting, and employee relations will be another. But I hope to spend a good chunk of my time helping each of you with organizational and people development as well. I'm working on getting on each of your schedules to do an initial review of what my team has on its plate for you now, as well as how we might better serve you in the months to come. Watch for that. Oh, and special thanks to Mary, who apparently saved me from making the legendary donut faux pas!"

There were knowing laughs around the table and a thank-you from Greg to Mary. Greg continued, "Okay, on to agenda item number one, our new project, the Troubled-Real-Estate Information Management system. We've had lots of activity on this the past few weeks, and we need to get this whole team up to speed. Neville, as you know, is chief engineer on the project. Neville, can you take it from here?"

Background on the TRIM Project—Why It Was Needed

"Happily," Neville responded.

I knew from my interviewing that Neville was the most senior chief engineer in what was now Cremins Corporation's Real Estate Division and the only chief engineer directly on the senior management team. That role, as defined here, was not one I'd seen before in my career. About 5 years ago, Greg and his team had settled upon the chief engineer role as a key part of a better way to drive software development. They'd learned about the approach from Toyota and other manufacturing companies that had been experimenting with, and relying upon, the role for several years. It was a tough role to fill because it was an unusual combination of market-ing manager, technical lead, and project manager. Neville fit the bill—he'd come to the States 20 years ago to get his engineering degree at Cal Tech up in Pasadena, where he'd married one of the few women attending the school at that time. He'd drifted from electrical engineering at Lockheed into the booming software field, and then into customer-facing and product development roles. Greg had found him 4 years ago as he was building his initial management team, and Neville had now become a key member of our leadership group and the point person for our most important development projects.

"Let's talk about TRIM—the Troubled-Real-Estate Information Management system," said Neville.

"What a name! I sure hope you are better at the software development part of your job than the marketing side," kidded Walt.

"Hey!" interjected our marketing manager. She joked, "I resent that remark. It wasn't easy to come up with an acronym that worked for this. Who doesn't want to be trim?"

"OK, Walt, so you don't like the name," Neville continued. "But the idea and the project are both very likable. To briefly summarize—yes, I can do that!—around the beginning of this year, say, February 2005, we began hearing from our realtor and broker customers that house prices were jumping up unsustainably quickly and that lenders were loosening standards in entirely new ways. Greg began talking to some of his ex-colleagues in the mortgage banks, and I checked in with some chums in the investment banks. We saw the possibility that home prices could stop growing, or even take a tumble, and that the unsafe lending practices could come home to roost in a very large way. At our March 2005 management offsite, we all—except you of course, Beth—spent a day exploring what business opportunity there might be in this for us, and the idea of TRIM emerged."

Walt, always eager to keep financial results at the forefront, turned to face Beth and added, "It appeared that we had a series of powerful unmet needs emerging and a lot of assets and skills that could fill the gaps. We just had to figure out how to make money from doing that, and I think now we have it."

Neville regained the floor. "I'm not really much better at money management than I am at marketing, so Walt has been a big help to me putting this together. Just yesterday, as you no doubt have already heard, the Cremins management committee approved the capital to enable us to begin full-fledged work on the project. This also permits us to sign the contracts with the first set of banks, multiple listing agencies, investors, and government agencies. I expect the contracts will be a mere formality now because they mostly negotiated; they were just waiting on us having the money to proceed. So it's rock 'n' roll, let's get going! I'm going to need all of your support and help."

After Neville, Mary was probably the most senior software professional in the division; she led the development of the sales tools for realtors and brokers, and she helped with the sales-oriented portions of the multiple listing systems. She was intrigued about next steps. She said, "Neville, can you tell us where you are on the project and how you intend to proceed? That would help us figure out how we might be able to help—although it's looking like I might be off to Corporate for Cremins United." Mary didn't seem entirely happy with that idea.

"Don't worry, Mary, I'll be coming directly to you all for help; you won't have to work too hard to figure out what I'll need! Nevertheless, I'll answer your question. We've spent the last 6 months or so listening to potential users, understanding needs, figuring out who would pay how much for what, noodling on what we would build to meet the needs, thinking through options on how to build it, and then putting all this information into two documents."

Neville elaborated, "The first is the concept document. In this case, I had to break it into two pieces, one for internal use and one for external. The external version is essentially a sales piece, used to get our partners on board. It provides the background of the problem, the need to address it, and the basic ideas of TRIM. The internal version has the financials laid out, including exactly who we think our users are, their value proposition, how much we think they would be willing to pay, how much we think it will cost us to build and operate the solution, and the risks and threats we see. You've all seen both versions of the concept document, the last time about a month ago on its way to Cremins Corporate for approval."

Mary nodded and said, "Very nice work, Neville. The concept looks great. But how are you going to get it done quickly? It sounds complicated, especially having to work with that unruly bunch of partners."

Greg chose to answer Mary's question instead of waiting for Neville. Greg was deeply invested in TRIM; he saw it as the best opportunity for the Real Estate Division to grow over the next few years—not only from the direct profits from TRIM, but also in helping us build new businesses with companies with whom we had very little direct engagement now.

"While we did the iterations of the concept document, we began working at the same time on the project statement of work (SOW). This laid out how we wanted to proceed, and it gave potential partners a detailed view of what they would be signing up for. As the concept matured and partners began to take an interest, Neville and I built a small lead team that included National Mortgage Servicing, Universal National Bank, the Atlanta and San Diego multiple listing services, the Federal Mortgage Finance Agency, and the Strothman Brothers investment bank out of New York."

"It's quite a group," Neville interjected. "We had to have several other parties as well—someone to provide public records information, address data, maps, and more."

"While these companies are all in generally the same industry," Greg explained, "they have never come together in this kind of cooperative group to solve a problem. The first challenge was getting enough agreement to proceed, both on the probable existence and shape of the problem and on the need to solve it. We wound up with these partners largely because they were the ones who saw the future as we did; many of the companies we approached had some concerns about what is to come, but didn't see any need for a response of this type or just preferred to sit back and wait to see what happens."

I wondered how we'd cajoled the group of companies into cooperating, and Greg was happy to explain. "It was our newfound ability to deploy our own capital, thanks to Cremins Corporation backing. We offered to pay for the entire system build-out, excepting the minimal costs each partner would incur. Our partners merely had to agree to do their modest part, commit to providing data under the negotiated terms, and agree to use the system in the future under certain conditions."

Choosing a New Approach to Project Management

Greg continued, "You all know what a nut I am about statements of work. And on this project we were fortunate enough to have Neville and his protégé Alex on point. They began laying out how this project would be run and continuously sharing it with the growing team. The concept document laid out the 'what' and 'why,' and the SOW laid out the 'how,' 'who,' and 'when.' Our partners weren't used to planning in this depth, and arguments emerged especially as we tried to get this loose group to define roles and responsibilities, milestones, management escalation, status reporting, and issue management. But the primary argument was about development approach."

Mary saw where this was going: "I suppose the big banks and the government agency wanted us to follow a document-heavy, strict stage-gate approach?"

I knew little about software development methodologies, and I knew that Greg's team had been taking their Lean and Agile path, but I was still surprised to hear in Mary's voice an aversion to what I thought was the best-practice approach to product development. In fact, the computer hardware company I'd just left had been very proud of its formal phase-end reviews and extensive documentation.

"Mary," I said, "would it be okay for a newcomer to ask what's wrong with that? Isn't it good to finish a phase before starting the next one, to be sure you have everything documented, understood, reviewed, and agreed?"

Mary looked over at Greg for guidance on whether or how to respond in this forum. Greg nodded to Mary, so she replied, "There are some good elements in that type of approach, Beth, especially in hardware development, where a lot of parts suppliers need to gear up to produce new components at the same time. Getting all the designs done on paper, or in design software, is a well-rehearsed and effective mechanism to reduce risk before undertaking the very expensive tooling."

"But in software development, we normally don't have such a step function of risk and costs to control, and we aren't as good at understanding and writing out all the requirements and designs before beginning to build. In large-scale new system development projects, there is usually a lot we don't know, and we need to accelerate learning as much as we can. It's normally much more effective in software development to get the overall architecture and a high-level plan in place, and then do requirements, design, build, and test in iterative phases, adjusting as we go along. Doing all the requirements up front, then all the design, then all the build, and then all the testing can result in a tremendous amount of waste, and it reduces success rates."

Neville interrupted at this point, trying to keep the meeting on track. "Great summary, Mary. Couldn't have said it better myself, although I might have given a bit more emphasis to the people and team elements. Beth, how about you and Mary get together offline, and Mary can give you her full Lean and Agile primer course? You'll need to have a pretty good understanding of that if you are to help us with organizational and people development. That okay?"

He looked first to me and then to Mary, and both of us nodded and smiled at each other. "Great. There is no one better to learn this from, Beth. But now, back to the SOW."

"Alex and I had to spend quite a bit of time talking with our partners about how our Lean and Agile development approaches work and reassuring them that indeed they give us more control, less risk, and higher quality code faster than the approaches they are used to. Alex documented our approach in the statement of work, so they were able to see exactly what we proposed and understand how they would be able to monitor and control progress at each step. Several had to take the SOW back to their own internal process and compliance groups for review. At the end of the day, everyone has agreed to let us proceed as we wish, mostly because we are paying for most of the development and refused to compromise in any material way."

"Neville was so great, you'd all have been proud of him," Greg said. "He gently cajoled in that soft British accent of his, and every now and then he'd just surprise folks and quietly say, 'It's our money and we won't budge on this.' So we've got the okay from our project partners, although it's a skeptical and tentative okay. All we need to do now is to deliver."

Neville basked in Greg's praise for a moment and then leaned back in his chair, smiled, and said, "And so we will. Now let's talk about our schedule. We're aiming at going live in 6 months with our first release, which will be limited function for just a couple geographies, but it will be useful and start bringing in revenue. Then we'll do releases regularly—probably quarterly but also some between the big quarterly releases—to add function and geography. By the time the loan crisis explodes, if that's what it's going to do, we should be well along to capturing the market.

"Right now," Neville was finishing up, "we begin a month of formal planning. By Halloween we'll have the next set of plans complete, taking the concept document and SOW to the next level. We already have our high-level technology architecture completed and a pretty good sense of what we need to do. We still have to flesh out our mythical users, our first-generation backlog, details of our first 1-month sprint plan, a general sense of the objectives of each sprint plan until our general release, and to nail down some details of the technical design. We also need to get our privacy/security policy and plan completed and our team structure and knowledge-sharing platform done. We're going to bring in a dozen or so contractors—most from TopCoders, a lot of whom have worked here before, plus a few others—because we need some more talent and more hands. Greg has given us the west side of the second floor, sorry and thanks to those of you moving—mostly Walt's folks."

I heard the words and partially understood; I did fully sense the confidence in Neville's voice. I was grateful that Mary had agreed to educate me on what this all meant.

Neville wrapped up, "Any questions?" Greg responded, "Let's hold questions for now; you all know the basic drill. We'll talk more in next week's meeting. Now, I want to fill you in on the Cremins United project."

Signposts   **TRIM project**

- The project was conceived to meet information and services needs for a possible real estate crisis.
- Greg and Neville assembled a coalition of companies interested in and capable of solving these needs and creating an ongoing profitable business model for all participants.
- An extensive period of analysis and planning was undertaken, culminating in a capital investment decision by Cremins Corporation.
- By providing the capital, Cremins was able to convince its partners to go along with its Lean and Agile development approach, despite their misgivings.
- Time lines and targets have now been set: 6 months to first delivery.

Cremins United (CU) project

- The project team was being assembled; Mary O'Connell, from the Real Estate Division, was being considered for a key role.
- Greg Allenby, the Real Estate Division president, was working with CU leaders to determine how else he could help.

Guides from Beth	• Prior to embarking on a major development effort, undertake a study phase to validate the business need and profitable business model, and resolve the major issues to establish a framework for success. Toyota calls this the *kentou*, or study phase.[1] Contrast this with many traditional software methods, where the first phase is concerned only with requirements.
	• Use chief engineers for major systems development projects. If that construct doesn't fit exactly, find a variant that does.
	• In the study phase, write a concept document defining the "what and why" and a statement of work defining the "how, who, and when." The documents are to facilitate the discussions and identify and resolve conflicts, rather than an end in and of themselves!
	• Create win–win business partner relations. Listen to what others need and find a way to align interests.
Coming up next	Our other narrator, Jim "Wes" Wesleyan, will kick off the Cremins United project tale at a meeting of the Project Control Authority taking place at about the same time as the meeting we just left.

NOTES

1. See, for example, James M. Morgan and Jeffrey K. Liker, *The Toyota Product Development System,* Chapter 4, New York: Productivity Press, 2006. This chapter explains one of Lean product development's principles: "Front load the product development process to explore alternatives thoroughly."

2

Kicking Off Project 2:
The Cremins United Project

SEPTEMBER 2005

Wes:

It had been a little over a year since I'd joined Cremins Corporation as chief of staff for the Cremins United project, and it had begun to feel like home. As a strategy consultant at Griffin Corporation for the past 10 years, I had typically been assigned to short projects, meeting new people all the time, and I had to remind them continually to call me Wes instead of James or Jim. Here, I was Wes all the time. I liked that, and I liked the sense of ownership and continuity I was achieving, just as I'd hoped when I'd decided to leave Chicago for St. Paul to join Cremins.

I'd come to Cremins at the request of Evan Nogelmeyer, Cremins CEO and a Griffin alumnus. He'd asked me to join the Cremins team following our consulting engagement that had laid the strategic groundwork for this project. I wished I knew more about system development because it was clear by now that that was where this project was heading. I hoped that my strategy, financial, marketing, and leadership skills would be enough to carry me through while I learned and that I could find others to provide the needed expertise I lacked.

Today's 2:00 meeting of the Project Control Authority—PCA for short— was a momentous one. The board of directors had just given us the green light to go to the next step in implementing the Cremins United strategy:

a more detailed proposal on specific scope, time frames, and costs for a Cremins United project. Evan himself was going to stop by and talk with us, to give us guidance on what he expected from us over the next 6 weeks as we crafted those details. Because Evan was so busy and had to squeeze us into his schedule, we were meeting in the Cremins boardroom, just down the hall from Evan's office. The boardroom was just what you'd expect from a 100+-year-old, very successful company: dark wooden walls, a huge, heavy wooden table, high-backed, broad, fine leather chairs, and dark maroon window coverings with a faintly moldy smell. Like Cremins itself, the boardroom had been brought into the twentieth century with teleconference and projection facilities; perhaps also like Cremins itself, it wasn't all the way to the twenty-first century and was missing video conferencing.

The boardroom did have large picture windows staring down from the 34th floor of the First Bank building. First Bank had long ceased to exist, but its big neon "1" on the roof had been a St. Paul landmark for 50 years and had remained in place. I wandered over to the windows to watch the slow, cold drizzle outside, incongruously gray on such an exciting day. The Mississippi River flowed slowly by, just a few blocks away, and barges pushing grain down the river and gravel up (for the icy roads not very far off) slipped past each other.

Creating the Project Control Authority

As I watched the barges, the other members of the PCA began to filter in. I usually got to PCA meetings first because I had to prepare the agenda, prepare any printed handouts, and set up any audio or visual needs. The PCA had four primary members and several others with bit parts, at least at this stage, such as human resources, deployment, and communication. The four were Tom Stillman, overall project leader and a direct report to Evan Nogelmeyer; Neil Gottschalk, responsible for project management and finance; Jamie Kawolski, the business line liaison; and Frankie Alexander, technology. Tom Stillman was the first to arrive, talking on his cell phone as he walked in, barely acknowledging my presence. All four were senior, experienced, trusted Cremins leaders, who had been successful in almost everything they'd done in their careers. Evan had insisted that the Cremins United project would be run by his best people because so much of our future strategy depended upon it.

Tom Stillman was close to and trusted by Evan. I'd been in many meetings with the two of them, as Tom's chief of staff, and was impressed by the openness of the dialogue and debate. Evan was confident in Tom's abilities, although probably not quite as confident as Tom himself was. Maybe Tom's opinion of himself was justified; after all, he'd already had a great career in marketing and communications, starting as a young star on Madison Avenue and then moving through two major financial companies before arriving at Cremins's St. Paul headquarters a decade ago. The assignment to Cremins United had the hallmarks of his last hurrah—he was nearing 60 years old, presumably already wealthy, and likely not up for another big challenge after he succeeded on this one for Evan. But while Tom was experienced, he gave no hint of slowing down. He still worked incessantly, was as outgoing and charismatic as ever, talked and moved quickly, and spent energy relentlessly. I had to work hard to keep up!

Tom had taken on Cremins United 2 years ago, while the strategy was just being formed and before it had even been formalized as a project. It had gradually become clear that our strategy of acquiring and merging with other printers wasn't going to succeed and that it had just slowed our gradual descent along with demand for printing. Evan had pulled Tom out of his line management position—marketing, strategic planning, and communications—and asked him to work with Griffin Corporation consultants and an internal team to come up with a new way forward. They did, and the result became known as Cremins United: Infuse our printing capability with information technology, grow our information technology–based businesses, and become intensely customer focused to provide all our existing products through all of our channels and drive fused product development to meet customer needs. The eventual results of Tom's strategy work, in addition to the strategy, included my movement to Cremins, the formation of the Cremins United project to drive execution, and the creation of the Project Control Authority.

I initially thought that "project control authority" was a somewhat heavy-handed name, but as I continued to think about it, it made sense to me. Evan is a smart and experienced leader, and he's seen this type of large, strategic system development initiative get off-track and fail at other companies. As we settled on the strategy and grappled to shape its implementation, Evan consulted formally and informally with several experts, and the guidance he got was consistent: Large projects fail due to weak leadership, poor understanding of requirements, and inability to control scope and execution. With so much riding on this project, Evan wasn't going to let it get out of control. Tom understood this, and he showed Evan and everyone else his understanding by choosing the "project control authority" name. The Cremins United project would not fail due to weak leadership or lack of control!

As for the Cremins United project, its goals were simply to build the systems to support the strategy. We needed a common sales system so that our sales forces could deal with the full range of customer needs, instead of just the products they now sold. That system would have to provide the needed product and other sales information so that customer-focused generalists could deal with most of our product sales without deep product-specific expertise. We needed improved customer information and financial systems so that we could manage credit across our units, bill for combined products effectively, and provide product bundles and discounts. We needed integration of our sales systems to our production systems so that we could effectively quote prices and delivery dates. We needed common production systems, especially in our printing areas, so that we could manage our capacity. We needed great management information so that we could analyze our customer behavior, spot trends, and support product development. It was a daunting list I'd assembled from the consulting engagements and preliminary planning, and we needed it all to be delivered in synchronization over several years at enormous costs.

Right as the clock's hands showed 2:00, Tom kicked off the meeting in his usual boisterous way. "OK, let's get going. We've got a lot to cover. The board approved our going ahead and putting some more meat on the bones of this project, like costs and time frames, and getting back to them around Halloween. That leaves us just 6 weeks to get this done. I want to be sure that we all understand what we are aiming for and what Evan expects from us, so I invited Evan to join us today. Unfortunately, he's very busy and couldn't give us a firm commitment on a time, so we're going to play this by ear. When he shows up, we'll stop whatever we're doing and resume when he needs to leave. I've asked him to give us a quick summary of what he expects from the Cremins United project and this group, as well as what the board will be expecting. That should all be familiar to you, but I want you to hear it from him directly. Then we can ask a few questions; I think Evan has only half an hour or so."

"After Evan finishes up, we have to go through our plan for the next few weeks and finish up our discussion on how we want to organize and run this project. Wes will lead us through that conversation. Any other items we need to talk over today?"

What Exactly Do We Need to Deliver?

Frankie Alexander, the PCA's technology leader, waited a moment to be sure no one else wanted the floor and then somewhat hesitatingly spoke up. Frankie was short for Frances and, indeed, Frankie was short—just a tad over 5 feet tall, and she couldn't have weighed more than 100 pounds. Frankie was usually quiet and her physical presence was unimposing, but she seemed competent enough from what I could tell. For the last 5 years, she had been the chief information officer of our Business Communications Group (BCG), one of only a hundred technical team members who remained with Cremins when BCG outsourced its technology management to Global Resources Inc. (GRI) several years ago. It hadn't been her choice to outsource; that decision had come from Pete Cremins himself, who had concluded that technology was not a differentiator for a printing company and succumbed to the temptation to get rid of a headache he had little hope of alleviating himself. Frankie had done an excellent job of managing the transition of most of our technical team members and our systems to GRI, as well as managing the vendor relationship since.

Frankie had initially struggled with the outsourcer as Cremins's business changed over the years, trying to get technology delivered and control costs to meet new needs in the context of a complex contractual relationship. She had successfully built a team and a development process that reliably controlled costs and predictably delivered changes to the systems GRI managed on our behalf. The process emphasized clarity and completeness of business requirements, clear and explicit handoffs to the technology provider, detailed and committed cost and time estimates with consequences for errors, and rigorous independent user acceptance testing of changes. Her skills, model, and team seemed just right for the Cremins United challenge ahead.

Frankie's experience and success made her selection as the technology lead for PCA a logical choice for the corporate CIO, Evan, and Tom. In her new role, she was in charge of all the technology development to be done, including all software development, technology architecture, integration, infrastructure, and technical testing; she reported directly to the corporate CIO with a strong "dotted line" to Tom. Many of the technology resources now reported directly to her, while some others, such as the Infrastructure Group, continued to report direct-line functionally in the CIO organization and dotted line to Frankie.

Frankie now posed a question for Tom, and it was entirely consistent with her focus on reliably meeting specific expectations: "Are we going to talk today about the details of the project—what we want to deliver, when we want to deliver that, and how much we think it might cost? I'm worried that we are agreeing to go forward without knowing what the specific requirements are. I can't estimate cost and time without a design, and I can't do a design without requirements."

"Good questions, Frankie. That's why we're here today," Tom responded. "We need to plan out the next 6 weeks so that we can get answers to those questions. We know the broad outlines of what we need; Wes has documented that in the board presentation that was approved yesterday. You each have a copy in the folder in front of you. I'd expect that as we bring in the next level of leadership and they work together under our direction for the month, we'll get those questions answered in time for the Halloween board meeting."

My sense was that Tom wasn't at all sure how to make the transformation from vision and broad project goals to the detailed expectations around delivery that Frankie needed. Frankie, I knew, wanted to avoid any projection of time or cost until she had detailed requirements, designs, and formal estimates. Evan and Tom weren't patient enough to wait for these before moving ahead. I was sympathetic to Frankie's goals, though, and would try to help get her scope questions answered in the coming weeks.

Transforming the Business to Keep Up with Market Changes

Just then the boardroom's heavy door opened, and Evan joined the meeting. Evan Nogelmeyer had been CEO of Cremins for 5 years, and he had another 10 ahead of him to retirement. He had begun his career as an industrial engineer, practicing that craft for just a few years before jumping into management consulting. He made partner at Griffin, excelling at strategic analysis and developing outstanding communication and customer relationship skills, even though he was somewhat of an introvert. I'd met Evan at Griffin while I was a beginning consultant, but I don't think he remembered me from that time; we had met again just a few years ago. Evan cultivated the Cremins business for Griffin when Cremins was mostly a business forms provider and seeking help in setting a path for growth while it still had resources to deploy. He'd helped Pete Cremins create the strategy that led to the acquisition of the Commercial Printing and Specialty Groups and set the overall direction toward full-service printing and electronic information publishing/management.

Pete recruited Evan to join Cremins as head of strategy and later moved him to run BCG to get operating experience. Evan had excelled at BCG, which was Cremins's poster child for integration of printing and information technology. While succeeding at BCG, he had joined Pete in the Griffin-led strategy work that eventually led to the acquisition of several information technology companies, including our Real Estate Division now embarking on the TRIM project. Of all Pete's direct reports, Evan became the most closely identified with the Cremins United strategy, the most articulate in espousal of its benefits, and the most enthusiastic about its envisioned implementation through the Cremins United project. When Pete recently retired from his role as president to be chairman of the board, Evan was the logical, groomed successor. The Cremins United project was to be his next step in the transformation of Cremins according to his grand strategic plan.

"Evan, welcome and thanks for joining us," said Tom.

"My pleasure. Thank you for making time for me today, and for being flexible about it," Evan replied. "It's great to get a chance to thank you all personally for your contributions and to talk about the compelling Cremins United vision and how we are going to implement it."

Evan continued, "Why don't we start with some introductions, and then I'd like to share some thoughts with you on where Cremins sits with regard to our marketplace and the very exciting things we hope to accomplish under the 'Cremins United project' banner. I believe you all know who I am"—Evan chuckled a bit—"so I won't waste your time on that. But I do want to convey Pete's thanks for your great work over the last year, and the board's strong support for the project. This looks to be the biggest and most significant investment we've made outside of an acquisition, and the board is looking forward to giving you a formal go-ahead in 6 weeks. Why don't we go around the table clockwise, starting with you, Tom?"

Tom replied, "I think everyone knows me as well, Evan, so let's skip on to Wes."

"Hi, Evan, I'm Jim Wesleyan, but everyone calls me Wes." Evan and everyone in the room knew me as well, so there was no need for more discussion.

"Frankie?" nodded Tom.

"I'm Frankie Alexander, from Technology.

"Sure, Frankie," Evan said. "Good to see you again. It's great that we have you and your BCG team aboard." Evan knew Frankie from his time at BCG.

"Neil Gottschalk, Project Management and Finance. I'm leading project management and finance." Neil had joined Cremins just 2 years ago, when we'd purchased a large regional magazine printer. He'd been chief financial officer there, responsible for all technology as well as finance, accounting, and facilities. Neil was a certified public accountant, had begun his career at one of the (then) Big 6 accounting firms, and been picked up by one of his clients. His role had been eliminated as his firm was absorbed into the existing functional structure of the Commercial Printing Group, but he was well respected in the company and thought to be a great fit for this role on the PCA. Neil had responsibility for the Cremins United project management office, which was responsible for all project planning, cost/benefit analysis, budgeting, project processes, and official status communication.

"Neil, it's good to see you again. It's great that we were able to spring you free for this job," said Evan. Of the primary PCA leaders, Evan knew Neil the least, but he liked what he'd seen so far.

Introductions continued through the Deployment, Business Liaison, and Human Resources/Communications PCA members (none of whom are central to this tale) and then it was back to Evan.

"We've come a long way in the 15 years since I first started working with Pete Cremins, back in my management consulting days before I saw the light and joined up. Pete was seeing the threat posed to the business by personal computers, electronic point-of-sale systems, computerized accounting, and do-it-yourself printing, and he asked us to help him assess the threats and opportunities and set a path forward. We saw a future in which the traditional business-forms business would essentially wither away and be replaced by three emerging, related opportunities: a transformed forms business—really an outsourced business communications operation; high-volume, high-efficiency commercial printing; and very targeted, vertical business communications and information management."

"Over the past decade, we've grown Cremins's revenue by a factor of 10, while acquiring more than 15 companies to build critical mass in these areas. We've transformed business forms into business *communications.* We spread our wings across the country, no longer primarily focused in the Midwest; we have major operations now in Baltimore, San Diego, and elsewhere. We've organized into three groups: Commercial Printing, Business Communications, and Specialty Communications. But we still haven't begun to tap the potential of tying this all together and delivering the profitability and growth our shareholders deserve."

Evan was very compelling when he talked about strategy. It was clear that this strategic vision was critical to him, and it seemed like a lot of the ideas and the execution to date were his babies. He conveyed a strong sense of clarity of mission.

"We have been successful, as many separate companies, focusing on our own niches, but that isn't good enough anymore. We are under tremendous pressure from new technologies, the migration of paper-based communication to the Internet, and lower cost foreign competition. We need to combine our closeness to our customer bases in each of our divisions with our breadth of capability, from custom low-volume marketing communication to repetitive customer communication, like statement printing, to high-volume, high-efficiency printing of magazines and annual reports to pure information management like our innovative specialty businesses in healthcare and real estate."

Fusing All Company Capabilities and Making Them Available to All Sales Channels

Having given us an overview of how the company had changed in the past few years, Evan went on to sum up our new challenges.

"Here is where you come in. Our work over the past 2 years laid out a compelling business case for fusing our printing and information technology capabilities and making them available to each of our sales channels. Think of the benefits: our sales force on Wall Street could leverage the high-volume skills of our commercial printing plants; our sales force catering to the ad agencies for newspaper inserts could sell our business communication skills; our folks in hospitals could sell the data management skills in our real estate business. Our operations managers could manage our entire capability portfolio and ongoing investments to best tailor our capacity to our markets. And together we all define and protect a Cremins brand, known for customer-focused reliability, efficiency, and innovation."

"We've tried a lot of experiments over the past 2 years, some cross-selling training, some sharing of capacity across our groups, and learned a lot. One thing we learned is the extent to which our businesses rely on our systems to facilitate the flow of information and the amazing degree to which our systems are built in tight silos, tying each sales channel to the operations that support it. These systems are both technological and procedural, and over the years, it's become hard to know which is which because they are so intertwined. As we tried experiments to link our groups together more strongly, the need to change our systems became apparent."

"Some of you were involved in this work and know what I'm talking about. We have over a dozen major systems to support our sales efforts and perhaps 20 or more systems to manage the fulfillment of orders, invoicing, and accounts receivable. We don't have a consolidated view of our customers, any common way to manage sales commissions across our groups, several major Web presences, and no effective way for a sales person to find out what products or service might be available to fit a customer need. Our accounts payable systems are so fragmented that we routinely forgo lucrative volume discounts because our separate divisions don't know what each is buying. We need to change this and have shared systems when it makes sense, without going overboard and crippling our businesses with systems that fit everyone to some extent but no one well."

"No business takes on something like this lightly. If there were another way, we'd take it. But in today's system-dependent world, we've proven that we can't get the benefits we need for our customers and shareholders without undertaking a fundamental redesign of our supporting technology systems. The costs of doing this are so great that we can't do this in our silos. We need to pull together and build the next generation of systems for Cremins Corporation together and we need to do it quickly and well."

"Let me stop here and take questions if you have some."

Setting Expectations for the Project

At this point, Tom jumped back in, perhaps reflecting back to Frankie's earlier probing questions on requirements and scope. "Evan, thank you so much. You paint a very compelling picture for us. We understand that our next step is to get a time frame and objective before you and the board in late October. Can you tell us what you expect from our first delivery?"

"Sure, Tom. We need to deliver a working system as soon as we can that supports at least some part of all three major business units and shows the viability of the approach. The benefits are very high, so I'd expect a fairly significant spend. And we need to show how we can do this while limiting the risks. The board knows about the high failure rate of this type of effort in other companies, and, given the buzz about board accountability for risk management, it will be very demanding on ensuring that we have a good plan and strong controls. I know that Frankie has good experience and thoughts on how to do that."

There was a knock on the door, which opened to reveal Evan's assistant. She walked over to Evan, where they spoke quietly for a few moments. Evan frowned slightly and then looked up at us. "Tom, I'm really sorry, but I need to cut this just a little short. Let me end by thanking you all for your hard work so far and say that I'll be looking forward to a review of the plan a week or so before the board presentation ... say, around October 23. Let me know if you need more from me before that. Sorry, but I have to run." With that, Evan left the room to return to other pressing business.

I was pretty jazzed up from Evan's talk. This was a well-thought-out effort, the result of years of work and strategic evolution. I was very lucky to have this chance to bring strategy to life with this great leadership and on this scale!

Tom brought us back together. "Well, let's get going. Wes, I think you are prepared to help us finish out the planning work so that we can get this into high gear next week. We only have a month to get ready to put the plan in front of Evan."

Signposts	Cremins United project
	• Vision was clear: Fuse the printing and information technology capabilities and deliver them to all sales channels.
	• The Project Control Authority was created to manage the project. Key leaders were Tom Stillman, Frankie Alexander, Neil Gottschalk, assisted by narrator Jim "Wes" Wesleyan. The great fear was to get out of control; people and structure were chosen to minimize this risk.
	• The technology model was derived from BCG: "technology as vendor," rather than "technology as business."

- The board of directors blessed the next step in establishing the project, which was to determine detailed costs, benefits, scope and time line in 6 weeks' time.
- CEO Evan Nogelmeyer established some expectations: Deliver a working system "soon" to serve all three major business units to show the board that the approach was viable. Expenses were expected to be high, and it was understood that this was very large and risky.

Guidance from Wes

- Developing a software system is not like ordering a pizza. You can't just set a great vision, specify your requirements, and order them up from the technology department or a vendor. This flawed conception drove many things in CU, including at this stage the selection of a PCA that lacked the necessary skills and experience to drive a project of this magnitude, even though it had no doubt that it could!
- Getting "out of control" is certainly a major risk in a system development project, but there are other equally critical risks: not having or building the capability to deliver, failing to develop knowledge quickly enough, and setting scope too large compared to what's known and achievable.
- For a very large effort like CU, it's not feasible to compress the "study phase" to just 6 weeks. The development of the strategy has been going on for several years; why should the board expect, and the PCA agree to, the development of scope, time, and cost projections in just 6 weeks? Systems development projects should not skip so directly from vision to plan; TRIM's 6-month study phase, which includes extensive consultation around the development of detailed concept documents and a statement of work, is a much better model.

- Converting from broad vision to specific implementable plan can be driven by one question: What is the smallest, most valuable functionality we can put into production along our long-term architecture path?

Coming up next

Beth will take over narration and recount how, immediately following the staff meeting, Greg recruited Mary to the CU project. Mary and Beth learn that CU will be organized and run very differently from the way Real Estate Division projects are run.

3

Two Different Approaches to the Two Different Projects

SEPTEMBER 2005

Beth:

After Greg's staff meeting ended, Mary and I joined him in his office to discuss Mary's new assignment as the technical lead for the sales system for Cremins United. Greg's office was on the first floor, steps from the entrance to our building, with a view of the courtyard from his window. The wall adjacent to the window was entirely covered by whiteboard; in front of the whiteboard stood a small, round table with chairs, into which the three of us settled.

Greg had broached the Cremins United idea with Mary a few days ago, and we'd just reviewed it with the management team. Their reaction was multidimensional: dismay at losing Mary, pride at having one of our team be a leader in the Enterprise effort, and anticipation to see the collision of Mary's fierce independence and strong commitment to Lean/Agile development with Corporate's ponderous ways. Mary's reaction was even more complex, which is why I was here with her and Greg.

"Well, Mary, you've had a few days to think this over. I hope you don't mind, but I've asked Beth to join us in this conversation. Beth is going to be involved in Cremins United as well, as a member of the Human Resources/Communications team, working on the organizational change aspects, although she will be just part-time. You two will be our primary contributors. I think Beth can help you navigate some of the situations you'll find yourself in over the next year or so."

"Glad to have her here, Greg," Mary said, nodding at me. "I'm sure I can use the help!"

"Well, what do you think?"

"First, I want to thank you for the confidence you have in me and in the applicability of the sales systems we've built to a broader purpose. You know how much I love a grand adventure; this one looks like such a challenge that I wouldn't want to miss it!"

"It's not quite driving your Harley over the Rockies, Mary, but it's not going to be boring, either!"

"I do have some questions and concerns. First, I can't travel all that much. My ex-husband and my parents can watch my kids, who are older now, so I do have some flexibility, but I don't want to be gone more than several days a month. I'd think that the central team for CU would have to spend quite a bit of time together, and I don't see how this can work for me logistically."

Greg had discussed this issue and others when he and I first talked about giving Mary this assignment, after Greg's boss, Gina Sebastian, the president of the Specialty Communications Group (of which the Real Estate Division was a component), required Greg to contribute some meaningful leadership to the CU project. Mary was such a great choice in many ways. She had the experience with sales systems, both functionally and technically; she could bring along the technology she already managed as a starter kit; and she was ready for a new challenge, having mastered her current role and not having anything major on her plate, given our coming focus on TRIM. The concerns were travel and the risk that she would have a lot of conflict over how the project should be run. If the assignment ended in a deadlock between Mary and other project team leaders, it would be a disaster for her and for our division. It was one of my missions to be sure that didn't happen.

Building a Virtual Team

"Mary," I said, "Greg and I had the same concern. I checked up through the HR lead for CU. He says that Cremins is a geographically diverse company now, and the plan is to limit travel for the project. We need to learn how to work effectively over distance, so we're going to rely on conference calls and maybe some video conferencing, rather than depend on getting together physically."

"Interesting. Well, I suppose that could be okay, depending on how we architect the system components and interfaces. If we allocate major sub-systems to geographically focused teams and do enough intense interface planning, design, and end-to-end simulations, we might make that work. But how about for my own team? I won't be comfortable building out the sales system over the phone or by passing documents around. I can't lead the sales system if I can't get my team and the critical interfacing teams together regularly."

Mary's rapid, thoughtful, and direct reaction was typical for her. She was very focused on getting results and quite set in her way of doing things. She could make compromises to some extent, but when directions from others threatened successful delivery, Mary would stand her ground. These qualities attracted Greg and Gina to the idea of putting Mary on Cremins United and also worried them.

On most topics related to how to organize and execute software development, Greg and Mary were on precisely the same page. They had, after all, worked together before in two other companies, and both of them would be happy to keep working together until they retired. On the topic of in-person time, Greg was completely with Mary. He believed strongly that there was no substitute for extended time in person for a team to function effectively. He had checked this out as well with Gina and had assurance that the budget and policies would allow Mary to get her subteam together as she needed but to expect limited in-person meetings for the larger project team.

Greg relayed Gina's support to Mary and assured her of the ability to manage her subteam as she needed, within certain boundaries to be determined. "Also, Mary, you can focus your development team here in San Diego; to the extent you need added people, you can add them here."

"Great, that solves my travel problem. Next, my role. I understand it is 'technical lead for sales.' How do they define that? Am I chief engineer? My understanding is that Corporate doesn't have this role, and I'm worried I might wind up being treated as a software coding vendor—given requirements and designs to implement instead of driving the development to meet the business goals."

A New Organizational Approach

This was another question for Greg to answer; I didn't fully understand what Mary meant by the question. "Well, Mary, the CU project is being organized somewhat differently than we would do it. Let me draw you a picture." With that, Greg got out of his chair, grabbed a marker, and drew a diagram on the wall (see Figure 6).

As he drew, Greg narrated, "Each major area—Sales, Finance, Production Management, Product/Service, and Management Information—is going to have a team of three leaders. I'll just draw out the Sales team here; the others look the same: one business lead, one technical lead, and one project lead. The *business lead* is responsible for dealing with the business liaison group around priorities and high-level requirements and then driving to detailed requirements and priorities within the area. The *technical lead* is responsible for technical design, build, and unit testing. Finally, the *project*

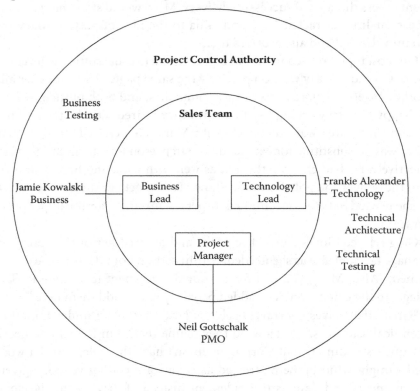

FIGURE 6
Cremins United team structure.

manager is responsible for putting the plan together and managing to it, keeping track of issues, and managing the money."

"Each of the three area leads reports up to an overall lead on the PCA: the business people to Jamie Kawolski, the technical leads to Frankie Alexander, and the project managers to Neil Gottschalk. Then there is a separate testing group—actually, two groups: one to do 'technical' testing that reports to the central Cremins Technology Testing Department and another group of business testers reporting to the deployment lead on the PCA to do acceptance testing. Oh, and there is a Central Architecture Group to ensure that all the technologies fit together and comply with the Cremins strategic technology plan."

This was the first time that Mary had heard how CU intended to organize, and I could see skepticism on her face. I knew that Mary had spent the better part of 15 years doing some pretty impressive software development projects. She had an intense desire to understand and improve how things worked, and high on that list was how to get software done effectively. The diagram that Greg had just drawn was clearly not how she would organize things!

"Well, this is another whole can of worms. Where is the leadership and accountability? It comes together vertically at the PCA in a committee? Greg, how can that work? Even just for my piece, who winds up to be accountable for sales? I'm not sure I can live with that. I also don't think I can let the testers be outside my group entirely or have my architecture be set for to me from outside."

"You are preaching to the choir, Mary, and you know that. I'm pretty sure Gina understands this also. The problem is that the PCA is led by people who haven't done a lot of hands-on technology projects; their two key folks putting this structure together are Frankie and Neil, both of whom are taking a highly control- and process-oriented approach. They believe this structure is the best way to reduce risks and ensure delivery, and the consultants from GRI they are using to help manage the project are reinforcing that belief. You and I know what a chimera that is. You'll have to do the best you can to deliver your part of the project, and you'll need to influence the other areas as best you can to help them succeed as well. In a way, you have a twofold mission."

"Wow. You know I'm not exactly a smooth politician. This is going to be very tough for me," Mary said, quite subdued now.

"I couldn't think of a better challenge for you now, Mary. You've proven that you can deliver great work when you are in control and in an organization aligned with your belief system. You want that next challenge, and you have the talent to rise to the next level in this company. You see the potential benefits of the CU vision, and you can see, like Gina and I can, how much they need your help. Now your challenge will be to get great work done when you aren't in full control, to balance your need for autonomy with being part of a larger effort, and to influence and teach others with different beliefs who may not really want to learn. I will support you every step of the way, as will Gina when we need her, and Beth will be with you as a counselor and, I hope, a friend."

Greg followed up, "More questions?"

"Will I remain a part of your team as well?" Mary sounded almost as if she were pleading as she asked this.

"Absolutely. Our team will support you in developing the sales subsystem, and you'll need to keep us in the loop as the other parts of the system impact us. So you continue to come to my staff meeting, and you might need to pitch in a little to help Neville with TRIM."

Mary liked this answer, but had one more question. "What if the whole project falls apart? What happens to me?"

At this, Greg paused and a somber look appeared on his face. "There is certainly some risk there. You will formally be joining the CU team, reporting to Frankie Alexander, and your salary will be coming from the project budget. Your immediate fate will be out of my hands, so I can't make any promises other than my personal respect and admiration for you and my eagerness to have you working with me whatever I'm doing. But I can't guarantee anything at all."

It was Mary's turn to pause. Her natural optimism was now tempered by the challenges and risks she saw ahead, but her belief in the basic rightness of the CU idea and her spoiling for adventure won out.

"There is a lot I don't like about this—the structure, my role, the risk to my job—but, OK, I'll do it. I don't see how I can miss out on something this big, and you're right, it's just the thing for me now with our focus on TRIM. Neville can get that done without much of my help, and I'd guess that'll take most of our development groups anyhow."

Greg leaned back in his chair and smiled. He'd believed that Mary couldn't resist this challenge and was happy to see her take the bait.

"Fantastic. I'll let Gina know. Beth, can you notify CU human resources? The PCA is in the midst of putting together the next layer of management for each area, and I think they want to put out a communication by the end of this week. Mary, you do need to be in St. Paul next Tuesday through Thursday; can you manage that?"

"I think so; it's my ex-husband's week with the kids. I just need to confirm that he doesn't need me for anything."

"Great; then it's a go."

If I was going to be of use to Mary, I knew I had to get more up to speed on what was so wrong with the PCA organizational structure; plus, I hadn't received my Lean and Agile primer yet. "Mary," I said, "can we schedule our primer session now? I can see that I'm going to need it. And maybe when we do that you can explain more of your concerns with the CU structure."

"Sure, Beth, I'd be happy to. Is your calendar up to date?"

"Yup."

"I'll send you an invite, and we'll get together for an hour later this week. OK?"

"It's a deal."

Signposts	Cremins United project
	• Mary O'Connell, from the Real Estate Division, agreed to join as technology lead for the Sales team. Mary's management wanted her to help that part of CU succeed, as well as influence the project as a whole.
	• The project intended to operate in a virtual environment as much as it could; Mary had permission to get her team physically together as she needed.
	• Mary and Greg were concerned about CU's organizational structure. Leadership and accountability were too diffused in functional groups (Project Management, Testing, Architecture) instead of relying on strong chief engineers.
	• Beth was also taking a minor role in CU, on the organizational change team. Greg wanted her to help Mary succeed on the CU team, so Beth needed to get a better understanding of what Mary's cherished Lean and Agile was all about.

Guides from Beth

- System development is about how teams of people transform ideas into working code, and people work best face to face. If your team can't be completely co-located, some options are:
  - By all means, use virtual tools—teleconference, video, shared Web sites.
  - Organize geographically by component or subassembly and integrate virtually. Ensure there is enough face time (initially, err on the side of too much).
  - Place intense and early focus on interfaces and end-to-end simulations.
- When projects are large enough to demand breaking into smaller teams, ensure that business-area-focused teams (such as Mary's Sales team) have clear and strong leadership, such as a chief engineer. In Toyotas's LPD, the specialized groups are known as "Model Development Teams."[1]
- Development teams need architecture and testing to be tightly integrated and directed by the chief engineer. The staff members can be organized in many ways (e.g., directly reporting to the chief engineer or to functional groups); what's important is a common focus on delivery of business value.
- Develop staff with "towering technical competence," like Mary. To do this, you need to leave people in jobs long enough to develop depth, and help them turn their eyes outward to the competition and to mastering their fields.

Coming up next

Beth continues narrating a few days later as she gets her Lean and Agile primer lesson from Mary.

---

[1]Morgan, J. M. and Liker, J. K. 2006. Building highly expert, well-led module teams can be a foundational, organizational strategy. *The Toyota Product Development System*. pp. 154 ff. New York: Productivity Press.

4

Understanding Lean and Agile Development

SEPTEMBER 2005

Beth:

When one begins a new job (which I've only done a few times), one can be immersed in a world with its own language, customs, and rules. That's what I was feeling after my first few weeks at Cremins. Greg and his team had been together for several years and adopted, or maybe built, a way of doing things that was quite different from what I was used to in computer hardware design and manufacturing. I needed a crib sheet to it all, and that's what Mary had promised to give me. She did so literally, over a couple of glasses of wine.

Mary's ex-husband had her kids this week, so I e-mailed her and asked if she'd like to go out for a leisurely drink and dinner. Thursday worked, so we agreed to leave work around 5:30 and head off to a restaurant in Del Mar. I'm originally from Kansas, so I love the ocean, and Jose's Fish Emporium has a nice outdoor patio right on the beach. We both drove so that we could each go directly home; she was waiting at a table, next to the railing, nursing a glass of wine when I walked in. I ordered a glass as well, and after some chit-chat waiting for it to arrive, we began.

"Mary, thank you so much for doing this. I've been thinking about what you said last week about the CU approach and really want to hear more of your thoughts."

"Well, you have a fair amount of experience observing technology development, albeit hardware not software. What do you think of the approach?" retorted Mary.

I hadn't expected to be asked this; I thought I was just getting a lesson, so I had to think a moment. I had a lot of ideas running around in my head that I hadn't pulled together yet, but I did have some early conclusions. "It concerns me. It sounds bureaucratic and fragmented. I'm used to development with the engineers at the center; here it seems that the engineers are viewed more as cogs in a big, tightly orchestrated machine."

"Sounds like you see some of the issues. How about I show you the model we've been using to describe our development approach, and I tell you about some of the key principles? Then I can give you a list of some more material to read at your leisure. Any chance you can attend Neville's planning session next week? If you read his statement of work and attend the planning session, you'll get quite a bit of the details of our approach, and I can stick to some of the principles today."

"Sure," I said, "I'll be around and I think Neville would be okay with me listening in. Greg's been encouraging me to spend time observing how we do things, so I need to do that anyhow."

"Well, let's get started. Here, let me give you our cheat sheet."

Getting Up to Speed on Lean and Agile

With that, Mary pulled a copy of a chart out of the folder in front of her (Figure 7).[1] "This is the current version of the chart we use internally to train new people and help our staff understand the nature of what we are trying to do. The basic framework originally came from Japan, especially Toyota.[2] We've tried not to use any of the Japanese words in our communication because we've found they build a barrier between us and people whom we are trying to teach."

I had been curious about where this all came from; Mary's explanation answered some of my questions—but not all. "I hadn't heard that Toyota was a great software company; in fact, I've heard that their software technology isn't as sophisticated as some of their competitors' because they are skeptical of benefits and tend to wait for proven technology."

"Well, I don't know about their software technology," said Mary, "but the Lean product development techniques they use for automobile development seem to fit software development equally well. Their car development

Lean & Agile Development

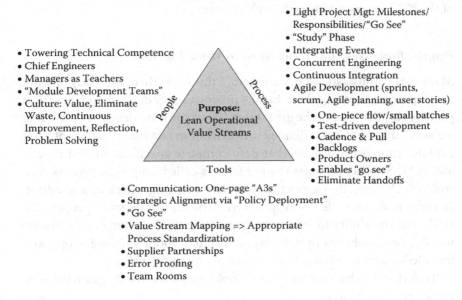

- Towering Technical Competence
- Chief Engineers
- Managers as Teachers
- "Module Development Teams"
- Culture: Value, Eliminate Waste, Continuous Improvement, Reflection, Problem Solving

People

Purpose:
Lean Operational
Value Streams

Process

- Light Project Mgt: Milestones/ Responsibilities/"Go See"
- "Study" Phase
- Integrating Events
- Concurrent Engineering
- Continuous Integration
- Agile Development (sprints, scrum, Agile planning, user stories)
  - One-piece flow/small batches
  - Test-driven development
  - Cadence & Pull
  - Backlogs
  - Product Owners
  - Enables "go see"
  - Eliminate Handoffs

Tools

- Communication: One-page "A3s"
- Strategic Alignment via "Policy Deployment"
- "Go See"
- Value Stream Mapping => Appropriate Process Standardization
- Supplier Partnerships
- Error Proofing
- Team Rooms

FIGURE 7

Lean and Agile software development. (Adapted from Morgan, J. M. and Liker, J. K. 2006. *The Toyota Product Development System*. New York: Productivity Press, p. 18)

has been the most successful in the world, and it's not an accident. Some parts of their Lean manufacturing approach also seem to fit well.[3] Of course, we don't just copy them; we've incorporated other good ideas that seem to fit us well."

This was intriguing. "Like what?" I asked.

"Well, before much at all was known about Lean, Greg became a devotee of the Microsoft Solutions framework.[4] He was doing project management then, and the division of the world into 'business' and 'technology' people didn't make any sense to him. He loved some of the ideas articulated there—small teams, six roles rather than two, teams of peers, overlapping responsibilities, and everyone focused on shipping code. He still has all of us read some MSF material; I keep some of those documents in a folder right behind my desk. More recently, the Agile Manifesto[5] spoke to a lot of what Greg and our other leaders believe, and it implemented some of the Lean concepts, like pull, flow, and cadence, for software development."

I wondered how this all came together. "Is there a unifying concept to all of this?" I was eager to hear Mary's answer.

People, Processes, and Tools Need to Work Together

Mary was enthusiastic in her answer: "I think so. There is a body of work about process control, which breaks processes into defined and empirical process control. One of the great tragedies of software development is that we've tried to treat it as a defined process, but in fact many aspects of it are actually complex processes that defy complete specification and repeatability.[6] Complex processes require what is called 'empirical process control,' which basically means that you do something, check it, and adjust. In order to do that effectively, you have to have great people—people with skills and the ability to work together effectively. Building great software to solve new problems in new ways is as much about building people and knowledge as it is about actually building the software."

"Describe the chart for me," I said, looking again at the diagram between us on the dinner table.

"In the middle of the triangle, you see the purpose of our work: to build Lean operational value streams. In the Lean manufacturing world, that has specific meaning about providing the customer with what she values—nothing more—and avoidance of waste. Everyone on the team has to understand what we are trying to build because everyone is making decisions every day and needs that 'true north.'"

"In order to build the value streams effectively, we need three supporting dimensions fulfilled: people, tools, and processes. They're the three sides of the triangle—like three legs of a tripod. *People* are the most important— expert people, with great leadership, assembled together in the right kinds of teams, with a powerful culture of customer focus, waste elimination, and continuous improvement."

Mary was rolling now; her passion shone: "But the people need to work together in a common *process* that helps them learn quickly and does not burden them with waste. So all of this information on the right side of the triangle that pertains to process is also important. For example, project management must be lightweight so that the teams can be flexible and not be overwhelmed with useless tasks and information. Management has to rely on seeing results, rather than on reports; they need to go see for themselves. We need integrating events to focus all our attention on common goals and reveal issues on the path, and we need to take time to study the way forward before jumping too quickly. We need to be sure we consider options, sometimes even going so far as to build the same function two different ways so that we can learn which one works better or to take the best from two or more approaches and integrate them into one best solution."

"I'd heard about concurrent engineering in my old company," I responded, noting that this was one of the components of process on Mary's chart. "We sometimes asked two or more of our suppliers to compete in designing a component for us, and then either chose the best one or asked companies to work together to build a hybrid."

Mary nodded approvingly. "It's sometimes a great approach, although within a single company, it's often viewed as wasteful, instead of being seen as a way to accelerate learning and reduce risks. Consideration of options is the same—often we see a single answer being given and the proper thoughts not being explored. Standard software methodology reinforces this: We hand off requirements to the designers, who give THE design to the developers. The need to explore and learn is mostly missing from the 'standard' software development approaches."

Mary paused a moment, took a sip of wine, and continued describing the core process elements listed on her chart.

"The next process group is straight from Lean manufacturing: We need to build software with one-piece flow, visual management, and cadence and pull. In manufacturing, this means the elimination of batches and pacing build to customer demand. So far in software, the 'Agile' techniques of sprints, scrums, and Agile planning are the best we've seen in providing an approach that does this. The critical commonality to manufacturing is the elimination of batches. We try to build one piece at a time, going from requirements through design, build, and test as quickly as we can and continuously integrating the results in software that is always ready to ship, even though it isn't functionally complete."

"Should I continue or do you need a little break here?" asked Mary.

"I think I'm following you. It doesn't seem like there is any magic here," I said. "The concepts aren't all that foreign to me, although I have no idea what on earth 'scrum' stands for."

Mary beamed back at me. "That is exactly right, Beth. There are no silver bullets in this; it's all just common sense. The trick is to take this common sense and build people and organizations that can execute. What do people say—common sense is anything but common?" Mary saw me nod and added, "Oh, and don't worry about scrum just yet. It's just what we call a special kind of team meeting, named after that weird sort of huddle they do in rugby."

Taking a breath and a sip of wine, Mary continued.

"The last dimension is about *tools*. This is the third side of the triangle, and it's just as important as people and process. Unfortunately, some companies that are trying to implement Lean, whether in manufacturing or product development, start with the tools and never get beyond them. That can help, but it won't result in a sustainable Lean enterprise. Anyhow, one of the key ones we use are the A3s. A3 is a paper size used overseas, a little bigger than legal size; it's just a way of distilling problems or proposals down to their essence and communicating effectively. Value stream mapping is a kind of process flow on steroids that helps you see and eliminate waste. The final thing I'll mention is supplier partnerships; this is related to expertise in the people dimension, but also concerns how we reach outside our company in win–win partnerships."

"Wow, that is quite an extensive set of ideas," I said. "Have you written this all up in a detailed guide? Something like, 'The Cremins Real Estate Division Development Manual'?"

Mary laughed. "That would be silly; why would we do that? By the time we wrote it up it would be obsolete, and if people really followed it, the process would freeze in place. Also, the details of its application are too complicated to make it into a cookbook. As I said, each project is so different and even each step within each project so complex, that it's too hard to specify the steps precisely. It really requires people who know how to do the work and how to work together. We need to improve and adjust what we do continually; we can't simply document a process and follow it. This chart is about the extent of it."

How Can You Improve If You Don't Standardize?

I must have had a frown on my face because Mary said, "What's the matter? You seem puzzled."

I was. "That doesn't make sense to me from what I know from Lean manufacturing. Our network equipment manufacturing group was religious about standardizing the work. They repeatedly said that if you didn't have standard work processes, you couldn't improve them. They went to great lengths to define standard ways of doing the work, even putting up big pictures at each factory station on what to do and how to do it. Then they measured, watched, and experimented, and only then did they make changes. Now you are telling me just the opposite!"

"Ah, yes, one of the great confusions. In some ways it's too bad 'Lean product development' got that name; because it came from Toyota and had some similarities to Lean manufacturing, the name stuck. Perhaps a better name might be 'knowledge-based product development.'[7] We need to be really careful to separate two kinds of work: predictable, repetitive work, which we need to standardize and continuously improve, and unpredictable, creative work in which we need to focus relentlessly on knowledge creation and application. Unfortunately, it's not a simple task to put efforts into one category or another because most things share elements of both. It takes smart, experienced people to apply the right techniques and approaches to the right problem; even then, different people, with different skills and aptitudes, can successfully choose somewhat different approaches."

I still wasn't completely following Mary on this. "So there is no room in software development for rigorous standardization?" I said. "That sounds so radical! I can't see how that can work. In order for us to sell our network gear to the Pentagon, we had to meet a lot of audit requirements. The development teams had a very standard, controlled path they had to follow, with milestones that had to be met before we'd get paid and they could continue forward."

Mary leaned forward and sighed. "Remember what I said about different approaches for different applications? The process you'd use to build, say, software for an artificial heart or a nuclear reactor control module would likely be much different from how you'd build an informational Web site. Even within a Web site, you'd take different approaches for a new type of user interface than you would for a series of control reports. The user interface would be about experimenting and learning, while you'd like to treat the writing of a large number of routine reports more like a standardized manufacturing task. It's not that we *reject* standardization of software processes; rather, it's that we want to use the *right* process for the problem at hand. When we have a highly standardizable process, even within a larger process that isn't so standardizable, we want it rigorously standardized. When we have something new, with many unknowns, we want to focus on knowledge creation and sharing, and constant evaluation and course correction. Unfortunately, most new system development projects are in the latter category."

"This gets back to how we help our teams understand and improve our development processes. We do a lot of information sharing among our groups on what works and what doesn't, and we put our deliverables and documentation online for folks to read and copy, if they fit. We encourage staff to read the literature on Lean manufacturing, Lean product development, Agile development, and whatever else can help us. We don't need to reinvent the wheel on this knowledge: It's being developed and improved by people all over the world. Oh, and we have quite extensive knowledge development plans for our teams, showing what they need to know at each stage of their careers and how to get it; people on your staff manage that program, don't they?"

"They sure do. It's a very impressive training plan and seems so connected to the line management," I replied. I'd been very happily surprised by the development plans that I'd seen. "How do our team members know how to apply this information? Seems like there would be a lot of ways to do it wrong."

"It's the accountability of all our managers to be sure their people are trained and to help them apply training to the jobs they are doing. Our managers are the keepers of our culture, our lead trainers."

The Root of the Difference in Project Management Approaches

I changed topics here, thinking about the differences between Mary's methods and those of Cremins United. "I think I see a difference between this approach and the CU approach already. In the CU approach, the 'technical' leaders are to build what the 'business' leads specify in accordance with tightly defined rules, while in this approach, the technical leaders really need to understand what they are building and build the people, culture, and knowledge as well. Is that why you didn't like the role slotted for you?"

"It's one reason, yes. In the Lean/Agile approach, my role is what we call 'chief engineer,' a very powerful and accountable position. I'll let you see that in action from Neville next week. I'm used to taking that broader ownership role and I'm just not sure how well I'll fit into a narrower definition. But it's not just that: I think it will be tough on me to operate in a non-Lean/Agile environment. I've been working with Greg and his team for years, building out the reinforcing legs of our own Lean and Agile triangle, continually improving down that path. I worry about how I'll fit into the whole CU endeavor, how I might help it build its own Lean and Agile triangle, and whether my contributions will be welcomed or flat-out rejected."

By now it was dark, and we could hear the waves but not see them. I could sense that Mary was getting a bit tired of talking about work and also was worried about what was to become of her in the CU project. So I decided we'd had enough work talk for the night.

"I'm sure you'll do fine, Mary, and I'll be there to support you. Greg will be, as well. Why don't we get another glass of wine and study the menu, instead of this brilliant chart of yours?"

With that, I picked up the menu that had been hiding on the table under my new chart and began looking for another kind of lean—maybe a steak.

Signposts	**TRIM project**
	• The project would be led according to Lean and Agile principles.
	• These approaches had been developed systematically in the Real Estate Division for several years and incorporated into business management mechanisms culturally applied by the division's managers.
	• TRIM's success would be determined by the quality of the division's people, the development of whom had been an intense focus.
	Cremins United project
	• The project would be led according to defined process control principles.
	• The principles would be enforced through organizational structures unifying each major function. Thus, the Testing Group controlled testing, PMO controlled project management, and PCA controlled it all.
	• People were viewed as interchangeable resources to accomplish specified tasks.

Guides from Beth

- Lean product development (LPD) is a set of ideas that have radiated from Toyota and other manufacturing companies. Many of the ideas apply equally well to software development. Agile software development, as articulated in the Agile Manifesto, came from a group of leading practitioners. Although it didn't intend to do so, Agile methods are a specific implementation of LPD process goals.
- Lean manufacturing also radiated from Toyota. Among other precepts, it seeks rigorous standardization to enable elimination of waste. Many of its principles also apply to systems development.
- Successful systems development requires understanding when to focus on the tools of Lean product development (for "empirical process control") versus the tools of Lean manufacturing (for "defined process control").
- Lean and Agile systems development is a three-legged stool, suggesting techniques for each leg. While there is value in implementing techniques independently, larger value is available by adopting multiple parts of the overall scheme.

Coming up next

My narrating partner, Wes Wesleyan, will resume telling the Cremins United tale the following week in early October. The second level of leadership is brought to St. Paul to create the plan for presentation to the board of directors in 6 weeks, and they learn that they will follow "The Process."

NOTES

1. Figure 7 is adapted from Jeffrey K. Liker's earlier book, *A Toyota Leader's View of the Toyota Production System. The Toyota Way*. 2004. McGraw Hill. The adaptation is to fit software development better and to highlight the items I think are most important. As Mary says in the text, this chart is just one team's summary of the approach; other summaries, such as the Poppendiecks' (see note 3), are equally valid and powerful.
2. The best overall exposition of Toyota's product development system is found in Morgan and Liker, 2006.

3. A good comparison of Lean manufacturing to Lean development can be found in Mary and Tom Poppendieck, *Implementing Lean Software Development,* Upper Saddle River, NJ: Addison–Wesley, 2007. The summary is on page 14, Table 1.1, of the book.
4. My favorite explanation of Microsoft's approach to software development is Michael Cusumano's *Microsoft Secrets: How the World's Most Powerful Software Company Creates Technology, Shapes Markets and Manages People,* 1st Touchstone ed., New York: Free Press, December 4, 1998. The book is getting a little dated now but remains very fresh to those who have not been exposed to the ideas. The current material from Microsoft is at (as of January 2008): http://www.microsoft.com/technet/solutionac-celerators/msf/default.mspx. I have found the team model to be the most powerful aspect of the approach and believe the team model carries directly over into today's "Agile" approaches.
5. AgileManifesto.org. See also Alistair Cockburn, *Agile Software Development,* Appendix A, Upper Saddle River, NJ: Pearson Education, 2002. See also Neville's presentation on page 179.
6. See, for example, Ken Schwaber and Mike Beedle, *Agile Development with Scrum,* Chapter 5, "Why Scrum?" Upper Saddle River, NJ: Prentice Hall, 2002.
7. Michael N. Kennedy, *Lean Product Development for the Enterprise,* Richmond, VA: the Oaklea Press, 2003. I owe a debt of gratitude to Mr. Kennedy for what he taught me in his book, plus the inspiration to try to do a good deed for software development similar to what he did for engineered product development.

5

The CU Project Team Will Follow "The Process"

OCTOBER 2005

Wes:

"Let's get going." It was early Tuesday morning, and Neil Gottschalk, the Cremins United project's Finance and Project Management Office lead, was standing at the front of the conference room at Cremins headquarters in downtown St. Paul, surveying 45 Cremins team members and consultants. He proceeded to manage the obligatory introductions, a lot of new names for almost everyone in the room. While the Cremins United strategy had been cooking along for almost 2 years by now, this was the first time this level of technology and project staffers had been brought together for the implementation project and given their mission. We had business leads, project management leads, and technology leads for each major area of the project, plus the overall project management leads, architects, and business liaisons—and, of course, me, in my role described as chief of staff for the Project Control Authority.

"Great," Neil said, smiling at the room. "This is our official kickoff meeting for the Cremins United project, finally getting around to implementation of our strategy. Many of you are new to this and to each other, which is an exciting sign of progress! We have taken strategy and planning well along in the past 2 years. We've identified the opportunity, made cross-business line connections, and created high-level visions and somewhat more detailed blueprints for where we want to go. We've learned that we need extensive system modifications in order for us to get to where we need to be, and we've reached out all over the company for you all, the people we think can make this happen."

"Let me lay out the next few days for you. First, for those of you from out of town, thanks for coming to St. Paul. We wanted to get this meeting in before the snow. We don't expect an excessive amount of travel in this project because we think we can be effective managing this virtually using a clear process, defined deliverables and reviews, and regular conference calls."

"This morning we will kick off the week with your marching orders and expectations from the PCA. Wes here has been working with us, and he will convey our basic expectations on how this project will be organized and run. Then my boss on the project, Tom Stillman, the overall PCA leader, will give you our first challenge, which is getting the PCA ready for a presentation to the board of directors in late October, which is just a few weeks away. The remainder of the time we have together—till the end of the day on Thursday—has been left open for you to use as you wish to get organized and do planning. We'll have meetings with this whole group and the entire PCA at the end of the day on Wednesday and Thursday to report on where we are and provide the opportunity for you to raise any issues or ask for any help you might need. We also have a nice dinner and drinks planned Wednesday evening at the hotel; I hope you all can make it."

"Wes, would you like to begin?"

Going for Broke instead of Starting Small

My turn. I'd worked for days on this presentation. I knew how important first impressions were from my days in consulting, so I wanted to get this off on the right foot. It wasn't always easy to represent the PCA in this sort of thing.

"Welcome," I began, and I started going through the PowerPoint slides. I began with some background on the project, summarized the visions and blueprint, described the project structure and the PCA's role and members, and laid out the initial objectives as Evan had provided them to the PCA a few weeks ago. I explained how we sought to fuse the printing and information technology capabilities and deliver them to all sales channels. I gave them Evan's challenge to us to deliver a working system "soon" serving all three major business units to show the board that the Cremins

United strategy is viable, as well as his expectation that this was going to be expensive.

There weren't many questions until after I'd explained the objectives. An attractive woman, maybe approaching 40 years old, raised her hand as I explained the initial goal.

"Hi, Wes. I'm Mary O'Connell, from the Real Estate Division, responsible for sales technology for the project. I understand that to get broad buy-in, you want to do an initial implementation that would include all three major business groups—Commercial Printing, Business Communications, and Specialty Communications—and that could have certain benefits in helping us ensure that the solutions we build are general enough to support the whole company. I'm wondering if it might be safer to pick something a little smaller as our first implementation: We could plan for the larger scope, but actually do something more quickly, with less risk, and with some earlier business benefits on the way."

"Good question, Mary, thank you. This very question was discussed rather extensively both at the PCA and at the steering committee. As I explained earlier, the steering committee is made up of Evan and the leaders of each business group, plus technology, legal, and finance. In order to prove the viability of the Cremins United premise, we need to get a system into production as quickly as we can that shows how the various sales channels can sell products and services from more than one business group and demonstrates how we can better manage our production capacity. Implementing something smaller might be useful as an interim step, but doesn't meet the basic objectives of the project. So, our mission will be to plan and deliver a solution that meets those minimal goals—nothing less."

Mary was frowning at this, and a woman at her side who I soon found out was Beth Dumas, director of Human Resources for Mary's division and my future co-author, was whispering in her ear, with her hand on Mary's arm. Mary smiled at the woman, shook her head, and looked back up at me. "I won't belabor the point, Wes, but we are going to have an awful lot of new technologies in this project being assembled by a group that hasn't worked together like this before. Everything I know tells me that we need smaller, interim goals to test out the system as we build it: not only the technology, but also the requirements and designs."

"Nothing I said precludes the establishment of interim goals and milestones, Mary. In fact, establishing those is one of the things we want to accomplish over the next few weeks. We can talk more about this offline later, if you wish. Okay for me to go on?"

Mary nodded, although I could tell she wasn't convinced. I'm not sure I understood her point completely, but her confidence was attractive. I made a mental note to be sure to get to know her a little better this week if I could.

Managing Project Risk

I continued with the next section of my PowerPoint presentation. "That was actually a nice lead-in to the next topic, 'risk management and project process.' As we began to move into this implementation phase, the PCA looked all over the company for best practices that we could adopt for the project, instead of trying to reinvent the wheel, so to speak. We were very fortunate to have found, in Frankie Alexander's team in BCG, a detailed methodology and people who know how to implement it. Frankie has been managing much of BCG's technology through their outsourcer, Global Resources; you all probably know them as GRI."

"In order to manage risk, priorities, and costs, Frankie and GRI together have specified a detailed technology process flow; each deliverable is clearly specified, with explicit, formal, documented sign-offs at each step. GRI has provided a set of tools for project management; they include the ability to document each requirement and trace that requirement through design, development, and testing to ensure that all requirements are met. They will also provide us a project management system so that we can keep a consolidated, complete project plan and be able to track whenever something begins to slip so that we can address issues early. I understand that the project system is so sophisticated that it can automatically generate the tasks required to follow the process correctly!"

I stopped to take a breath and look up at my audience. The PCA had been very excited to embrace Frankie's and GRI's contributions to management; Neil, in particular, was enchanted with such an organized, methodical, and controlled approach. I was a little surprised when, in surveying my audience, I saw Mary O'Connell again in somewhat agitated conversation with the woman next to her.

"Mary, do you have a question?" I asked her.

"No, thanks Wes. I'd like to hear the rest of the presentation."

I think her self-control might have had a little leak at that point because she hesitated and then went on. "I am concerned that the approach you are proposing isn't appropriate for what we are trying to do. But I'll just listen to the rest, and then perhaps we can talk it over in the next few days."

At this, Neil Gottschalk, who had been quietly leaning against the counter along the inside of the conference room, walked up to the front of the room and assumed center stage. "Wes, I'd like to emphasize something on behalf of the PCA at this point. I think Mary said the word 'proposed' with respect to the project methodology, and we need to be clear that isn't what we have in mind. This is a large, risky, and important project, and we want everyone to understand that following the CU process is not a proposal; it's a requirement. Each of you probably has his or her own favorite way of doing things, and we do want you to bring into the project your talent and experience—that's why you were chosen. But we can't all be doing things in different ways or we'll have chaos. We need to have an organized, methodical, predictable method that can keep us all on the same page and ensure that we know at all times exactly where the project is."

Neil surveyed the room, almost as if he were asking for objections now. I was worried about what Mary might say; it was pretty clear that she had some serious issues with what she'd heard so far. But it wasn't Mary who spoke up now; it was the woman sitting next to her.

"I'm Beth Dumas, Real Estate Division Human Resources, helping the organizational change team. Neil, thank you for the clarity; it's great to get such good communication on what is firmly set and what remains open. Wes, what do we call this process we will be following?"

I was grateful for Beth's intervention; Mary was back to doodling on her notepad. "Its formal name is the Cremins Development and Risk Control Process, but everyone calls it 'the development process' or just 'The Process.' I think those of you who haven't seen it yet will be pleased by it; it draws on industry best practices such as the capability maturity model, the project management institute, and the rational unified process, and it supports those ideas with some added innovations from GRI and Frankie's team." I saw some heads nodding in the audience; some of these folks knew about these best practices. Because I'd had only tangential involvement with software development projects of any scale, I hadn't worked with any of them; however, I'd done some research and they seemed like respected and widely used methods, and I was comfortable representing the PCA in this decision.

I continued through the PowerPoint presentation, every now and then taking a look at Mary to see her reaction. I thought I saw actual sneers when I described the project management audits to ensure that the process was being followed, and when I talked about traceability. She listened intently and made some notes, but didn't speak up again. She did periodically confer quietly with Beth. I wondered what she might be thinking. I knew that it wasn't enthusiastic agreement.

Signposts	**Cremins United project**
	• A broader team charged with implementation was brought together in St. Paul.
	• Evan's objectives were communicated: rapid implementation of a system that serves all three major units; cost shouldn't be a barrier.
	• Neil made it very clear that The Process had been established to guide the CU project and that following it was not optional.
Guides from Beth	• Setting boundaries clearly, as Neil does with his expectations to follow "The Process," can help a team avoid spinning. Just be sure they are the right boundaries!
Coming up next	Beth continues narrating immediately following the meeting. The CU leaders break up into their functional teams. Mary and Beth attend the Technology breakout and hear about the technology architecture.

6

The CU Project Imposes Technology Architecture from the Top

OCTOBER 2005

Beth:

After the kickoff meeting Tuesday morning, Mary and I had time to stop by a coffee shop for my necessary latte. Mary was pretty upset with the approach and with Neil's dictatorial insistence that The Process be followed. As we walked, we chatted about how she should approach this. I counseled her to hold her criticism, to keep an open mind, and to think carefully about how she could help. I was growing to like and respect her more and more, and the last thing I wanted to see was for her to burn her bridges to the CU leadership prematurely by seeming to be a know-it-all or too critical. Plus, Greg would probably push me off the Coronado Bridge if I let that happen so soon. Mary seemed receptive to my counsel. She was a big believer in what CU was trying to accomplish and excited to get going, but a bit bamboozled by how this was all going to work. Well, more was about to be revealed, as we walked over to Frankie's first CU technology staff meeting.

"Welcome to the first staff meeting of the Cremins United Technology team," Frankie kicked the meeting off. Once more, we did introductions— this time, names, organizations, roles, and, for good measure, one thing we each thought was critical to ensure success of the project. One by one, the technology leads for the business areas of Finance, Production

Management, Product/Service, and Management Information (and, of course, Mary for Sales) introduced themselves. Then the "pure" technical areas of Architecture, Testing, Data, and Infrastructure took their turns. Over half of the group came from Business Communications, which I found a bit strange, given that they had outsourced most of their technology development.

Frankie had asked me to keep a list on the board of the critical items, and at the end of the round she asked me to summarize. Looking at the list, which I'd tried to organize as we went along, I said, "Looks like the number one concern you all have is the need for good requirements. The second is change control: Once we have agreed upon requirements, we don't keep changing them, so we can get our software done. There were a couple of concerns with integration across the business areas, and one that getting the teams constructed and engaged together around code deliveries is most important." That was, of course, Mary.

"Good. Thanks, Beth; it's nice to have you here to help us. I think the most useful thing for us to do this morning is to share with the business-aligned technology leads the plans of the technology area leads in architecture, testing, data, and infrastructure. You will need that guidance as you work to put your plans together over the next couple of days and then as you refine them through the end of October. As much as Neil emphasized this morning on the need-to-follow-the-Process, the plans and standards from these areas aren't going to be a subject of argument. We need to have a common architecture and it has already been agreed upon. Similarly, we need to manage our data consistently, and we are fortunate to have our Data Group, which has developed an enterprise model to guide our development. Similarly, our Testing team will ensure that we have tests traceable to each requirement, and our infrastructure group will ensure that we use common hardware, operating systems, and monitoring."

I could tell Mary was chafing again. I'd learned from our lesson in Del Mar that she believed that technology architecture should be driven from the development team based on meeting business goals rather than given from afar, but she didn't say anything. Instead, the technology lead for management information, who I would learn shared some of Mary's perspectives but was much less polished politically, asked a question.

"Frankie, I'm Amit Banerjee, out of Commercial. I'm new to this project, having just joined last week, so forgive me if I ask a dumb question. But how do we know that the standards that these groups have selected—or is it 'will select'?—are right for the problem we are trying to solve? I'm used to picking the technologies I think are appropriate for the business need I'm trying to address. I don't see how this is going to work."

I stole a glance at Mary and saw her smiling; she'd found an ally.

"Amit, that is an excellent question, and it goes right to the heart of why we are having this meeting and why we are doing this project." Frankie had a slight look of annoyance in her eyes, but managed to keep a smile on her face and in her voice. "Today, we have dozens of data warehouses and data marts, many different query tools, and lots of kinds of hardware and operating systems. All this diversity and duplication cost a lot of money and create differences where we don't need them. This team needs to come together around common architectures, common data, and common technologies. You are no longer solving problems for your individual silos; instead, we need to solve problems for the entire company now. Why don't we have Janice do her architecture deck for us? Hopefully, your concerns will be addressed."

The "Cremins Architecture Specification" Controls the Process

Janice Neustal had worked for Frankie for several years, leading the BCG architecture team. That team had several members assigned to each of the major parts of BCG's technology. Their responsibilities had been detailed precisely in both The Process and the GRI contract, which ensured that no technology decision was made without their approval. Neil and Frankie liked how that had worked because it gave them strong control over every technology decision being made in the group and ensured that rules were made and then followed.

Janice explained: "An architect will be assigned from my team to each of the business areas. They will be accountable for the conceptual architecture and then the system architecture specifications—the two major architecture deliverables specified in the process. These documents will be reviewed and approved by the architecture council to ensure congruence with the CAS—Cremins Architecture Specification—and to approve any exceptions." This was all laid out on a very complicated PowerPoint slide being projected on the screen.

Mary was intrigued by this and inquired about what the CAS was. She hadn't yet seen it; because she was in a recent acquisition and had been focused on enhancements to her products, the topic had not yet come up.

Janice replied, "CAS has several pieces. There is the list of technology standards, which you can find on our Web site. For each technology area, we have enterprise standards, for what is approved, and an exception process built into the deliverable review steps in the process. For example, the approved technology for databases is Oracle; if someone wants to use something else in a project—say, an object database or open source—that would be specified in the project's conceptual architecture document along with the reasons for it, and then approved or disapproved by the council."

"CAS also has a high-level model of the major systems and interactions at what we call 'end state.' This is the approved vision for where we want to be. Once again, we manage exceptions through the architecture document review process in the council."

Amit asked, "Can we get a briefing on both the standards list and the end-state model? I'd like to see some samples of the architecture documents as well."

"Sure," replied Janice, "although you probably won't need to understand them in depth. Your architect will understand them, and it will be his or her responsibility to do your architecture deliverables."

That didn't sit well with Amit.

"I'm planning on setting the architectures and designs for CU management information," he said. "I'm planning on just extending the work we've already done in commercial. It's pretty new and I've got folks who really know it; it should do the job quite well, with some upgrades and modifications. We're the experts in this. We don't need an architecture department that knows nothing about our systems telling us what to do."

"We'll have to see about that," Janice replied, as politely as she could muster. "It's too early to make decisions on that yet. Once we get the requirements complete and understood, we'll start work on conceptual architecture, and you will be one of the primary contributors to the document. I don't know much about what you have or how it fits or if it complies with our standards, but we always like to leverage existing solutions if we can."

As Janice was talking, Mary had pulled on my sweater and pointed with her pen toward a doodle she had drawn. It showed an airplane with the CU logo on it flying toward a mountain labeled "The Process." I frowned warningly at her and turned my attention back to the meeting.

"Janice, can you take a few minutes to share with this group the high-level conceptual architecture for CU?" said Frankie, who wanted to keep the meeting moving along and get past the emerging Janice–Amit confrontation as quickly as she could.

"Sure, you can turn to, oh, page 6 of the deck." Janice fumbled with her PC and got the slide projected. It was a very complicated slide, full of circles and arrows and with lots of colors. "Our fundamental approach is a service-oriented architecture. We plan on leveraging the common service facility, or CSF, that business communications built to abstract the legacy systems that GRI manages. The idea of CSF was to build Web-based business services, using a standard set of data definitions that would enable us to rebuild all the legacy systems gradually and let us unwind GRI at low risk over time. CSF was planned to be the common interface from our internally owned and managed systems to the GRI legacy systems, as well as among our internal existing and new systems."

"What's the status of the CSF?" challenged Amit. "I've heard that you'd spent millions of dollars on it but couldn't get it to run."

Wow. I resolved, as the Human Resources person here, to have a chat with Amit. He needed some time at charm school!

"Well, it was fairly costly," Janice responded, holding her anger well. "It was a lot of new technology for us, and we had to build out the common data model and map all of the BCG data into it, and then build the transformations from our remaining internal systems to the legacy systems at GRI. GRI had to build its own set of interfaces for us as well. That high cost is exactly why we are going to reuse the facility and data model for CU: We won't have to reinvent this particular wheel."

Janice continued, without precisely answering Amit's question about how much was already running on CSF. "We built the CSF using application and Web server technology, set and followed standards, and ensured that all the data flowing over the CSF is in a common, well-understood and -documented format. We have development, integration test, user acceptance test, production mirror, failover, and disaster recovery environments. It's ready to be the centerpiece of Cremins United."

"We have identified a preliminary list of services that we'll need to build for CU, such as 'place order,' 'check credit,' and so on. They will all be standard Web service calls, very open. Calling systems will invoke the service on CSF, and CSF will in turn access the system of record with the data needed. All the required rules will go into a separate rules engine that we'll manage in CSF as well."

Mary jumped in now. Amit's open hostility had given her cover to ask challenging questions politely, without seeming oppositional. "Janice, I have two questions. How will we know which rules go into the rules engine and which get contained in application logic? Are you saying that all system-to-system connections will go through CSF and get translated coming and going into CDM format? Are you confident that the CDM data format can support all the variety in the other divisions?"

Janice replied, "Regarding the rules, we have a rules architect on our team, and she will work with our team's application architect assigned to you in order to decide. Generally, if a rule can benefit from the rules engine infrastructure or might someday be called by more than one application, we would want to abstract it and put it into CSF. And, yes, our plan is to have CSF be the hub for all real-time system-to-system interactions and to use CDM as the common syntax. We believe it is extensible to whatever we need it to accommodate."

Amit responded, "Won't that add a lot of cost and hurt performance? How do you know that mechanism is the best for all interactions? What do you think the business benefit of that is going to be?" I was now wincing every time Amit spoke out, as was the rest of the room, even though he was asking questions the others were thinking.

Janice appeared to be supremely confident. "Doing the translations is very fast—only a few hundredths of a second—and if we find that we have performance issues, we can always add hardware. So we're not worried about that. On the business benefit, we can't quantify a specific dollar benefit, but there are great long-term benefits: the ability to swap out individual systems more easily, be less dependent on vendors, have better control of our data, and implement security more effectively, as well as all the benefits that service-oriented architecture can provide. We've reviewed this architecture with some SOA specialist consultants, and they've said that our conception is an excellent design consistent with best practices."

Janice continued, "So, to summarize, each of you simply has to worry about the systems within your functional area, whether it's Sales, Production Management, Finance, or whatever. Determine what your business rules are and let our architects decide where they go; build out your interfaces to CSF transactions and CDM data."

The room was now silent; this was a new approach for many of the technicians present, and Janice seemed to have it all figured out, with little or no room for argument. Just to be sure, Frankie capped off the architecture discussion by saying, "The Project Control Authority is making great efforts to provide clear and consistent guidance and control for this project. Just as The Process is not optional or open to debate, neither are the CU architecture and its associated processes. We need to have consistent data and functions, which we will get from the service-oriented architecture that Janice has described, and toward which we have such a good start in the CSF and CDM. Your jobs are to focus on the needs of your individual business areas and let the architecture and the architects support you."

Frankie continued, "Now let's hear from Data, Testing, and Infrastructure. We will have similarly excellent common support provided to you by each of these functions as well."

CYA Processes?

An hour later, Mary and I were walking out of Frankie's meeting, on our way to lunch. Amit sidled up to us and asked if he could walk with us. He introduced himself to Mary, and he asked her what she thought of the project so far. I lightly touched her arm. She understood that I was signaling her to use caution.

"Well, I love what we are trying to do. The business vision seems compelling enough. How about you?" Mary replied.

"I think it's a huge load of crap," Amit said. "These BCG technology guys have been trying to get control of our stuff for a couple of years, and now they seem to have it. They haven't developed anything that provides real business value in years—some of them maybe never! They spent millions of dollars on that CSF of theirs and, for the life of me, I can't see any return. And that process of theirs! It's basically a way to get nothing done at all and have an excuse for not doing anything." He was pretty worked up about this; clearly, he'd had some negative experiences with Frankie and her team.

Mary saw a like-minded leader in Amit, but his aggressiveness scared her a little. She had known, at least to some extent, what she was getting into when she'd agreed to join the project, and she was going to play this out as best she could, as she'd promised Greg. So she responded carefully, "I am a bit concerned about the approach as well. We've been doing Lean and Agile development for several years in our group, and this is about as foreign to us as it would be in Slovakian! But I'm hopeful that we can learn about the current planned approaches and modify them as we need to as the project proceeds. Frankie seems like she would listen to reason, and I've been promised by my management that I'll have some degree of autonomy within the sales technology."

"That's very optimistic of you, Mary O'Connell," Amit said. "I hope you're right."

Signposts	**Cremins United project**
	• The Technology team was told that it would follow a tightly controlled architectural model and process, much like the broader team would follow the broader "Process."
	• All transactions and real-time intersystem communication would go through the common service facility (CSF) and use the common data model (CDM).
	• Similarly tight controls and services would be provided to the business-focused technology teams (e.g., Sales) for infrastructure, data, and testing.
	• Amit, a technology leader peer of Mary's, expressed grave doubts about the architectures and architects. Mary shared some of those concerns but, being more politically astute, kept them largely to herself.
Guides from Beth	• All large-scale systems development projects need guiding architectures, and getting this right is a critical success factor.
	• Leaders need to balance prescriptive specificity and the degree of ongoing control against their confidence in the solution architects and the extent of knowledge of the problems to be faced.
	• For a known problem and high confidence in the architects, a detailed prescription and tight controls are appropriate, as long as you continue to listen to your teams for new findings.

- For something like the Cremins United project, where many of the specific problems are not yet known and the architects haven't proven their ability to understand and solve them, the up-front architecture should be left at a high level, and its evolution should be a cooperative endeavor over time of the central architecture group (if there is one) and the several application development teams working to solve business needs.

Coming up next

Wes takes over narration as planning for CU continues after lunch in preparation for the upcoming board meeting. The newly forming team struggles to set specific scope, time, and cost goals. Mary steps up to help.

7

Setting Expectations for the CU Project: How Iron Is the Triangle?

OCTOBER 2005

Wes:

It had been a long morning, and now I was on again in the afternoon. All the CU leaders were gathered back in the same conference room in which we had started this morning. After Neil's kickoff meeting, the leaders split up into their three functional teams for some planning. The Technology group met with Frankie, the project managers with Neil and Trevor McDonald (the lead PM), and the business leads with Tom and Jamie Kowalski (the business liaison lead). While they were meeting, I caught up on e-mail and prepped my deck for the afternoon meeting.

Our goal this afternoon was to lay out expectations for the building of the plan. I was going to kick the meeting off; Neil, Frankie, and Tom thought it best now for the team to start forming on its own, without their direct involvement all the time. Then, Trevor, a senior consultant from GRI traveling weekly to St. Paul from his Chicago base, was going to explain the details. He was one of the authors of The Process, and he was acting as the lead project manager, reporting directly to Neil. We were lucky to have him on board.

"Well, here we are, midday of day 1 of the Cremins United implementation project. How was your morning?" I got a few murmurs and nods and thought the crowd was still interested and eager.

"We are all excited by this project, and knowing that we picked the best people from around the company to be our leaders—that would be you! I'm sure you're eager to get going. You should now have a pretty good understanding of what the project goals are, its organizational structure, and the process we will be following. The technical team has spent time today going over the high-level technology plan, and the business team has had a few hours to specify what they want in a little more detail. I'm sure you have a lot of questions, but from this point on, my guess is that you'll be supplying a lot of the answers yourselves."

I flipped on the overhead to display a time line of the next 2½ days. "Let's see, we're here," I said, pointing to midday Tuesday. "This afternoon, we are doing this meeting, and then we are unscheduled until the end of the day, when we have a get-together with the PCA to review today's progress. Tomorrow is also not yet scheduled, except for the end of the day, when we have another PCA meeting. Thursday we've also left open for us to do what we need to do, and those of you from out of town will likely be traveling Thursday afternoon. So, we have a couple hours here to plan our attack for the rest of the week."

"Attack on what exactly, Wes?" came from the back of the room.

"Our charge is to have a plan for the board of directors meeting at the end of October. That has to include our specific business deliverable, a time frame, and a cost estimate. We don't need to present business benefits because the high-level business case has been made. We just need to be on the path and have the costs of what we need to do to be consistent with the overall cost estimate in the business case."

Again from the back of the room, "Can we know how much that would be?" This time I saw the questioner; it was Amit Banerjee, the tech lead for MIS.

"Suffice it to say that we expect this to cost quite a bit. We don't want to give you a target at this point; we'd rather that you do your plan and figure out what it will cost. That way, we have a reasonability test, instead of your potentially being limited by a preset budget."

Mary O'Connell spoke up now. "Wes, we usually prefer to have a good understanding of the value of the business case before we get into designing solutions. There are lots of ways of doing a project, so we need to make trade-offs of cost, features, performance, flexibility, and a host of other characteristics."

I was rescued at this point by Trevor. I really didn't have the expertise in technology projects to go toe to toe with Amit and Mary on procedural issues like this. Trevor did.

"We really don't want technical designers making trade-offs like that, Mary. We want to identify the functional and nonfunctional requirements, such as performance and scalability, clearly. Then we'll have you design to that set of requirements. You can identify any trade-offs you see in that process and then the business will make the trade-off decisions."

I stepped in to prevent what looked like a dustup because we had to get on to the planning.

"Between now and the end of the day tomorrow, we need to come up with the highest level plan that we can commit to and share it with the PCA. They will review it with us and let us know if it meets the broad parameters they have in mind. If it does, then we will have 2 weeks to flesh out the plan and identify any serious issues or caveats we might find, prior to the PCA presenting the plan to Evan. Evan will then review it, and if he finds it acceptable, he, along with Tom, will present it to the board around Halloween."

Mary spoke up again. As she spoke, I could see how, now that she had a charge, she turned to the practical. "What people can we use to help us put the plan together? Is there some funding for us to use outside resources to help as well?"

"Each business group has committed to helping on this. You are all senior leaders with internal and external networks. I suggest that you recruit whomever you need, using whatever resource management process you'd usually use to get staff assigned to a project. If you have any issues, you should first escalate to your management chain, up through the heads of the three business groups, and then to me. If you want to use external resources to help, send me an e-mail with what you want to do and how much you want to spend, and I'll take it to the PCA for approval."

Trevor added, "The project managers who are now assigned to your teams will help you with the financial management, and they will track how many people we have on the project in what roles. They will also have access to other GRI experts under a master agreement we have to support you."

Mary smiled—the first time I'd seen her happy with an answer I'd given her so far. My bet was that she'd be working on an e-mail to me, rather than a request of Trevor.

"Any questions on our mission before I ask Trevor to talk about what the plan needs to look like? He'll address the mechanics." No questions were coming yet, so I turned over the stage to Trevor.

The Difficulty of Estimating Time Requirements

"One of the first things we need to do is to educate you on the basics of The Process," Trevor announced. "I'm handing out a brief 'cheat sheet' on The Process's stages, with the required and optional deliverables at each stage. I'm also handing out a somewhat fuller description of the same things. If you'll look at the cheat sheet, you'll see the internal Web address of The Process Web site, which has a lot more details, including templates of all the deliverables, audit criteria, and role definitions."

I couldn't help much with the substance here, but maybe I could help communication flow a little more smoothly. I said, "Why don't we do The Process introduction after this meeting is over? Say at 3:00? Trevor, can you do it in an hour?"

"Sure, Wes," Trevor responded. "Most of you will find it familiar, at least in outline. Pretty standard flow, with high-level requirements, detailed requirements and use cases, high-level design, detailed design, master test plans and test cases, data requirements documents, data design documents, implementation plans, risk management plans, and project gate and signoff definitions. Within 2 weeks, we want to have a high-level plan completed that can help us be sure we can get the project done, in the chosen scope, in the committed time."

"Fortunately, we have automated a lot of the building of plans based on The Process. Once you identify the software components and interfaces, the project management system will automatically generate a plan with the required process artifacts and allow you to choose additional optional artifacts. Based on your assessment of complexity, the system will insert a default number of hours and, based on your specification of development priority and dependencies, put the deliverables into a pretty decent order and give us an end date. Then, you'll need to adjust the plan to fit your specific knowledge better by adding deliverables or tasks or by modifying the dependencies. The system will provide you with a total number of hours, which you can sort by resource type to determine the size of your teams. We simply do the math—number of people by type multiplied by the cost per type—and then we can determine people costs, which will be our biggest expense. Add in some money for hardware, licenses, travel, and so on, and we have our answer."

Mary seemed puzzled. "How far out are we planning? Through design or all the way to production?"

"To production," I replied. "Neither the PCA nor the board is interested in design; they want to know when we'll get into production and how much it'll cost."

"How will nondevelopment tasks be estimated—most importantly, testing?" Mary continued.

Trevor answered, "Testing is a percentage of development, based on historical averages for GRI's engagements, based on number of components, number of development hours, and number of interfaces."

"Wouldn't it depend on how we test?"

Trevor had the answer. "Yes, it does. Fortunately, we're going to test the same way on this project as on most of the projects in the sample, according to The Process specification. So we should get a pretty decent estimate."

"Sorry to monopolize the questions," Mary said. "I only have one more, I think. If we don't know what the components will be yet, how will we do the estimate?"

This question stumped me. "Why wouldn't you know the general components yet? I thought the technical architecture had been completed, shouldn't you be able to estimate the components from that and the high-level requirements we have?"

Mary laughed a little, and in this she was joined by several of the other technical leads.

"Well, Wes, this gets back to the trade-off discussion we had a few moments ago. If we need to build this very quickly, I'd likely hard-code more of the options, rather than build abstract structures with flexibility to change outside a software release. I might buy more components, or even entire systems, instead of building them. I might reuse existing systems or components that I'd rather not use if I had more time. I might use more contractors, which might limit my choice of tools to some extent. All these options would be within the technical architecture that has been proposed."

"That makes a lot of sense, Mary," I replied. "What do you need in order to figure out likely components, remembering that we only have"—I looked at my watch—"27 hours until we need to tell the PCA our target date rough cost and 2 weeks until we have to share that with Evan?"

"For me," Mary stated, "the most important thing is the target date. If we are aiming at a year from now, it's one plan; if it's 2 years, it's probably a completely different one."

Now one of the business leads spoke up. "Wes, I'm Ken Fong, business lead for Production Management. I guess I'm agreeing with Mary on this.

It makes a big difference for us in production if we have a month to get ready, or 6 months. It affects our tooling choices, which presses to use, potentially paper or ink choices. I understand what Trevor is getting at with the project plan determining the end date, but in reality, it's a bit of back and forth."

The Problem with the "Iron Triangle"

Trevor clearly didn't like where this was heading. "One of the goals of The Process is to avoid forcing a project into a predetermined time frame. We all know the 'iron triangle' of project management. Just a minute, I actually have a picture here." Trevor opened a PowerPoint deck titled, "Cremins Development and Risk Control Process—Overview," and, sure enough, there on page 4 was the iron triangle (see Figure 8).

"The triangle shows the relationship among cost, scope, and time. If one side of the triangle changes, at least one of the others must as well. If you fix two sides, say scope and time, the third—cost—is determined," Trevor explained.

"Too often," Trevor went on, in his element now, "our senior leadership traps us into cost, scope, and time objectives that just don't add up. The Process helps us make sure we have a balanced triangle up front by clearly identifying scope, with rough estimates of cost and time. Then, whenever something changes, we can clearly identify what's changed, whether it was a scope or requirements issue or a particular component that cost more than we had expected."

I saw that Mary had turned to Beth, sitting next to her, and was drawing something for her. I had the clear sense that Mary didn't buy most of what she was hearing about how we were pursuing CU, but that she was consciously being "well behaved" about expressing her opinions. I'd

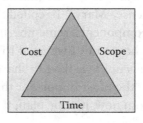

FIGURE 8
Iron triangle.

already found her questions and comments to be on target and wanted to encourage her to say more. I hoped she wouldn't mind my trying to draw her out a bit.

"Mary, any more to say on this? You okay just putting the plan together and seeing where it falls?" I asked.

She looked up from her huddle with Beth, and it looked like Beth gave her a "go-ahead" wink. At least, that's how it seemed Mary took it.

"Well, our approach in the Real Estate Division is a little different. We don't have very high confidence that we can get the scope clear in much detail early on in the project, and we tend to think that building a speculative project plan and trying to manage to it is a lot of waste of resources we'd rather apply to development. We do quite a bit of up-front work thinking through business value, typical user scenarios, and testing out technical options until we are settled enough to start coding. Then we put together a rough iteration plan, make sure it looks like we'll get business value from the cost and time frame that we seem to be facing, and then get going."

"We only plan in detail for the coming month. We look ahead to some end point of business function, usually a release, in as much detail as we need to be sure that the investment we are making will be justified by what we anticipate delivering, and to be sure that we identify any long lead-time items we need to start working now. Then, we build code and test every month from the inception of the project, and we keep adjusting the plan as we go."

Mary continued: "I would draw out our iron triangle a little differently from yours. First of all, with a leaner approach, the relationship among the three sides is quite different; with less waste, we deliver more scope for less money in less time and with higher quality. But we really only fix two sides of the triangle—money and time—and how much we can deliver begins as a rough estimate and becomes really clear only as we move along the project. I wish we could fix all three sides, but we just aren't good enough at what we do to be able to predict everything well enough to make it worthwhile to add all the management overhead."

Now I understood where Mary was coming from; in fact, I'd been mentally drawing out her triangle as she spoke. She had a completely different set of assumptions than the PCA had and a completely different approach. The PCA implicitly believed that it could accurately specify what it wanted in business terms and, essentially, contract with the technology group to deliver it. The CU technology leadership members believed that if they followed a proven, repeatable process, once they got good requirements it was just a mechanical set of steps to deliver what they were asked, as long as they could limit change during the build process. I knew there was no way the PCA would ever accept an approach like the one suggested by Mary; it would require it essentially to trust that what was delivered for a set of cost and time was the best we could get. The group would believe there would be no way to plan and hold people accountable effectively. I could only hope that Mary wasn't right about it being simply impossible, and highly wasteful, for the PCA approach to work well.

"That is certainly a different approach," I said. "Let me see if I understand what your triangle might look like." I stepped up to the board and drew out the diagrams (Figure 9).

"Here is Trevor's triangle, with fixed sides implying that up front we know scope, costs, and times fairly accurately and can make explicit trade-off decisions. Here is Mary's, which shows the same types of estimates and trade-offs up front, but also ongoing scope iterations that continually update what to do in the next iteration, and cost and time estimates. Does that look right, Mary?"

"Nice diagram, Wes; that's very good. The only adjustments I might make would be to show that the costs in my triangle are going to be less than in Trevor's because there is less waste, and to note that, in my triangle, up-front work is limited to the amount that is reliably knowable at that time. We wouldn't do as much detailed planning and systemic estimating as Trevor proposes."

"Any comments from others on this?" I asked.

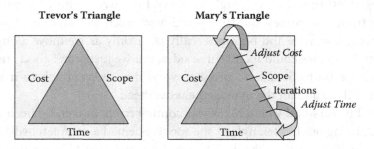

FIGURE 9
Competing iron triangles.

Ken Fong, who continued to show his leadership skills, proposed a compromise solution. "I'm not seeing how we can finish Trevor's approach in just a few days, so how about for now we try to set the plan both ways? We let Mary help us do a high-level—what'd she call it—iteration plan and try to get a usable date projection. Then, we follow up with Trevor's approach to confirm or reject Mary's dates. Hey Mary, could you help us think through quickly what the iterations should be, how long they'd take, what they might cost?"

"I could," Mary volunteered, "if you all wanted to try that, although we don't have all the right preliminary work done to be very reliable." She looked up at Trevor and me, not wanting to take this in a direction in conflict with us.

"Trevor," I asked, "what do you think of Ken's suggestion? Would The Process be okay with some high-level top-down planning, in addition to your project management system's calculations?"

Trevor was surprisingly open to trying this: "The Process is not at all against high-level, top-down planning, as long as it is balanced with the detailed plan before we make any commitments or implement change control. Mary, would you be ready to do this tomorrow morning? We need to have an answer for the PCA by the end of the day, and there really is no way to build the detailed plan we'd need by then. The PCA is demanding a date for the Board even though we aren't ready. Maybe you could help us get something reasonable to propose?"

Mary thought for a moment and then said, "Let me be clear on what I could help us do tomorrow. First, we'd start at the end—what exactly we want the system to do, for whom, at the end of our planning horizon."

Ken agreed, saying, "I think we have a pretty good idea of what that is, so that shouldn't be a problem."

"Then," Mary proceeded, "we'd work backward on each major milestone and build a very high-level time line, based on what we all think might be possible and reasonable. We wouldn't have much detail or evidence—just our experience, but from what I know of you all we should be able to make a pretty good guess." Heads nodded. "I'd like to get us thinking about doing some number of iterative code releases and integration testing; we can talk about that more tomorrow. The end-of-the-morning deliverable would be our plan, turned on its head: the number of iterative code deliverables that we would integration test, a rough schedule for when they would each be done and what would be in them, and the path from code complete to first use to full deployment of initial scope. I can facilitate, but I'll need others to document it and put together the presentation for the PCA."

Heads nodded all around. It seemed everyone was thinking that this was a good proposal for how to spend tomorrow and that it was our best hope of getting something of significance to the PCA by the end of the day. I asked the group for a moment and then pulled Trevor aside to be sure he'd be okay with the plan. He was; I think he was relieved because he really had no idea how to give a date and cost tomorrow without putting the whole project plan together, which could take a month or more. He added that once the team had a proposed flow, he'd ask each lead to estimate team sizes and other costs so that he could get an immediate rough order of magnitude cost. I turned back to the group, and gave them a break.

"Let's get back in 10 minutes and get The Process overview from Trevor. After that, I'd like each business area—Sales, Production, and so on—to get together and do some preparation for tomorrow. Project managers, can you get your business and technical leads plus yourselves and the technical architect together? OK, 10 minutes."

I was very pleased with the outcome of the meeting. It wasn't at all where I expected it to be, but it seemed a better place than we would have been without Mary's leadership. It seemed as if this group of individuals, from all over the company, was starting to form into a team.

Signposts	Cremins United project
	• The second-layer leadership learned about The Process's estimating model. Some doubts were raised about its linear nature, and the team's ability to use it to get estimates as quickly as the PCA was demanding.
	• Mary proposed another planning approach based on Lean and Agile concepts.
	• The team agreed to try to use both mechanisms. The immediate approach was to try Mary's because it could give them *an* answer for the PCA meeting the next day. Following that, with some more time, The Process's mechanism would be done to provide what would appear to be a more reliable answer.

**Guides
from Wes**

- Making the right trade-offs among scope, time, and cost is an iterative process that requires growing knowledge.
- LPD guidance is to set a clear concept up front (the concept document) and have an extensive study phase prior to beginning the project officially. During this time, knowledge is grown, alternatives considered, and trade-offs socialized among decision makers.
- Asking engineers to design a complex function without enabling them to think through costs, benefits, and constraints is a waste of their talents. There are multiple ways to accomplish most things, and it's usually worth considering the trade-offs among them.

**Coming
up next**

Wes will continue narrating on the following day as Mary presents the team's planning results to the PCA.

8

Don't Shoot the Messenger: The CU Project Team Meets with Management

Wes:

The Wednesday morning meeting had gone very well, all things considered. Mary had prepared overnight and came to the meeting room with some structured exercises to make people think through the steps that would take us from here to there. Remarkably, Ken was able to articulate fairly well what "there" looked like. The hottest arguments were between Trevor and Amit over the need to do all the "artifacts" and steps that The Process required. Mary had stayed silent on that, taking her job seriously as the facilitator of the group, rather than its leader. The group, with the prominent exception of Amit, had gotten the message from Neil and Frankie that they had no choice but to do as The Process, the architecture, and other "givens" of the project specified, so those items were built into the plan.

Mary had us start at the end and work our way back to the beginning. She had posed questions and let the group, organized into small teams that split apart and got back together to compare results, work through them. In this way, the group had thought through the issues from Trevor's vantage point and, to a somewhat lesser degree, from Mary's. The result was an answer that the whole team could support. Unfortunately, once I saw the time lines and costs they had come up with, I doubted whether the PCA could do the same.

Trevor and I had spent a frantic lunchtime putting together the material for the PCA update. Our last step this morning had been for each team lead to estimate costs, and we had to aggregate and validate that before the PCA meeting. We had assembled a formal PowerPoint presentation with the approach and time line information that Mary had driven out, as well as the cost information that we had just calculated. Now we were back in the conference room where we had started yesterday, after two very long and hectic, but productive, days. I planned to provide some overview comments and then ask some of the team members to provide color commentary because this was primarily their work.

Tom Stillman, the PCA lead, kicked the meeting off with a story, as he was wont to do. "I was talking with some of our steering group members this morning about next year's technology budget. We have a problem beginning to grow, in that we want to fund Cremins United without a dramatic increase in total spending, mostly by cutting spending on legacy systems that will be replaced. So getting this done quickly is extremely important; we need to be able to show the lines of business that this is real, that they can depend on it, and that they can start to cut their investment in their legacy systems. I hope you have taken a good hard look at what we can accomplish."

That was a tough start to the meeting, putting us right on the spot at the beginning. I knew I couldn't let Trevor take the heat on this because he was a consultant. I'd have to be the one to deliver the news.

"Tom, PCA members, we have had a very productive two days of planning." I went on to describe what we had done, from Neil's kickoff to the "vertical" meetings (i.e., all the PMs, all tech leads, etc.), the overall planning meeting, the overview of The Process, the "horizontal" meetings (all parties for Sales, etc.), the planning meeting Mary had facilitated that morning, and finally the cost estimating and consolidation. Neil, Frankie, Tom, and the others asked a couple of polite questions, and then Tom got right to the point.

Management Asks for a Target Date

"So, what's the bottom line? When do you think you can have us in production and what do you think it might cost?"

I guess I was not getting to the point very effectively as I tried to explain Trevor's approach, which would get us a good level of detail and reliability but not for a month or more, and Mary's approach, which gave the early answer we were going to review today. Tom interrupted me again and said, "Enough with the back story. What's the answer? Did you come up with a date or not?"

At this Mary, bless her heart, felt compelled to rescue me.

"If you don't mind, I'd be happy to explain what we did yesterday, which will give you a sense for likely dates and major milestones. Then Trevor can give us the tally from the first rough cost estimates we made this afternoon."

"Thank you, Mary, that's great." For the benefit of the PCA members, I added, "Mary has a lot of experience doing this kind of high-level planning, and she did a great job helping us work this through this morning."

Mary got up at the board, ignoring the formal PowerPoint that I'd put together. She went to the far right of the whiteboard and put an X there (Figure 10). "This is the end—when we have sales people in at least some units of all three business groups using the common sales system to sell some of their own products, as well as to sell some products provided by the other groups. We also have some production management going on in the new systems, including some capacity management activities. We thought the ability to leverage the commercial group's high-volume print capacity to do some of the annual report work from Specialty and business communications would be a good target, along with commercial and specialty-finance able to sell BCG's print outsourcing capabilities. At the start, we've deployed the CU systems throughout the BCG, Commercial, and Specialty-Finance Sales teams, to be used alongside legacy systems, but giving them new capabilities they will want to use, even though they'll need to use more than one system."

"OK," said Tom, "that sounds like a good target. How do we get there?"

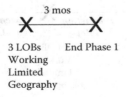

FIGURE 10
CU time line, phase 1.

"We figured that we need at least a quarter to roll this out nationally once we have it working in a more limited geography. So here," and Mary drew another X a foot or so to the left of the end, "is when we have the system working well in limited numbers for all three lines of business" [see Figure 10]. Mary wrote "3 months" on the line between the two Xs.

"Why so much time?" Tom inquired. "Couldn't we roll it out faster?"

"We could," Mary replied. "But as the group talked it over, we were concerned that we would probably find some functionality and scaling issues as we rolled it out, and we'd probably have some bugs or required enhancements from the earlier phase that we'd want to fix before we put the whole company on it."

"OK," Tom hesitantly agreed, "that might make sense, but we might want to speed that up. I suppose the next step left is one LOB working well?"

"Right on," Mary nodded. "Let me draw a couple more milestones, back to code complete." [see Figure 11].

"Before we begin going national, we need to be running pretty well in a smaller geography with all three lines of business, and before that we'd have to pilot with a single LOB, with one line of business in a limited geography—say, a couple of states—for a quarter or so before we could extend to all three LOBs. Of course, before we can begin a pilot, we have to integration test after code complete. We had a rousing argument on how long that would take (mostly between 3 and 6 months), and we settled (at least, for this presentation) on 4. The amount of time to integration test will depend a lot on what happens up to code complete—how much continuous integration and testing we do on the way there. If we do a lot, we can keep formal integration testing to a short period, perhaps 3 months. If we don't get much integration done until code complete, integration testing could take an indeterminate amount of time: 6 months could be optimistic."

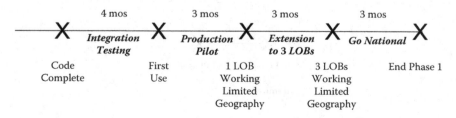

FIGURE 11
CU time line, code complete to end.

By this time, Tom and Neil were looking anxious, and Frankie had her eyes looking down at the table, obviously not taking ownership of the plan that Mary was laying in front of the PCA. The other project leaders who had participated in the planning were nervously watching, glad that Mary, rather than they, was doing the presentation. Mary's time line looked like over a year from code complete to national rollout of limited functionality—how long to code complete? That was what Neil asked next.

Mary turned back to the board and finished the time line (Figure 12).

"Whoa there, Mary, are you saying we need 18 months to get to code complete? How did you determine that? If this is right, we're"—Neil was counting up the months—"almost 2 years to first use, and then 9 months after that to national rollout—2½ years!"

It was quite a performance by Mary. The rest of the group was afraid to tell the PCA how long they really thought it would take to do something this big, and the official project lead, Trevor, had a planning mechanism that would require a lot more time to execute than we had available. Here she stood, in front of the entire PCA, calmly explaining the team's reasoning:

"The group thought that the best approach was to stand up the integrated system as quickly as we could and then do two iterations of fixes and added functionality to get to code complete. I'd normally recommend a lot more, smaller iterations. However, we talked it over and, given how much new software and hardware we have involved here and how new the group is at working together, we didn't think we could get the first iteration up prior to a year or so. Then, given how much there is to test—and, again, the newness of the team—we didn't think we could handle synchronized releases much more frequently than quarterly."

Mary was walking a very fine line, I could tell: working hard to keep fidelity to the group consensus worked out earlier, while conveying some

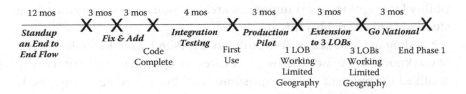

FIGURE 12
CU overall time line.

of her ideas and emphasizing the iterative approach to which she had subtly led the group.

The tension in the room was so thick I could just about feel it. This certainly was not what the PCA wanted to hear. Neil was about to pop a cork.

Can You Do It Faster and Cheaper?

"I appreciate the thinking you've done here and thank you for presenting the group's thoughts, Mary," Neil said. "This gives us a starting point; at least we now have some reference point. But I didn't hear any real FACTS, and plans like this can always be improved. Wes, Trevor, how do we go from this very rough, and way too long, plan to something that is FACT BASED? We need to figure out the barriers to getting this done much faster and then work those through so that we can get this done faster."

Trevor saw his opening and jumped in. "Neil, Tom, Frankie, that's exactly right. Our next step is to put the project plan together based on The Process, get the estimates done, and then figure out what things we can do in parallel and how to speed this up. We should be able to get that done in a few weeks. Then you'll have the facts. Right now, this is just our best educated guess of what we can do."

Tom, who had been quietly listening to the dialogue for most of the meeting, now spoke up. "You know, I respect this group deeply, and I'd like to hear any thoughts you might have on how to get this done faster and cheaper. While we haven't talked money yet, I'm willing to bet that news isn't good either."

"It isn't," I confirmed.

Tom solicited, "Any thoughts?"

Neil's reaction to Mary's presentation didn't exactly set a welcoming tone, so I wasn't surprised when the room was silent. After what seemed like a very long time, Ken Fong spoke up. A "business person" with responsibility for one of the most important areas (Production Management), he stood up and cleared his throat.

Nodding in particular at Tom Stillman, the PCA leader, Ken said, "Many of you know me. I've worked my whole career in operations, so I'm not really qualified to comment on your question, Tom, but I'm going to anyhow. It seems to me that one reason this time line is so long is because of The Process and to what sure looks to me like an overcomplex technology design. As we put the time lines together, the time to do all the required documents, review and approve them, and then do the next set—all before we are building anything in earnest—seemed to consume most of the first year. As I listened to these brilliant technology folks talk about what it would take to do the data mapping, transaction definitions, and testing, I kept wondering why we didn't just connect up a sales system to a couple of our production management systems and then get on with it. I can only compare this to our projects to set up and improve new plants and such. We try to get going and get machines running just as fast as we can and document it afterward."

Frankie responded on behalf of the PCA. "Thanks, Ken; those were interesting comments, and we can consider taking shorter paths through The Process. The risk we'd run is that if we get a requirement wrong, it is very expensive to fix after coding, so we need to be very careful to get requirements approved, base design on the full set of requirements, and then do development based on complete designs. We also need to ensure we have traceability from requirements through testing, for audit purposes. I'm sure we can find a way to cut this time frame down and still do the best practices represented by The Process."

I noticed that Frankie had ignored Ken's comments on the complex architecture. The PCA wasn't exactly proving open to input on how this project should be done or how long it should take, so other comments were not forthcoming. With that, Tom called the meeting to a close and asked the PCA members, Trevor, and me to stay behind for a closed-door consult.

Signposts	Cremins United project
	• Mary led the team on a top-down, backward-looking planning exercise and presented the results to the PCA.
	• The team incorporated the PCA's requirements around The Process and architecture, despite some misgivings of some team members.
	• The PCA was not interested in hearing about those misgivings, and was not receptive to the planning results. Neil in particular felt that the plan was short on facts, which Trevor promised to get in the next few weeks.

Guides from Wes

- The PCA adjourned its meeting with the delivery teams to consider what to do about the team's too long, too costly plan.
- Top-down, backward-looking planning is a great way to get a quick, rough cut on what a project might take. Its quality depends entirely on the expertise of the people involved and the quality of the exercises that bring their knowledge and judgment together.
- Following up this type of planning with a more detailed step, as Trevor proposed, is an excellent next step.
- As a leader, if you have time frames and cost constraints that you are expecting, don't hide them from your team! If a system or new feature is only worth, say, $X, tell the team and ask them if there is any way to do it for less than that.

Coming up next

Beth wraps up the tale of the initial planning of the CU project. What will the PCA do with the team's input?

9

Cutting CU Project Development Time—by a Year

OCTOBER 2005

Beth:

Thursday morning: I'm going home today! St. Paul isn't such a bad place, at least not on a beautiful fall day like today. I'd gone for an early walk with Mary early down by the Mississippi River. Overhead, birds were flying south in noisy formation.

I'd told Mary what a great job she was doing, helping the team think through how to do this project, respectfully pointing out issues, and avoiding any confrontations that would undermine her ability to help. She was feeling quite pessimistic about the possibility of success for Cremins United. The long time frame she'd presented yesterday seemed to her a possible way to succeed, but she sensed that the PCA would never accept that much time and cost. As it neared 8:00, we turned from the river path back into the city and into Cremins HQ for a wrap-up session with the PCA and the project team, to find out what had happened.

Management Balked at the Long Lead Time

It turned out to be a short meeting. The PCA did not show up—just Trevor and Wes. Wes explained that the PCA's direction to us was to bring in the time frame, even if we didn't cut costs equivalently. Trevor told us how we were going to do it: Instead of three iterations, we would just do one, at 1 year. We'd follow The Process, with the exception that the technology groups would be allowed to put in hardware and rough out the software, to go as far as they could while waiting for the requirements and software designs to be completed. The PCA expected that there would be some limited rework and waste from this, but that would be OK. The test period was to be cut from 4 months to 2 by using testing support in India; that way, we could test around the clock and get it done twice as fast. Rollout would be shortened by doing all three LOBs at once and cutting the pilot times to 2 months each. Wes handed out the new time line (Figure 13).

The project had magically shrunk by over a year! The reaction of the group ranged from groans of resignation to Joe Karras's statement, "We'll have to go figure out how to do this." Joe was the technology lead for production, Ken Fong's technical partner, who seemed a particularly compliant and optimistic fellow.

Trevor explained that we had 2 weeks to put together a detailed project plan, based on The Process, the project management system, and the accepted architecture, that met this time line. We had to provide cost estimates and proposed staffing plans. We were to raise any issues with meeting the date with the PCA as soon as we saw any, and they would help us figure out a way to deal with them. Wes cautioned that the PCA would be more than willing to help, but that they insisted that any issues be based on FACTS, rather than speculation or guesses. In essence, the team was being told they had to do a plan to meet this schedule unless they could prove it could not be done.

After just 45 minutes, the meeting ended and Mary and I walked out side by side. Wes hurried after us and asked if we could stop for a cup of

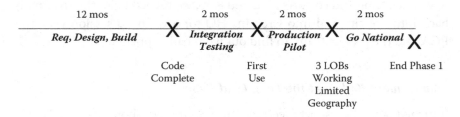

FIGURE 13
CU time line from the Project Control Authority.

coffee with him. We couldn't because we'd already decided to head out to the airport and catch an earlier flight to San Diego.

"Do you mind if I just walk with you for a while then?" Wes asked. We didn't, so he did.

"So, Mary, what do you think? Can we get this done on the revised schedule?"

Is It Doable?

Outside the large group, Mary felt a bit freer to be frank. "This project could get done in 18 months, if all the stars aligned, Wes. But we have some basic pieces missing. The group doesn't seem to have the technical or project skills we need; it's being run by people who have spent the last 5 years managing an outsourcer, rather than doing very large-scale software development. We're being forced into a slowly moving, rigid, big-bang development process that creates enormous risk. On top of all this, we're being asked to implement a highly abstract architecture, which, according to Amit, doesn't seem to work very well."

Wes nodded. He was not surprised by her comments, but he did want to know more. "What can we do to help?"

"I'm not sure. It seems the PCA doesn't have the same view of the situation as I do, and maybe they are right; there is some chance we can get this done on that schedule. Maybe they are playing chicken, picking unreasonable dates to get us to commit to and execute on a faster schedule than we would without the pressure. But I don't see any actions to address the gaps, and it doesn't seem like the PCA really wants to hear from us."

"Maybe not," agreed Wes. "What are you going to do? Can you get your piece done in a year?"

"A year is quite a bit of time," Mary responded, "and I've got a head start as long as I can use some of my current team and some consultants and contractors I know. I've got an idea on how to accelerate the time frame, if I can get my new team to agree to it. So, I'm going to focus on building out my piece, ensure it's a great piece of software for this company, and stay out of the rest of it as best I can."

I laughed and said, "I find it hard to believe you'll keep that pledge for long."

Signposts	**Cremins United project**
	• The PCA unilaterally cut the time frame by a year. They gave permission for a few shortcuts to justify the decision.
	• The delivery team reacted with resignation and resolved to go forward and build the detailed "FACTS" that showed they could do this.
	• Mary was now doubtful that CU could succeed, but resolved to do her part and to try to avoid broader leadership in the project.
Guides from Beth	• Ordering it so does not make it so.
	• Leadership of knowledge workers must create conditions that support team commitment and rigorous decision making.
	• Once leadership shows it cares about neither of these things, team members may still continue to do their best to accomplish tasks, but the full flow of information, ideas, and knowledge stops. At that point, decision making becomes reliant solely on the formal leaders, the integrity of the information they take in, and the wisdom they can marshal on their own.
Coming up next	We turn back to TRIM. Beth describes the TRIM planning session occurring a few days after the CU session, and we see a very different type of leadership in action.

10

Planning the TRIM Project

OCTOBER 2005

Beth:

I'd been back from St. Paul for just a few days. The weekend had passed in housework and a little gardening. I found that I had somewhat enjoyed the fall days in Minnesota, although I was glad I didn't have leaves to rake or face the prospect of falling snow. I had 1 day to catch up at work on Monday, and then it was another immersion into my learning. Tuesday morning, bright and early, Neville kicked off his TRIM planning session. This looked to be quite different from the CU planning I'd attended last week in St. Paul. From Neville's opening line, after introductions were completed and we'd done a get-to-know-you, what-are-you-expecting/hoping/fearing exercise, it certainly was.

"Problems Are Our Friends"

"The first thing we all have to agree upon is that we don't know exactly what we are building or how we are building it," Neville began. "That is not to say that we don't all have beliefs about it or that we don't know what to do next. But we have to be humble, acknowledge that we have a lot to learn together, and get on with it."

"The second thing is that we love problems. Problems are our friends, kind of like pain is your friend. Without pain, we wouldn't know we'd just jammed our finger in the car boot and might drive off like that! Problems will be this project's pain."

"Anyone who thinks they know enough to plan this project out in detail, could you help us 'plan the work and work the plan'?" Neville surveyed the room of 30 or so people, finding no takers. "I always hope to find someone who could do that for us. We do need to build a plan, and we'll do that this week. But we'll build a high-level plan, focused on specific user value, and not waste a lot of time planning in detail things we just can't yet foresee. Then we'll get to work building code, and each month we'll check to see if we got done what we said we were going to do and reset the plan for the next month or two. Everything we do will be focused on delivering working code and will be measured by what we actually deliver. We'll do documentation only when we need to; if we can just code something that we know will meet the need, we'll do that and document it for maintenance or support."

Neville had the rapt attention of the group. Overall, they liked what they were hearing, although there seemed to be a few skeptics. But Neville wasn't done with his show yet, and he left no opening for interruption at this point; he was on a roll.

"How can we work this way? Who will decide when we need to document something and when we don't? Our development team will. We need to build our team, across all our organizations, as a single coherent project relentlessly focused on code delivery, vigilant for problems to raise. We need team members who are truly excellent at what they do, and who are willing to admit when they are in areas in which they are not expert. Cremins will be supplying major parts of the team—the project management, much of the systems analysis, development, and testing—and I can attest that this is a group of truly excellent talent and commitment. Each of you needs to ensure that your people on the project are of the highest caliber and capable of delivering. You must be willing to tell us—Alex and me—when we have gaps in Cremins people or anywhere else. One of the surest ways to failure is having people trying to do things they don't know how to do without the help they need."

"So, the big takeaways are right here, on the table: a Lean project plan and approach, with constant focus on results and adjustment; outstanding people with the right skills; and a unified team, without handoffs, all working toward common goals. We've agreed that this is how we are going to do the project, even though some of you," Neville said, looking up at a gentleman I'd seen looking somewhat concerned as Neville ranted on, "may not be entirely comfortable with this approach. Your companies or organizations have agreed to this in the contracts and agreements establishing the project, and this is how we are going to work." Neville was telling the TRIM people how they were going to work, just as Trevor told the CU group, although the instructions couldn't have been more different.

The Primary Goal: A System That Delivers Value to Our Customers

Neville had a bit more to say about how the TRIM project would work: "Let me explain a little about my role, and then I'm going to turn this over to Alex Fuegos, our project manager, to go over the agenda for the day. I'm called the chief engineer for TRIM. This is a role that you probably haven't seen before, unless you've spent time in product development in manufacturing. Anyone? No? Basically, I have one ultimate responsibility: delivering value to our customers.[1] For TRIM, that includes several of your organizations, including real estate buyers, brokers and agents, lenders, providers of service for troubled properties, and government agencies, investors, and journalists. It is my job, with the help of our team here, to understand what our customers want and then turn that into reality."

"I've been leading this project since well before it really began, all through the study phase. Many of you were also involved in that phase, as we explored business needs, put together some initial thoughts on technology design and business models, identified and, I think, solved some tough problems like privacy management. So far my primary work has been the product concept document, which has been the basis for the agreements and contracts among our companies, and the statement of work, which Alex authored. I've also been working to figure out our team structure in more detail; Alex laid it out in concept in the SOW, but we needed a little more tinkering to be sure we had the right talent on each team and the teams broken out the best way. We've got a good start on the technology architecture, which we'll finish up in the first sprint, and we've got a good start on the overall schedule."

"While we were working on the SOW, Alex and I were in a meeting with several people from one of the lenders here. As we reviewed the roles, I was asked whether I was the overall business lead or the overall technical lead. My answer was a simple: 'Yes, I am.' My background is as an engineer and project manager, much of it in the real estate and financial services fields. I've had a turn managing operations and supporting sales, and I have worked hard to understand the business operations and financial dynamics of our businesses. I spend at least half a day a month with actual users of our systems. In preparation for the TRIM project, I spent a week in the collections and workout areas of two different lenders and several days in the field driving around with appraisers, property preservation workers, and realtors trying to sell foreclosed properties. Most of the other leaders on our team did similar stints; Alex here was out buying ugly houses! I'll never be the expert in each of your businesses that you are, but I promise I will listen to what you need, be your voice in this project, and ensure your voice is heard in every decision we make."

Mary had promised me that I would learn a lot more about the Real Estate Division's approach to system development by reading the concept document and statement of work for TRIM, which I had done on the airplane returning from St. Paul. She had also said I would learn by going to see the planning session. I was sitting in the back of the room with my copies of those documents and the Lean/Agile diagram Mary had given me a few weeks ago, trying to continue to check off items as the session went on. In just a few minutes, Neville had already touched on many of the key principles, including towering competence, chief engineers, teams, problem solving, "go see," and the "study" phase. There had been no discussion yet of a detailed process to follow or even any PowerPoint presentations!

I couldn't help but begin to compare Neville to Tom, Neil, and Frankie. There was no doubt at all that Neville was in charge of TRIM, accountable for the full delivery of value. In CU, the PCA was in charge, but it felt like the "business" people were accountable for requirements and Frankie's group for the technology, leaving the PCA or The Process or something I didn't really understand accountable for ultimate delivery of business value. I realized I'd never heard any of the PCA members engage with precisely what the CU systems would do, or how they would do it; they were totally focused on the project organization and process. This was not the case with Neville: He had a single-minded focus on what and how we were building in TRIM, the value, and its engineering.

Neville was wrapping up his introduction, taking a few questions from the group. They were mostly about some lingering open issues from the study phase, which Neville deflected for later consideration. He wanted to keep the session moving ahead because there was a lot to accomplish. Getting this many people together, he said, was one of the most important resources at the project's disposal, and we had to be very careful to take maximum advantage of our time together. He used the opportunity to ask everyone to think about the proper forum to bring up issues and problems, as well as to ensure that every meeting is carefully planned to respect people's time and get rigorous, accepted outcomes. Then he turned the meeting over to Alex.

The "Scrum Master" Describes Agile Development

"First," said Alex, "I want to make sure that you have all read and are comfortable with the concept document, the statement of work, and any agreements or contracts your company has entered into with regard to this project. After this week, I'm going to assume that all of you have done that and manage to the understandings documented already. Could I have a show of hands of those of you who are not fully familiar with these documents?"

Fully half the room raised their hands. "I was afraid of that. If you need a copy, please look on the TRIM project Web site. I'm going to ask this same question again next time we get together, and there will be a $5 fine for the party fund for each raised hand. I would also be willing to do a briefing on these topics for anyone who wishes. If anyone needs help in any way to avoid the fine, please let my assistant know, and one of us will be in contact."

I could see how Neville and Alex were laying the groundwork for this group to become a team. Neville established the leadership and culture, while Alex was ensuring understanding, agreement, and laying out the organization. They projected a sense of confidence that they knew where we were going and how we were going to get there, without knowing all the details and while really listening to the group. The extended study phase had laid a strong foundation on which Neville and Alex were constructing this project infrastructure.

"This week, our primary objective is to put together the high-level plan for the project and then lay out the beginnings of detailed plans for the next month. We're going to use a process known within the software development community as 'Agile development,'[2] although that can mean a lot of different things to different people. For those who follow this type of thing, the buzzword description of what we'll do is primarily 'scrum,' plus 'user stories' as our basis for building our 'backlog.' My formal title, according to Agile, would be 'scrum master,' and I'll be leading the 'scrum of scrums.' Could I see hands of those of you who know what I'm talking about, at least a little?"

All the hands from our company were raised, plus maybe half the others.

"I think I'll take a few minutes to describe this scrum approach to take the mystery out of it for you. It's really pretty simple, and I have this handy one-page diagram for each of you." With that, Judy started walking around the room, handing out the scrum overview (Figure 14), and Alex played a short video of an actual rugby scrum from his PC. For those who hadn't ever seen a rugby game, it was quite an unusual sight.

"Don't worry, our scrums won't be anything like that," Alex reassured the group. "Let's start in the middle of the diagram. At the center of the scrum are the actual scrum meetings, a structured 15-minute daily team get-togethers where we update the plan and ask for any help we need. This usually starts a cascading series of short talks among team members, normally immediately after the scrum. Scrums assemble into what we call 'sprints'; we're going to do roughly 30-day sprints in this project."

"Now, look at the left column, which is the planning. First comes the scrum planning, which we're going to do today. To do scrum planning, we need our overall release target, a date, and rough scope. This was determined in the study phase and memorialized in the concept document."

"We then make a list of features, which we call 'user stories,' prioritize them, do rough sizings, and make a rough allocation of them to sprints. Again, we are fortunate that in the study phase, we did a lot of work to understand the features we needed, and we did some planning around how long we thought it would take to build them out based on the designs we choose. We'll do another evaluation of feasibility when we finish this step as well. Everyone with me?" Alex looked around the room, saw no objections, and proceeded.

"Following the down arrow, you'll see something called 'sprint planning.' We are going to do that tomorrow. Here we take the first few sprints and plan them out in more detail. We're going to focus mostly on sprint 1 tomorrow because this is the first time this team is doing this sort of planning. Each user story is broken into its component tasks, and they are estimated. We use "ideal days" to estimate, but other agile teams use other mechanisms. Then the whole sprint is re-evaluated for feasibility, and if there is too much or too little, we adjust it—or perhaps we find a way to add team members, if we care more about time than money. Finally, we confirm the sprint goals, and we plan what we are going to demo at the end. We always try to show actual running software, but if that's not possible, we do something else visual, like a simulation."

"Back through the middle, our scrums, we have the demo at the end, and then some sort of reflection activity. We always want to evaluate

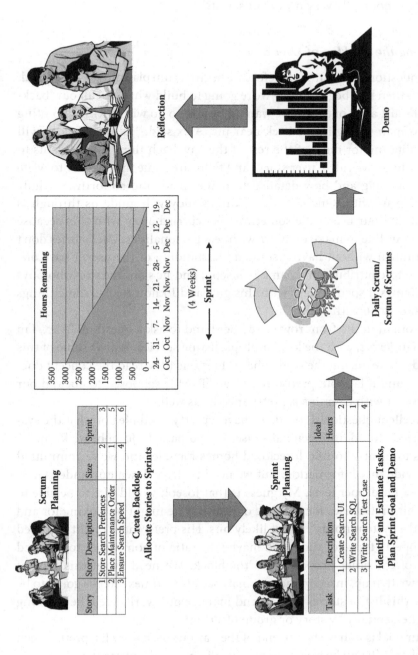

FIGURE 14

Scrum overview.

continuously how we are doing and what we can do to improve. That's about it—not really very mysterious, is it?"

Building the Backlog of User Stories

"Any questions or comments before we begin scrum planning?" Alex asked. "If not, then let's begin. Today we're going to build what we call our 'backlog.' It's just a list of things we want to be able to do with TRIM." Pointing to a woman sitting in the back near me, Alex said, "Judy Hollendar will be facilitating for most of the rest of the day. Each thing a user wants to be able to do we call a 'user story,' and there are some tips on how to write them, how big and how detailed to make them, and so forth that Judy will help us with. One of the fun things Judy will guide us through is identifying our users. We sometimes get carried away with this because some of us like to make up users with real personalities. User stories don't mean much without having some understanding of the user. I have one I'd like to contribute; his name is Joseph, and he's an investor who buys ugly homes. I spent 2 days with this guy, and I know he has some things he wants to do with TRIM!"

A woman in the front row raised her hand to ask a question. "Alex, I'm Sybil Gutierrez, with the local multiple listing service. Wasn't some of this already done during the study phase? I for one have read the concept document, and it lays out pretty well what TRIM is supposed to do, and our agreement with Cremins is pretty specific as well."

"Excellent question. Indeed, we have a pretty good idea of what the system needs to do, in a general sense. If I go back to Joseph, we know he wants to be able to find foreclosed homes for sale, and we've committed to provide that information. But we need to drive down our understanding to a bit deeper level. My guess is that Joseph would like to be able to enter his preferences for the type of property he might be looking for and have the system notify him of likely hits. His preferences might be based on property type, location, and maybe the ratio of home price to assessed value of the other properties on the block. We need to get this type of story written up, in a common format, because our next step is going to be to use this list of stories to plan and manage our work. We'll be building TRIM essentially by story or group of stories."

"Our goal is to have by the end of the day our user story list pretty much complete. It'll still be pretty messy, mostly in a bunch of cards and stickies, but afterward Judy will take all the results and put them into something coherent for us."

Sybil had another question. "Alex, is this the same as doing requirements? Are we going to do use cases also?"

"Not exactly.[3] We aren't really going to do requirements the way some of you may be used to. The user stories are just enough to provide us the skeleton of our plan and to kick off the completion of the conversations around what the system has to do. Once we get into that conversation, the developers and the product owners—in my example, it would be Jack Spence, our team member from Home Renovators for Resale—would determine if they have enough information to complete the design and development, or if they need to spend some more time fleshing out requirement details and immortalizing the results in a document. I've found that use cases tend to have too much detail on the technical solution and often send projects off-track or lead to a lot of waste and rework."

Sybil wasn't quite done. She didn't seem sold on Alex's approach, but she seemed willing to go along. "Alex, can I ask one more question? I fully agree with Neville about respecting all of our time, so I can talk offline if you like."

"Go ahead; we have a few minutes left until break. Your question is…"

"It's actually two questions. If we don't document requirements in the detail of, say, a use case, how do we know that what is built is what we wanted? How do we test if we don't have a use case to write test scripts from?"

"Sybil, you've obviously done software development before. What's your role with the MLS here?" asked Alex.

"I'm the technology director. I worked at a military contractor before coming to this job 4 years ago, so I do have experience doing software development that had to meet Department of Defense documentation and testing requirements. You'd never get away with this in that environment!"

There was a burble of laughter, including from Alex and Neville. Neville responded, "Actually, the Department of Defense officially endorses the basic approach we are taking, which is an iterative one.[4] I can certainly believe, however, that it has more documentation requirements than we will."

A new voice was heard from the left side of the room—Jack Spence, the team member from HRR, the investor in distressed properties. "Can I try to answer at least part of Sybil's question? I have read the SOW, and I read the book on Agile development you sent to us as well. I've never been involved with building a system; my experience is in buying, renovating, and selling foreclosed houses. My understanding is that once we get to working on my user story, I will be sitting right with the developer, making sure he understands what I want, and I'll be responsible for dealing with my company back home in Houston and the other property buyers involved in the project to be sure I can speak for them. I'll have to write tests that the system has to meet, based on what I tell the developer we need. In a way, we skip right over the detailed requirements document and do the code and tests at the same time, just by sitting with each other and talking. After all, aren't the tests pretty much the same thing as requirements documents anyhow?"

Neville really liked what he'd just heard, and he said so. "Jack, that is right on; you've got it. It's really quite simple in concept, isn't it? Unfortunately, it can get quite a bit harder depending on how complex the requirements are and how firmly someone like you, whom we'll call a product owner, can speak for his entire constituency. But you've got the basics down, and for many parts of this project, which is going to be quite heavy on the user interface and reporting, your description will be largely correct. We're going to have an overall test manager for TRIM; he's sitting right over there [pointing]. Janani Mugombe will put together an overall master test plan for TRIM, and he'll work with each team to ensure the system is adequately tested. He'll also own our test tools and make sure we do things like try to attack the security and privacy, and test for scalability. So it's a little more complex and formal than what you laid out."

Neville then turned to Sybil to check her reaction. I was finding that he was always doing this kind of gesture. Even though he was clearly in charge, he showed great respect for his teammates. He really wanted the whole group to feel this was their project and that they were being heard. "Sybil, does that answer your question? You feeling confident that we'll build what we're supposed to build and that we'll know that it works?"

Sybil wasn't quite willing to give a complete thumbs-up, but she said, "I can live with it for now." She joked: "But I'm watching!"

Alex stepped back in and wrapped up.

"After break, Judy will give us instructions in this room for about half an hour. Then we'll break into groups to work on user stories for the rest of the day. Back in this room, we'll have the loan servicers and the people associated primarily with them, like appraisers, home preservation, and the like. Across the hall, it'll be the home buyers and associated, including realtors, multiple listing service providers, etc. Around the corner will be government agencies, investors, rating agencies, and journalists. Fifteen minutes!"

I was able to sit in on the lender session for a few hours before I had to leave for the rest of the day. Alex had been leading the session and it had been a lot of fun. Everyone got cards and stickies, and the walls were filling up nicely. Our first task was to identify our prototypical users, like Alex's "Joseph" who bought the ugly houses. We had quite a few user characters at first, but we eventually figured out that several consolidated together. As the group moved on to identifying the user stories, I stepped into the other rooms for just a few moments before I had to leave and I found similar scenes. In general, everyone was contributing, although the product owners—the designated representatives of the various business partners—plus some of the special invitees just for today were doing most of the talking. They definitely had business tasks they wanted to be able to do that they just couldn't do today or that were prohibitively expensive. That boded well for the success of the project! I was also struck by the way the stories, while focused on things users would want to do, also touched on technical design questions, like how frequently the data needed to be updated, privacy management, and system performance. The developers were making sure of that by asking questions and writing some of the stories themselves.

Checking In on CU Planning

My afternoon was full of my "day job" activities, dealing with some staffing and employee relations issues. Late in the afternoon I stopped by Mary's office to see how she was doing and tell her about what I'd learned by watching Neville's session today. She was on a conference call with George Giordano (GG), her CU project manager, and Sam Baker, her "business" leader, so she couldn't chat for long.

She put the call on mute for a few minutes, listening to the meeting with one ear while talking and listening to me with the other. The CU group was working frantically to put together a project plan that showed they could meet the date set by the PCA. The debate of the moment was around when the "phase gate dates" should be and what had to be done by them. The Process called for finishing all the requirements for the release at one time and then putting them through quality assurance and handoff checks. Mary was trying to convince her peers that it would be better to work more like TRIM did, without explicitly drawing the comparison. By this time in the call, Mary had come to realize that she had totally failed, and she was resigning herself to finding a way to get her requirements complete in 2 months' time (although, formally, requirements were Sam's problem, not hers). They were launching into a discussion on how to do this and Mary shushed me, waved me off, and went back to the call. I was sorry I couldn't stick around and listen.

Signposts

TRIM project
- The project team conducted the scrum planning session, aiming for first release in 1 year.
- Neville explained his role as chief engineer accountable for value delivery to customers. There seemed to be no similar role in the CU project, other than that of the PCA committee.
- The Agile technique called "scrum" was explained. It comprised compiling a backlog of functions, allocating them to monthly development periods (sprints), doing daily meetings (scrums), wrapping up with a system demonstration and reflection, and iterating on sprints until code was released to production.
- The project adopted user stories as the items in the backlog. User stories are a simpler, more flexible form of requirements than the more formal and detailed use case that many companies use. User stories avoid overspecifying the implementation, a common risk in use cases, and provide "just enough" information to spark the next set of conversations.
- User stories were identified that are ready to be estimated and allocated to the upcoming sprints.

Cremins United project
- Phase gates were set: Requirements complete would be due in 2 months, with quality assurance and handoff checks required before beginning design.

	• Mary tried to convince her peers to do a more iterative flow, but was foiled by the PCA's insistence on following The Process.
Guides from Beth	• The chief engineer is a powerful position. Building or recruiting these people is a primary task for leaders. The role can be customized for different situations, but the skill set—engineering, customer focus, project management, and leadership—is the same. • It's hard work to get a team to have "fingerprints" on the entire plan for a project, but it's worth the trouble.
Coming up next	Beth completes the tale of TRIM's project planning. The team estimates user stories and allocates them to sprints, plans the first sprint in detail, and establishes the teaming and tracking mechanisms.

NOTES

1. See James M. Morgan and Jeffrey K. Liker, *The Toyota Product Development System,* New York: Productivity Press, 2006, p. 118 and following pages, for a description of the chief engineer role at Toyota.
2. A lot of literature on Agile development is now available. This section draws, of course, on the Agile Manifesto (see Chapter 17); Alistair Cockburn, *Agile Software Development,* Upper Saddle River, NJ: Pearson Education, 2002; Ken Schwaber and Mike Beedle, *Agile Software Development with SCRUM,* 1st ed., Upper Saddle River, NJ: Prentice Hall, October 15, 2001; Mike Cohen, *User Stories Applied for Agile Software Development,* Boston: Addison–Wesley, 2004.
3. See Cohen, p. 137.
4. Craig Larman, *Agile and Iterative Development, a Manager's Guide,* Boston, Addison–Wesley, 2004, p. 87 and following pages.

11

Planning and Managing TRIM's 1-Month Sprints

OCTOBER 2005

Beth:

Day 2 of the TRIM planning session dawned a beautiful fall San Diego day, sunny and crisp. The group had regathered in the conference room, and Judy and Alex were kicking off the meeting. Neville leaned up against the wall with his cup of coffee, a hovering presence ready to jump in if he thought he was needed.

Planning the Sprints

Judy started. "Today we are going to do two things. This morning we will all be together in this room, doing our best to take the user stories we did yesterday, do some rough estimating, and allocate them to the initial or subsequent releases of the system. Remember, release 1 is a year away, November 2006. We usually don't like a year-long period until release, but we have a big system to build. Any items that we allocate beyond release 1 go into a 'hold' bucket, and we won't be dealing with them any further today. Our goal is to build the smallest, useful first release, please try hard to keep non-essentials out of it."

"Next, we will take the R1 user stories and allocate them to the sprints. For R1, we plan on doing 11 sprints. One starts next Monday and continues through year end; we're going to make that one a little longer than the rest because we are just getting going and to accommodate the year-end holiday season. The rest will all be 1-month long, from the first Monday of the month to the last business day before the first Monday of the following month. The last sprint won't have any items allocated to it yet; we will use that for final testing and hardening of the system and for preparation to deploy."

"Finally, we'll do the detailed planning for sprint 1. This afternoon, we will split up into our subteams, and a few more people will join us from the development groups. By the end of the day, we expect to have the outline of the detailed plan for our first sprint, and a somewhat rougher sketch for our second sprint. Then, tomorrow morning, each of the teams will present its plans to the rest of us, and we'll work to harmonize them into an overall coherent plan. Finally, after lunch tomorrow we'll spend a couple hours talking through how we will manage the project—covering our meeting schedules, status reports, issue and change management, and the plan for our next get-together."

"Before I get started on some guidance on prioritizing and allocating the user stories, Neville, do you have anything you'd like to add?"

Neville walked to the front of the room and said, "Sure, I can add a few things. First, the general outline of the first release has already been set, as you've read, or will read, in the concept document and the statement of work. It'd be tough to change that foundational agreement at this point, but not impossible if you really think it necessary."

"Second, especially for those of you used to less iterative development approaches," with a friendly nod to Sybil, "as you put the plans together for the sprints you need to focus on actual, tested software deliveries. There can be a temptation to allocate requirements to the first sprint, design to the second, and so on, which doesn't do the job. Our goal is to come up with a plan that gives us enough technology architecture and infrastructure early on that we can test it, and then keep adding tested units every month until we have enough to ship. Every month we should have a working system, even though it won't do a whole lot for a while."

"As you put the plans together, remember that at the end of each sprint we'll all be meeting here for demonstrations. Each team will demonstrate its results so that everyone can see the progress and have an opportunity for input and to make any adjustments in their own teams that might be needed. Think about what the demonstrations look like as you do the plans. A sprint must have a visual, tangible outcome, preferably code;

especially in early sprints, however, there may be noncode work done that you'll need to find a way to demonstrate. As we move ahead, the demos become focal points for our intersystem assembly and testing as well. I'll warn you in advance how bored I get with walking through detailed system design diagrams!"

"Finally, you'll need to think through long lead-time items and be sure we get them started early on. One of the concerns I have is around our information privacy management. I think we've got an approach that will work well, but we need to get the design of user profiles and functional restrictions figured out in detail early because it will affect how all of our data and transactions are developed."

"I went over the backlog results from yesterday with Judy and Alex early this morning, and I want to congratulate you. It looks like a great foundation for TRIM. I'd also like to acknowledge the work Judy, Alex, Sybil, and Jeff did last night sorting out the stories into the organized list you'll have to work with today."

"I will be rotating through the individual team planning sessions this afternoon, to answer any questions you might have and to help you on anything you get stuck on"

"Judy, Alex, that's it for me. Let's get started!"

The morning session was spent taking the major user stories and allocating them to the 11 sprints and estimating the first sprint in detail. Alex had prepared the room by putting the refined user stories on cards along one side of the back wall of the room, and he had laid out the sprints and the teams along the rest of the wall (Figure 15). He split the room into six areas, one for each of the teams: Lender, Buyer, Watcher, Information

User Stories	1	2	3	Sprints 4	5	6	7	Team
								All
								Lender
								Buyer
								Watcher
								Info Mgt
								Sec/Priv/Billing
								Property

FIGURE 15
Allocating stories to sprints.

Management, Security/Privacy/Billing, and Property Preservation. He began the conversation by asking everyone to bring their chairs up to the front of the room, in a semicircle around the back wall, for the sprint definition exercise.

Along the top of the chart, Alex wrote the major themes of each sprint in erasable marker, as far as they'd been laid out in the concept document and the statement of work. He then facilitated a discussion to clarify and adjust the sprint objectives: Were we building the items in the right order, did we deal with long lead times and risky items early, did we have items in the later sprints that we could sacrifice for R1 if we got behind? Was each sprint a coherent, coordinated set of functionality across the several subteams? What would the demonstrations be? After an intense hour, we had a set of sprint objectives that seemed to work, and Alex gave us a break to recover and get refreshed for user story allocation.

When we were back together, Judy took over facilitation. Our next task was to take the user story cards on the left side of the wall and distribute them across the sprints. Judy grabbed a few cards and demonstrated the thought process: "Here we have 'send system usage invoices to users' for the Security/Privacy/Billing team. That would seem to go into sprint 7, when we start to flesh out our administrative functions. Got it?" She moved the card into its selected box on the wall and checked for understanding.

"Now, take your chairs and your cards back to your areas and start spreading. Each team should select a facilitator and a recorder. Go ahead and put the cards up on the board as soon as you allocate; let's do this task with flow instead of batch. Remember all the teams are right here in the room, so feel free to walk over to the other tables to confer and line up your plans. Alex and I will be wandering about to help."

Following Judy's instructions, each subteam began its work, and several hours of active, fluid discussion began. Groups talked at their tables, tables were rearranged into ad hoc cross-team conferences, and recorders went to the board and taped up their cards. Periodically Alex or Judy would call everyone to the board to talk over sticky issues or just to review our progress so far. By midafternoon, almost all the cards were spread across the sprints, leaving Judy just a few stragglers for which some more analysis was required. Our final task of the day was to do the detailed plan for sprint 1.

Back at our tables, with just the cards for sprint 1, each team began estimating the user stories. Following instructions and a demonstration from
Alex, user stories were broken further down into tasks, and tasks were
allocated and estimated. Each team had to do a reasonableness test that
the tasks fit into the sprint period and adjust if they did not. By the end
of this very long day, each team had a plan for sprint 1 and was ready and
raring to go the following Monday, the official beginning of sprint 1 and
the first scrums of the project.

Establish the Agile Management Regime

The following morning was the wrap-up session. After the teams shared
an overview of their overall and sprint 1 plans, Alex laid out some of the
teaming mechanisms. The critical ones he spent time on included:

- the knowledge-sharing platform—a series of Web sites, blogs, document repositories, and project planning and tracking tools;
- daily 15-minute meetings for each team and the "scrum of scrums"—
  the afternoon session of the scrum masters and other project
  leadership;
- the "Big Room," where each team would have wall space to track
  progress and our senior leadership team would meet weekly; and
- "A3s," a one-page format developed by Toyota and used in many Lean
  implementations, to help us be more efficient in problem solving.

There were a lot of questions, and Alex did his best to answer them. The
team had absorbed a lot of new ideas and was getting tired. As the noon
breakup neared, Neville reacquired control of the meeting to wrap it up.

"I want to congratulate you on what you've accomplished over the past
few days. I hope you all feel as good as I do about our progress, both sub-
stantively on our planning and on how our large team and subteams are
beginning to form."

"I know you all have a lot more questions on exactly how this project
will function," he said. "I want to encourage you to leverage the framework and tools we are providing, but also to keep a thoughtful and critical

eye open. Every project is different, and no doubt we'll need to adjust and innovate to make these tools work for us."

"I hope you now realize our basic approach; as you can see, Lean/Agile project management as we practice it is anything but the caricatures you may have heard. Our commitments are strong and firm; our plan is detailed and rigorously managed. The difference is that we will not over-plan, we will avoid wasteful activities and rework, and we will honestly know where we are, surface problems quickly, and deal with them swiftly and with integrity and rigor. Our progress will be measured by actual integrated and tested code delivery wherever possible; we need to have continual integration of working software be our common focus. All of our tasks need to be aimed at that, as well as thinking through what we need to do to ensure that users are prepared to use the software productively and that our team members are prepared to maintain and enhance the systems we build."

"We will have no detailed, consolidated central plan in the way some of you may be used to. No one ever reads those things, and I don't want to waste my time or yours calling you onto the carpet for missing dates for low-level tasks you planned months in advance. We will minimize intrateam information flows to avoid clogging our information arteries with too much detail. We'll bring the critical information forward to the forum where it makes the most sense, and we'll use the daily scrums, integrating events and the sprint-end demo to tell us all where we really are at all times. Of course, we will rely on you to tell us where you are and to identify and raise problems, using the forums and tools we provide."

"Finally, you should understand that while we have extensive governance established through our contractual relationships, the statement of work, management teams, and so on, I have overall accountability for the success of this project. Any issues or concerns you have that are not being addressed another way you are expected to bring to me. Leadership will determine the success of the project, beginning with me and including all of you."

With that, the meeting broke up, splintering into small groups that lingered or headed off to lunch.

Signposts	**TRIM project**
	• The team completed identification of user stories for the first release (ending in 1 year) and then allocated them among the 11 sprints that comprised it.
	• Detailed planning for the first sprint was done; teams were ready to scrum!
	• The management regime—meetings, communication, information sharing—was set.
Guides from Beth	• The user story—more than a "requirement," less than a use case—works well as customer-focused planning granularity.
	• Scrum establishes a cadence to the flow of development. This makes problems and slippages evident quickly.
	• Teams need leadership to structure interactions that enable them to succeed. The various exercises and props that Alex and Judy used helped the teams to use their time effectively, inject rigor into their decision making, and take ownership of the results.
Coming up next	Beth continues narrating. The Real Estate Division reviews the status of both projects as October 2005 comes to an end.

12

Status Update for Both Projects

OCTOBER 2005

Beth:

Greg Allenby looked a little tired this afternoon. He'd just returned from St. Paul, where he had presented an update on the TRIM project to the Cremins leadership team at CEO Evan Nogelmeyer's staff meeting. Gina Sebastian, president of the Specialty Communications Group and Greg's boss, had requested permission for Greg to give the update for two reasons: because TRIM was a fairly significant investment for Cremins, especially given the recent acquisition of the Real Estate Division, and as a low-impact way to start educating the group on some better ideas on how to do software projects.

Gina was quite concerned about the approach being taken on Cremins United, but didn't have any better ideas on how to go about addressing them. Tom Stillman was too highly trusted by Evan for any sort of direct confrontation on something as seemingly arcane as system development methods, given Evan's leadership style in areas he didn't personally know well. Technology was one of those areas, and Evan had been very successful managing gaps in his knowledge by relying on his sense of people. Until evidence arose to put Tom's judgment in doubt, Evan would trust him to manage the details of the Cremins United project.

Greg had brought Neville to St. Paul with him to give the update. Greg often brought others to do presentations. It allowed them to get exposure and development opportunities, and allowed Greg to keep one step removed from the content, watch the audience, and jump in with clarifications and additions when needed. Greg kicked off his staff meeting today by asking Neville to give a report on the St. Paul meeting.

Good Support for the TRIM Project

"I've handed out the presentation I used," Neville began. "As you can see, it's just a few pages. I started with the TRIM business plan, here on page two. It shows the market forces and changes that have created this need and who will pay us how much for what, and why us and not other competitors. This went over very well; that group really understands business planning and asked a lot of tough questions. Someone asked about supporting bulk home auctions; another was concerned about potential channel conflict if a bank or investor chose to bypass Realtors and sell directly to consumers, given the involvement we have with multiple listing services."

"On page three, I've laid out the project schedule and approach, with each sprint marked and an idea of what the demos at the end of each could be. I talked over some of the risks and how this approach helped us ameliorate them by giving us feedback every month. There wasn't much discussion on this, other than nods and okays. That was about it."

"Basically, we have good support for TRIM and there's no issue with how we want to do it; that's basically our call," said Greg. "There wasn't much engagement with the method of how we do it, pretty much what I expected, because they don't see development method as an issue they need to be concerned with at this point. This brings us to Cremins United. Neville, you had the pleasure of being able to hear Tom Stillman's and Neil Gottschalk's updates on CU; do you want to share that with the team? Mary and Beth, I'm sure you'll be interested in this."

The CU Project: Committing to a Wishful Schedule

Neville began, "I wasn't at any of the previous meetings on CU, so I don't know the background of what's been talked about already. The purpose of this update was to give a completion date and cost estimate for the phase 1. There wasn't much debate about what phase 1 would be: Basically, each business line wants its sales and production areas to be included, and it seemed pretty well worked out which areas would be involved. Tom had Neil explain the planning process the team had been through, using The Process and project plans based on the steps it defines. Neil said that the team had initially wanted to take almost 2 years till first release, but that by working the plan to do some activities in parallel, use offshore testing, and some other techniques, they were able to bring it down to about 14 months—a year to finish the development and 2 months to integration test."

Mary had been listening raptly, and at this she gasped. "Wow, that's amazing!"

Neville, who hadn't been involved in CU at all, wondered why.

Mary gave a brief explanation of what had occurred to date: her planning session, the PCA's direction to cut the time, and the creation of the Process-based plans. "I guess we do now have plans that show us finishing on that schedule. I just find it hard to imagine that Neil and Tom actually believe them, or that they would commit to them in front of Evan and the rest of the leadership team. The plan wasn't reworked down a year; it was directed down. Saying so doesn't make it so!"

"Well, Mary," Neville continued, "Evan still wasn't happy with the time frame or cost, although he was more concerned with time than cost. Neil said that we weren't done with the planning, that we were still working some ideas to try to move it up."

"Move it up!" Mary was stunned. "Greg, what did you say then? You know how impossible that is."

"Think about it, Mary. What could I say? I can't prove that it can't be done. All I have is your belief, which of course I share. In that forum I can't contradict Neil and Tom because I just don't have the data to do so. I did talk with Gina after the meeting and conveyed your concerns, so it will be up to her on how she manages the risk. Looks to me like there is a lot of wishful thinking going on, but we can't thrust help on people who don't want it."

Mary shook her head. "Do you think they really believe we can get it done on that schedule, or are they doing some sort of sneaky management upward? Like if they said it really would take 2 years, the project wouldn't be approved?"

Greg responded, "I really don't know, Mary. I find it hard to imagine because I'd never do that and could never trust anyone who tried to play me that way. But I'm new to the Cremins corporate culture, so I can't say."

"So, Mary," Neville continued, "what exactly did Tom Stillman commit you to?"

"Go-live with users is December 1, 2006. Isn't that around the time when you are planning your release 1 also?"

"Yes, about the same time," Neville confirmed.

Greg wanted to explore the CU due date and where Mary's part of the project sat. He asked her to relate to the group how she got her part of the project to come in on time after a year had been shaved off it.

"It wasn't easy. The Process has distinct phases, with phase gates between them when the artifacts are reviewed for quality and understanding by the recipients—essentially the people who are accountable for the next phase, plus a central QA/Audit group. In order to meet a December go-live date, with just 2 months of integration testing, the code complete date is September. The PMO set a requirements complete date of January 30, less than 3 months from now. We're not supposed to start design until the requirements milestone is complete or start coding until design is complete."

Walt, the CFO, had seen this kind of plan before. "That sounds familiar. That's how we used to do projects when I was in public accounting! It's a design to reduce risks to the integrator. Once you have the requirements documents reviewed and approved, you can update the time lines and the cost estimates based on what's new—usually a lot of things that weren't included in the initial estimate on which you got the job. Then, after the design, if you learn new things that cause you to have to update the requirements, it's a change order, which allows you to increase the cost and move the completion date again. It's not your fault—it's the client's, for not getting the requirements right. Then you can build right to the design, test to it; anything that is found in testing that won't work in actual practice, as long as it wasn't in the design, is another change order and more time and more money."

"Walt, the problem here is that we're not a consulting company trying to protect our behinds and our margins. We're all in the same company, presumably aimed at the same goal."

Mary continued, "Here's how we built a plan to meet the date. The Process requires that you identify all the documents that you need to do, and then it assigns an average number of hours to do each document. It then does the same for design documents and then for each component you have to build, like a report, a database, or an interface. My project manager, GG for George Giordano, is a wizard at The Process! He kept adjusting the number of use cases, their complexity—you name it—until he had a schedule that worked. It shows us getting done right on time, and it fits with the number and types of people that we have in our staffing plan." Mary was very proud of herself.

Greg had a puzzled look on his face. "He did all that in 2 weeks and now you're going to follow it?"

"Oh, no, I don't think we'll follow it at all. When GG started the project plan, our architecture was to take the sales software that my group has built for realtors and extend it to deal with everything CU needed. That's what the central architecture group had chosen; they said it was the best sales software in the company and it met their technical requirements, like Java, plain old browser-based, app server, and Oracle. So our plan, as we submitted it, is based on that technology. But, as I looked at what we needed to do, after spending time with my business partners, time in the field with BCG and Commercial salesmen, and playing with that horrendous schedule and process, I thought there was no way to build this out by next December. So I'm planning on changing the architecture, and then we can change the plan. I do wonder what the other teams might be thinking, though."

This was the first time Greg was hearing this, and I could tell that he thought this was vintage Mary. Count on her to find a way to get things done, but also count on her to find a way that is adventurous and rebellious at once. "So what *is* your plan, Mary?" asked Greg.

Buying Off-the-Shelf Software to Speed Up Development

Mary was happy to answer that question: I could see that she had spent a lot of time trying to figure her way out of this dilemma. "Our sales system was primarily built for lone rangers, which is how most realtors work. They jealously guard their contact lists and might have, at most, a couple of assistants. It was never built to support, in one instance, anything like the number of users we'll need for CU or to have the extensive interfaces, security, privacy management, and reporting we'd have to build. Also, because it's our own proprietary software, getting a lot of people to work on it at once will be impossible. We'd have to train people in it, which would take our expert staff away from development for months, and our development environment and code control mechanisms aren't designed for that many developers working at once. The architects were right that we do have many of the needed elements and it could be made to work, but we couldn't get enough changes done fast enough, and it's not likely it would be worth the money compared to what we could buy."

Neville caught the hint. "You're going to buy something?"

Mary smiled again. "You betcha, Neville. Hey, I'm sounding like a Minnesotan, how's about that? Too much time in St. Paul."

More seriously now, Mary explained. "There are a couple of mature sales systems in the market that could fit us better than our own software. They can support thousands of users, have sophisticated role-based security, and if we couple them with an integration/orchestration layer, can connect up with services very nicely. I can get consultants who have implemented the system several times before. The software vendor will even host the system for us, if I run into trouble with the enterprise hosting department."

"Oh, one more thing," Mary continued, "the consultant or vendor professional services group will have an implementation methodology that they've used multiple times before with this software, so I hope to get an exception to The Process. We can go with a product and an implementation method that is relatively standardized and proven, with people who know how to do it. Beats the heck out of trying to get my people and a bunch of contractors to follow The Process for the first time!"

This was the first I'd heard this from Mary as well. It sounded like it could really work—get the job done, and keep Mary sane by somewhat isolating her from the rigors of the specified, rigid Process. I asked her how she expected to get approval for the idea and what her next steps were.

"Amazingly, here is where The Process really helps out. It turns out that the overall architecture was approved in a conceptual architecture document about the time I was joining the project. The next architecture document isn't due until after the requirements phase, which wouldn't be until sometime after January. That means that to change to conceptual architecture, we need to submit a change request, laying out the reasons for the change, the cost, and the expected impact on cost and time. If the impact of the CR isn't a significant increase in cost or time, it doesn't need to go to the PCA; it can just be approved by the appropriate governing body, which in this case is the Architectural Council. So, I just need to convince Scott Diggs, the architect assigned to me, and then he presents to the AC."

"Scott's just about there; he's a practical guy, and he's helping review a couple vendors against the enterprise architectures and the requirements gathered so far. I've done some revised estimates of what it would take to modify our software—of course, *after* GG submitted our first plan— and they show something more realistic based on more time to get more developers involved. We're getting some quick formal proposals from the two leading vendors. I told them roughly where they'd have to be on cost to get the deal, and we'll see how they come in. Either one would do, and there are good consulting practices for both in San Diego and LA. I should be able to get a CR to the architects by the week after next, and Scott has warned Janice, his boss, and I alerted Frankie, the technology lead for CU and kind of my new boss, that it's coming. Frankie doesn't seem to think the PCA would care much; they are mostly leaving the technology choices to the technologists."

I had one more question. "If you don't get approval for a couple of weeks, you're all the way out to Thanksgiving. How could you get requirements done by end of January?"

"You've got me there, Beth. No way to do that. We'd have to get an exception to the phase gate, based on the development process of the vendor we choose. Both vendors are quite happy to do incremental development, and the consultants are comfortable working that way too. If we can get a contract by Christmas, we can start intensive work right after the first of the year. We'll stand up the software vanilla, do requirements, design, and build in the order the vendor recommends. We can get some requirements done by the end of January and keep doing them through, say, June or July, as long as we get the right foundational ones done early. I think if we explain that we really need services like pricing, product selection, and customer information well defined before we finish our own requirements, they should let us do it this way. Plus, they have a lot of other problems to worry about!"

Greg was quite impressed, I could tell. Mary continually surprised him, mostly in good ways, like today. She was never boring!

Requirements by the Book

Greg was still thinking over Mary's idea and was puzzled by something. "Mary," he queried, "let's say you weren't going to be your usual maverick self on this and thought the right solution was modifying our current sales systems. How would you have gone about getting requirements completed so quickly? Come to think of it, what are the other teams doing?"

"I'm not sure what all of them are doing, but I do know what the Production Management team is doing. Ken Fong is the business lead of that group; he is a very savvy, experienced guy, and he has had some bad experiences with technology people telling him what he could and could not get, based on what the system could or could not do easily. He is taking his role very seriously and has come up with a method to get consensus requirements on time. It's really quite brilliant of him, although it's sure to be a disastrous start for the project."

"Don't tell me," said Neville, "I can guess. Some sort of visioning how Production Management should work in an 'ideal state'? That way he wouldn't have to deal at all with any of the constraints of the production management systems, nor would he have to worry about the time constraints. He can do what he's supposed to do and claim victory."

"You've got it, Neville! Seen this before, have you? Ken is taking his role exactly as defined, giving requirements totally independent of any technology solution or any other constraints, getting ready for handoff to design at the end of January. He has hired consultants from one of the big firms to come in and facilitate visioning and requirements definition meetings, and then the consultants will write up what they hear into the use cases and other requirements artifacts that The Process demands. He really doesn't know any better, and I'll bet he'll do a pretty good job. I just pity the poor design team that is going to get his requirements in a big batch at the end of January!"

Neville scowled and directed his remark to Greg. "Is there anything we can do to help Ken or the PCA understand what they are getting themselves into? You can just see the inventory Ken will be building—something he'd never do in the plant."

"I really don't think so, Neville. PCA is completely committed to the methods and schedule they've chosen; they are going to have to learn for themselves. I think the best we can do is to help Mary and her team get the freedom to implement in a somewhat different way, while looking as much as possible like they are following the same processes that everyone else is. In the meantime, we have some other things on the agenda today we need to talk about."

With that, we went on to talk about next year's budgets, strategic planning, and the next generation of our training plans.

Signposts

Cremins United project

- The PCA committed to the new, shorter schedule.
- Mary had met the Process-imposed deadlines so far and planned to deliver by using a vendor product instead of building upon the Real Estate Division's architecturally approved sales products.
- Other areas planned to meet the first Process gate, requirements, without regard for how that affected what came afterward.

TRIM project

- Cremins leadership, at Evan's staff meeting, expressed support for the TRIM business case but evinced no interest in its development methods.

Guides from Beth

- A handoff-oriented plan can look right on track for a long time, as each group does what it needs to meet its handoff date and specified deliverables. Watch out for what happens when it finally gets to the people who have to build it!
- The phase-gate approach for requirements is going to result in a massive inventory of undesigned ideas. We know that large in-process inventory is a problem in our manufacturing plants; we need to learn that it is equally pernicious in systems or product development.

Coming up next

Wes takes over the tale. Next: Mary's challenge to the CU architects.

13

The CU Project's Buy versus Build Decision

NOVEMBER 2005

Wes:

Tom Stillman had asked me to sit in on a meeting of the Architecture Council meeting to represent the PCA. The Sales team had submitted a change request (CR) to the conceptual architecture, asking to buy a sales system instead of enhancing the sales systems sold by the Real Estate Division. My instructions were to ensure that the technology folks were considering business issues as well as just technical ones; Tom had some concerns in this area from previous experiences at Cremins. Other than ensuring a full consideration, the PCA didn't have a strong opinion on whether this should be a build or buy, or, if we did buy, what we should buy. I had to update the PCA on what the decision was, but as long as we had agreement between the AC and me, the presumption was that the decision on this CR was delegated to this team.

Several members of the Sales team were present at the meeting. Actually, by "present," I mean either in a conference room in St. Paul or on the phone. GG, the Sales project manager; Mary, the Sales technical leader; and Scott, the Sales architect, were ready to go.

"We Had a Lot More to Do Than We Originally Thought"

Scott, as the architect, was leading the presentation. "You should all have in front of you three documents: the change request itself, the revised new conceptual architecture document based on CSMPro, and a one-page PowerPoint with the key architectural issues we need to consider. Anyone need me to send them to you?"

Hearing nothing, Scott continued. "Most of you know that the approved CU conceptual architecture envisioned extending the Real Estate Division's sales system to support the enterprise. That is also the basis upon which we made our plan and were able to commit to making our dates. However, when we dove a little deeper into the changes we would need to make, we found we had a lot more to do than we initially thought. This put the date at serious risk."

Scott continued to lay out some of the problems his team was facing. "Our technology team also came to the conclusion that the requirements we have for CU are sufficiently different from those our current sales systems meet, even though on the surface they are similar, that it would be better to start our development from a commercial code base. As shown on the CR, we don't believe that this change affects either cost or time frame materially. We believe it is beneficial to both and that it would be a permanent improvement to our ability to deliver functionality and performance while containing costs."

Janice, the lead architect and head of the council, guided the conversation. "Scott, why don't you go on and describe the basics of the CSMPro product, and then we can deal with the architectural issues?"

I sensed some tension in Janice's voice; it was hard for me to pick up on anything more subtle. I wondered where Janice was on this question. But I didn't have time to think about it because Scott swiftly answered her question.

Buying off the Shelf

"You have the new conceptual architecture document in front of you, and you can read it for details," Scott began. "I'll just go over the highlights of the product, the company, and the technology. Interrupt me with any questions."

"CSMPro is short for "Consultative Sales Manager Professional," which is one of the top two or three sales management systems in the industry.

The product was initially built 20 years ago or so and had tremendous growth throughout the '90s. Its initial competitive advantage was that it was a pure Microsoft solution, begun for small- to medium-size companies, but as the Microsoft technology became more scalable, it gradually worked its way up to larger and larger companies. The product was bought by ERPro 4 years ago and integrated into its suite of enterprise resource planning tools and given the 'Pro' designation."

"In the last 4 years, CSMPro has been regularly updated to .Net technology. It now has a very friendly, rich user interface, is highly configurable, and is extensible. ERPro has a large and capable professional services group that could help us, and there are third-party integrators with good experience and methodologies for implementation with people in Southern California."

"We have checked out CSMPro with our external technology assessment services and found that it is well respected for vision and execution, and we also did brief reference calls with two companies larger than we are and got generally good feedback on the product and the company as a partner. Mary O'Connell knows several of their development managers and thinks highly of them. Their financials were pretty solid before they got bought by ERPro, and we have no reason to believe that in the intervening years anything substantial has changed. ERPro is a solidly profitable company with global presence, and Cremins already has an enterprise agreement with them because we have a couple of their other products in house."

"Finally, because our target architecture is Java and Oracle based, we had to deal with the issue of CSMPro being completely a Microsoft-based product. We are recommending that we outsource the hosting of the system to CSMPro, and rely on them to manage the infrastructure. We will still manage the development and integration, with help from their professional services group and probably a third-party partner. They are doing this for several large clients; increasingly, their new customers and older customers going through upgrades are taking this option."

While I didn't understand much about the technology issues, it sounded like a well-thought-out plan that could help us get to where we needed to be, when we needed to be there. From what I'd seen, I could trust Mary and her team, especially when they were being scrutinized by Frankie, Janice, et al. as well. I wanted to be sure that this solution would meet our business needs also, so I asked Mary's business partner, Sam Baker from the Commercial Group, what he thought of the change.

"Thanks for asking, Wes. I'm definitely not a technologist, so I can't speak to any of the architectural questions you guys are talking about. I can speak to the functionality of the system, though. I've had several people from the Sales focus group, which includes people from all three lines of business, and from more than one area within some lines, helping me look over the options. We all agree that the software that the Real Estate Division has, which is supposed to be the base for the CU solution, is missing a lot of key functions. We also spent some time with a developer on Mary's team who showed us what it would take to make modifications and integrations, and then saw the same type of thing from CSMPro and the other contender we looked at. Those systems are designed much more for configurability—I'd guess because they are being sold to a larger, less specialized audience than the specialized software in Real Estate Division."

Sam continued, "We also went out to one of CSMPro's clients. We liked what we saw and heard. We know there are some things it doesn't do well, especially around supporting the complicated sales process needed for custom quotes, but their product manager has committed to building those functions out because other customers have been asking for that as well. The Sales focus group is comfortable with the CR."

"Thanks, Sam," I said. "Sounds like you've done your homework. Janice, back to you; it appears we have some technical considerations to discuss as well."

Now it was Janice's turn. "Wes, if you or Sam want to drop out of the meeting now, as we get into the technical issues, you're welcome to do so."

That was annoying. Did she think I couldn't understand the conversation? I could see what Tom was worried about. "Thanks, Janice, but I think the PCA wanted me to listen in to the whole discussion, and besides it's a great opportunity for me to learn. I'll be quiet and not ask stupid questions, I promise."

"Ok," Janice replied, sounding surly even over the phone. "Scott, can you walk us through the architectural issues slide?"

"Sure. You should all have in front of you a diagram titled 'Comparison of CSMPro to Enterprise Standards' [Figure 16]. You all have it? OK, let's take a look."

Ref	Standard	CSMPro	Enterprise
1	Development Tools	Microsoft .Net, Software Factory	Java, Eclipse
2	Database	Microsoft SQL Server	Oracle
3	Integration/Orchestration Middleware	BizTalk	BusinessWorks
4	Hosting / Hardware	Outsourced to ERPro	Cremins Hosting Services, HP Blades
5	Data Definitions	Proprietary to CSMPro	Cremins Central Data Model
6	User Interface Design	Proprietary CSMPro, based on Microsoft Style Guides	Cremins UI Guidelines
7	MIS	Proprietary MIS Environment based on Microsoft Tools	Enterprise Data Warehouse
8	Development Methodology	CSMPro Accelerator, proprietary system-specific	The Process, generic and common method

FIGURE 16
Comparison of CSMPro to enterprise standards.

Making Off-the-Shelf Software Fit Company Standards

Scott then walked us through the chart he had prepared. "What I've done is to identify what seemed to be the biggest violations of our standards. You can see how it violates essentially all of our standards, including development environment, database, integration middleware, hardware platform, data definitions, user interface, reporting, and methodology."

"Other than those items, Scott, how does it fit?" That was Mary, trying to add some levity. She'd been very quiet up until now. She'd been very effective in getting Scott to carry her water to this point; I wondered if she saw a battle brewing. "Just kidding," Mary said.

Janice wasn't happy with Mary's jest. "There are some serious issues here that we need to consider. This product just isn't a fit with our target architectures. We have several options: we can work with them to try to get them to change some of their underlying technologies; we can consider other products on the market that meet our target architecture better; or we can look at the cost and time of modifying the Real Estate Division's software and determine whether the better fit to the target architecture merits the higher costs."

At this point in the meeting, I have to admit that I was completely sold on going with CSMPro; I just didn't see any downsides. As I looked over the list of items, I didn't see how any of these differences would matter, especially because we would be outsourcing the management of the infrastructure. I'd heard enough about our overworked hosting group to think the outsourcing idea a bit of inspired genius; it could help us in Sales and, by reducing the enormous workload on the hosting team, other areas as well. But perhaps there were some issues—I couldn't imagine that Janice would want to enforce uniformity for its own sake. I suggested we go through the areas one by one and talk about what problems a lack of conformity would cause for us.

"Let's start with number one on your list, the development tools," I suggested, immediately violating my oath of silence. "Scott, what is the downside to using tools different from the rest of our systems?"

After a pregnant pause, Scott tentatively answered. "Wes, I'm not sure I see much problem with this one. The..." At that, Janice interrupted; she wasn't happy with where Scott was going. "Wes, Scott, we need to consider the bigger picture. If this application uses tools different from those of other systems, we will have a harder time sharing developers among our teams and less effective internal code review and standards enforcement. We could also have some issues with interoperability for things like single sign-on."

"Mary," I asked, "as development manager, how would you respond to that?" By now Janice must really be regretting that I had stayed on for this discussion.

"Speaking as development manager—just about the sales system— I don't see either of these concerns as material deficiencies in this case. Development in this system will require extensive training and experience, not only in the underlying technology, but also in the factory framework, the CSMPro application, and the businesses we support. I'd anticipate a permanent development team for this, as well as supplements when 'surge' needs would come from either CSMPro Professional Services or from a third-party specialist. I don't see a problem on interoperability either; we already use active directory for authorization from Microsoft, and ERPro has integrated its hosted services with internal directory services of their clients several times. Janice, does that make sense to you?"

"Yes, in general it does in this specific case, but it usually does in specific cases. It's just when we wind up with many different silos of development environments; each case doesn't hurt in and of itself, but where is the grain of sand that finally breaks the camel's back? Let's go on to item 2: the database. The issues here include the uniqueness issues we've already addressed, but also some others, like monitoring tools, backup and recovery management, and disaster recovery."

Sam answered this one. "That's the beauty of the outsourcing. They take care of all of this; we shouldn't really have to care at all what technology they are using as long as we have a good contract and it's a technology that is safe—you know, not something weird that will become obsolete soon."

Janice replied, "We do have a risk with the database, operating system, and such that the outsourcer fails to meet our requirements. When an outsourcer is using technologies with which we are familiar, we always have the option of bringing the application back in house. When the technology isn't supported by our teams, our options are much more limited."

Mary could agree with this one, so she did. "You are right on with that, Janice. We'd still have options of getting another outsourcer to run it or building the skills ourselves. But I think the probability of CSMPro failing to the point where we'd need to make a change is pretty low."

Janice appreciated Mary's agreement and went on to the next items. "Let's cover a couple of more serious barriers: the proprietary data design and the proprietary integration software—I'm looking at numbers 3 and 5 on the chart. The CSMPro data structures are proprietary to them, so we will need to translate all data flowing in and out into our standard formats. That will create more mapping, transformation, and testing work, and it poses some risks to performance. Also, using BizTalk instead of our standard integration toolset adds another hop and potential points of failure and lack of operations visibility."

"Good comments, Janice; we've definitely talked this over and considered these issues," Mary responded. "Let's deal with item 5, their proprietary data model, first. We have a couple ideas on that. First, we believe that any sales system we implement will have data models that differ from the standard common data model—certainly anything we buy, and even our own system in the Real Estate Division. We had estimated the cost to change our own system's data model, and it was totally prohibitive. Second, addressing issue 3, we've talked through the costs and risks of doing the translations and believe we have a way to avoid that entirely. We propose to skip the central data facility and the translations in and out of it and connect directly from CSMPro to the production management system. I know that isn't completely in line with the target architecture, but it would eliminate costs and risks and leverage the inherent integration capabilities of CSMPro to the maximum."

Now the battle seemed to be joined; Mary had hit a nerve here. "Going through a common, standard data bus is fundamental to our strategies, Mary, regardless of which sales system you use." Janice's voice was stern and uncompromising on this point. "You have to connect to something in any case, so it's better to connect through CSF than go directly to the production system."

Mary disagreed. "We really don't see it that way, Janice. The BizTalk integration delivered with CSMPro can connect directly to the production system as easily as to CSF, and doing a direct translation of the data instead of relaying through the CDM will give us higher fidelity. It will also ease change control; we won't all have to dance together whenever a field changes in CDM, and our team will be able to work directly with the Production Management team on what's going to be a very extensive and complex integration."

Janice wasn't willing to debate the CSF and CDM issues in this forum with Mary. She seemed flustered and angry as she said, "We can agree to disagree on that for now, Mary. We don't have much time left, and I'd like to summarize the options now, if that's okay. Wes?"

"Wait a minute, I have one more thing to say," interjected Sam. "Going back to item 6 on the chart, I see that you have a concern that the user interface design wouldn't meet the design guides. We don't care about colors or logos, and even if we did the CSMPRO salesman said we could adjust them. You haven't noted the positive side of the difference: that the CSMPro user interface is a lot more responsive and flexible than anything I've seen us build yet. It doesn't seem as slow as most of the Web-based systems we seem to be building these days."

Mary endorsed Sam's thought. "Sam is onto item 6, the user interface design, for those of you counting. On the technical side, CSMPro was initially built as a client/server application and then migrated to a browser-based platform. When they did that, many of their clients refused to upgrade due to loss of functionality and performance, so they've been working very hard to get their browser system to work more like their client/server system. We've seen their next release, which is using Microsoft's newest generation of user interface technology, and it's very impressive. I hate to admit it, but it's much cooler than the sales system the Real Estate Division is now offering."

"Mary, doesn't the use of that technology mean that CSMPro is Windows only?"

"Yes, it does. I don't see a problem with that; aren't all our users on Windows machines?"

"They are now, but one of our strategies is to keep our user interfaces vanilla so that we are not limited to a single operating system."

"If that's a serious concern, then we'd give up a lot of functionality. CSMPro is committed to having user interfaces that are simpler and work in cross-platform browsers, but they are planning on maintaining that function only as customers request it. My recommendation would be that, if we don't have any non-Windows users, we take full advantage of the platform-specific capabilities. If we find later that we need to support non-Windows platforms, we'll deal with it then."

I was really enjoying this debate. Mary was sharp as a pistol; she obviously wanted to get a sales system that she had control of, to connect it up as she saw fit to the other systems, to make it really rock, and to finish it on time. She wasn't afraid to challenge Janice in a way I hadn't seen before in the technology group, where Janice and the architects seemed to make up some sort of high priesthood. Janice was not about to let Mary challenge her control, especially her beloved "data abstraction layer," as she called it. I wondered if Janice would have the guts to deny the CR based on the flimsy issues raised so far, compared to the strong arguments in favor of going with CSMPro.

Considering Other Software Options

I checked to see that we were done with this user interface/platform independence issue for now, and then I moved the conversation back to our options. "Janice, I think you said we had three options: Get CSMPro to adopt some of our standards as shown in the chart into their product, like maybe our data model or moving to Oracle and Java; choose a different vendor; or stick with our initial plan and modify the Real Estate sales system. Did I get that right?"

"You did. Scott, can you answer the first question? Could we ask CSMPro to use more of our standards, whether it's using Oracle and Unix, Java, or modifying their internal data model?"

"I'd hesitate to ask them to do anything like this. They have a coherent and complete set of technologies, and they have integrated them in a way that works well for what they are trying to accomplish. Anything that they might agree to do for us would cost us money and raise our risks."

"How about other potential vendor solutions? Anything out there that better fits our standards?"

Mary took this one. "I've been in the sales systems business for going on 10 years now, competing head to head with everything from Act! to Siebel to SAP. Without exception, every solution out there will violate Cremins architectural standards. Any system that is rich enough to meet the needs of a large number of potential customers has to have a lot of proprietary elements to enable configurability and cut the time from sale to implementation. We did look at another option because it does run on Oracle, but we don't think it's a good a fit for a number of reasons we can go into if you'd like."

Scott spoke up to support Mary on this. "Janice, I did some research as well, and I'm much convinced that CSMPro is the best option. Anything we'd gain by having more aligned technology would cause us to lose more in other areas."

"So," Janice summarized, "that leaves us with the option of enhancing the existing sales system. Do you have an estimate of how much more it would cost to enhance this system versus going with CSMPro? Also, do you have an estimate for how long it would take and if there is absolutely no way to get it done on the CU schedule?"

I could see where she was going. If, indeed, there were value in aligning with the enterprise standards—although I got the feeling that neither Mary nor Scott believed that—how much was that worth?

Re-estimating Costs and Time Needed for the CU Project

GG, the Sales project manager, had been silent most of the meeting. I'd forgotten he was on the call. But now the magic PM words—cost and time—had been raised, so it was his turn. "This is George talking. Once we'd figured out that the cost and time to modify the Real Estate Division's system would blow our schedule and determined to check out the option of buying a system instead, we didn't complete the estimates. It didn't seem to be a very close call."

Janice wasn't giving up. "George, I'd like to get an estimate so that we can do the analysis as to whether the benefits of following the enterprise standards would be worth what might be added costs. How long would it take to get a rough estimate?"

"Mary, what do you think?" GG queried.

"We could probably get a quick estimate in a day or so; in fact, if you insist on our pursuing this, we'll have to. We need to get this decision made this week if we are going to have a chance of kicking off the development right after the first of the year. We have some contract work to do, and that's going to take at least a few weeks, best case; it'll be over the holidays and you know how little happens then. How about if we get the estimate to you by day after tomorrow, Janice, and then schedule a follow-up meeting to go over it and to talk through the data interface questions? I don't see any value in all the data transforms and intermediaries you are proposing, so I'd like to discuss that further. How about if I do some estimates on how much more doing that extra layer of transforms will cost, and then we can consider both cost/benefit issues?"

Scott answered for Janice. "That makes a lot of sense, Mary. I'll schedule a smaller meeting—how about just me, Janice, you, and GG? Then, afterward, we'll loop the business folks back in."

"Sounds good to me, Scott," I said. "I'll run the issue past the PCA at tomorrow's meeting so that I'm sure I have their temperature, and I'll expect to hear from—whom, maybe GG?—the day after tomorrow."

The Technology versus Business War Continues

The PCA meeting the next day had an unexpected agenda item. Frankie called me first thing in the morning and asked to add "data standards" to the agenda. I had a pretty good idea what that was about. I decided two could play at this game, and if the Technology Group was going to go behind Mary's back to the PCA on the data issue, I figured I'd go behind their backs directly to Tom to see if I could clear a path for Mary to CSM Pro. I was convinced that the Technology architects were in love with their standards for their own sake; after all, that was their job and their power base. It seemed to me that the Sales team had thought this through well, and we needed to do what they suggested if we were to have a chance of success, both short term and longer term. It was hard for me to imagine a serious downside after the weak arguments Janice had put forth. She didn't have a lot of credibility with me anyhow, given the high costs and limited results of the systems that she'd been shepherding for the last 5 years.

Before the PCA meeting at 10, I stopped by Tom's desk and related the events of yesterday's meeting. Tom had no love for our technology group. Like a lot of business leaders who don't know technology, he found the technologists frustrating, expensive, unwilling to commit and take accountability, lacking in a sense of urgency, and confusing—plus he hated the fact that he was stuck with them and couldn't shop the services and get treated like a customer. He didn't have the knowledge, skills, or taste to get into substantive arguments with them, but he loved the idea of outsourcing a chunk of the project. He told me that, unless the cost and time difference of the architect's preferred option was minimal and Janice could specifically identify and quantify offsetting benefits, I was authorized to approve the Sales team's CR. He didn't want to get into a debate over this in the PCA and felt he didn't have to, given the PCA's previous delegation to the people in the meeting yesterday. One win for the good guys.

Signposts	**Cremins United project**
	• The Sales team and the Architecture Group, led by Mary and Janice, respectively, went toe to toe over the buy–build decision and the demand that all interfaces go through the common service facility and the common data model.
	• Wes and Tom intervened and approved the decision to buy the CSMPro product as the Sales team recommended, even though it "violated" many architectural standards.
Guides from Wes	• There is a serious risk that architects, especially when they are in groups separate from the development teams that have missions to support specific business objectives, put excessive emphasis on the purity of their visions and enforcing the standards.
	• Business leaders need to be aware of this and demand concrete explanations of value in terms they can understand. Generalities such as "that's our standard" or "we can't support one of everything" can be smoke screens for lack of understanding of the true costs and benefits of the rules they are promulgating.

- One way to ameliorate this risk is to have architecture subservient to development; if that is not possible (e.g., when architecture is at a broader organizational level), leaders need to ensure that there is proper tension in the system so that alternatives get vetted in business terms.

Coming up next

Beth relates the resolution of the argument over the common service facility and common data model and the Sales team's decisions on development methods.

14

Drawing Boundaries and Tailoring Methods

NOVEMBER 2005

Beth:

Mary was livid. I'd joined her team meeting today, part of my own "go see" pledge I'd made to myself. I figured I needed to observe as much of the leadership of the CU and TRIM projects in action as I could. GG, her project manager; Scott, her assigned architect; and Sam, her "business" partner were on the phone; Mary and I were in her office.

"What!" she yelled at the phone. "The PCA decreed what?!!?" I jabbed the mute button, lightly touched Mary's arm, and said, "Cool down, Mary. Inside voice." Mary took a deep breath and unmuted the phone. "Sorry, Scott, I'm not yelling at you; I'm just surprised." I winked.

Scott answered, and if a voice can be sheepish over the phone, his was. "The PCA reiterated yesterday that all interfaces must use the common service facility, and all transactions must be in the common data model. It was documented in minutes from the meeting that Janice sent to me this morning."

Mary muttered under her breath, "Damn that woman," no doubt referring to Janice. It was said quietly, but not quietly enough. Scott had picked up Mary's comment, and he responded, "I'm really sorry, Mary, but I don't think it was Janice's fault. She talked with Frankie about our meeting on the change request, and Frankie wanted to stop any swirl about the integration strategy. I must have heard 'It's not open to debate' a dozen times this morning."

"Damn, we're really screwed now. This is going to make it really tough to get this done. Well, I guess we'll just have to play by the rules. What exactly are they, anyhow, for our interfaces?"

GG knew the answer to this one. "There is a document specified by The Process called the 'interface specification.' We write this up with the transactions we want, describing the data elements we need, and give it to the data team. They will map our data elements to the standard elements, create a standards-based transaction, and then they'll do maps and transforms from our data elements to the standard ones."

Mary cackled. Not just a laugh, a real cackle. "No way. No way! That can't work; it's just not that simple! We need to get together with the developers for the production management system at least; the interface is too complicated for a separate group to have any chance of getting it right. We need to map the transactions through, make sure we have them right, continuously integrate and test and tune the heck out of them for performance. What's wrong with these people?"

I muted the phone again and made a face at Mary; that was enough to get her to calm back down.

"No choice about this, Mary," said Scott. "We'll just need to draw the boundary at our specification requirement and deal with any issues once they deliver the transaction. We can code and integration test against a mocked-up interface we can build out. No choice."

"We just worry about developing the code on our side of the CSF, huh? I guess we can do that," Mary conceded, shaking her head.

A moment of silence, and then GG spoke up. "I do have some good news, guys. Wes called me yesterday afternoon and told me to forget about doing the estimate of building out the Real Estate Division standards-compliant sales system; we don't have time. He said he'd talked to Tom about the CR, and Tom gave us the go-ahead for CSMPro."

Scott added, "Janice was really steamed. I guess you've both won a battle now."

"I hate to get in the middle of this war," I said, "but somehow we need to remember that we're all on the same team here."

"Spoken like a true HR geek," GG retorted. "You're right, of course, Beth, but it often doesn't feel like that. Dates and rules are set without our input, yet we remain accountable for delivery. It sometimes feels like we're being set up to fail."

Sam, who'd been quiet the whole meeting, now spoke up for the first time. "Let's try to pull this back together, team. This project is too important for us to screw it up. I don't fully understand the technical architecture issues you guys are dealing with, but what I hear is that we need to do our own jobs and trust the others to do their jobs also. We can't control everything in the project, so let's just worry about what we're being paid to worry about. OK?"

A round of murmured OKs and, "I guesses" ensued, and the team was ready to move on. Sam followed up with, "So what do we need to do next?"

Next Steps to Keep the CU Project Moving

Scott, true to his role, said that we needed to finish up the architecture. GG said that we had to get going on the requirements and the contract with CSMPro. We agreed these were the three major items and tackled them in turn.

Mary wasn't sure what Scott meant when he said we needed to "finish the architecture." Scott explained that he'd like to complete the system architecture specification document.

"Why do we need to do that now, Scott? Do we have some areas where the cost of change would be high so that we need to make decisions now?"

"I don't see any obvious ones. With the decision to go with CSMPro and the mandate on how our interfaces should work, most of the big issues are resolved."

"Is there anything in the way of our getting going or any long-lead-time issues that we need to start now so that we are done on time?"

"I don't see any right now, Mary," replied Scott.

"Then how about you just put together some high-level diagrams of the system, keep answering the questions I ask each week, and gradually build out the documentation we'll need to communicate the system design as we finish it? When do you actually have to have the document done?"

GG, the whiz at The Process, answered, as usual. "It's due right after the requirements are complete, before the high-level design is due. That puts it in mid-February."

Mary proposed, "How about you figure out how little we need to do to minimally pass the document QA check and support the development team, and then spend the rest of your time doing some coding? I'd hate to waste energy documenting things we don't need to document yet and putting things into stone before we're ready. Maybe you could skip it and start coding with the CSMPro team."

Scott said he'd have to think about that and get back to GG and her. He was pretty skeptical. I could tell he was comfortable with his job being the preparation of the architecture document, while Mary was trying to push him into a more connected, hands-on role. I doubted that was going to happen.

The discussion moved on to the requirements completion. Sam was formally responsible for the requirements, and he had a team of analysts and SMEs (subject matter experts) who had been nominated for his use from each of the lines of business. Sam had been put through a couple days of training in The Process, and GG had process coaches available to help Sam and his team. Some of the other groups, most notably Production Management, had gone so far as to hire outside consultants to come in, facilitate multiday requirements meetings, and do the documentation in proper Process-compliant formats for them. From what I knew of Mary, Agile, and Lean, this wouldn't be how Mary wanted to do things. I was, however, surprised at Mary's take on this.

"Before we discuss this," Mary proposed, "would you mind if we tried to get Jennifer on the phone? I'd like to hear what she thinks we should do." Jennifer Phillips was the account manager from CSMPro's professional services group whom we'd all met a couple of times during the vendor analysis process.

"I suppose you're going to want to do user stories instead of use cases," GG said. He'd been reading up on Agile software development and was resistant to any change that wasn't supported by The Process. He wanted to avoid being caught in the middle of a battle between the process police and Mary. I thought he had a good reason for concern because I doubted the ability of a team to absorb a new way of doing things, especially one that wasn't the official approach or supported widely by the team members.

"No, actually, I doubt that would be a good idea. I'd like us to understand what requirements, design, build, and test approaches Jennifer will recommend. They've been doing implementations of CSMPro for a dozen years and have probably done it over a hundred times; Jennifer has a lot of experience. Because they started with small companies that couldn't afford a lot of process and they usually don't get paid until it's up and running and used, I'd bet they have some pretty good ideas."

A lightbulb went off for me in my understanding of what Mary had been trying to teach me about Lean product development and Agile methods. There isn't one approach that is right for every problem; as Mary had explained a few months ago, we must first understand to what extent a problem is repetitive and therefore amenable to detailed process definition and optimization, or unique and therefore must be managed more empirically by doing, checking, and adjusting. Our development of our sales system would have elements of both: We could draw on the process expertise specific to CSMPro and then ensure we did enough empirical process control to deal with the unknowns specific to our own implementation. I think I was beginning to understand!

We couldn't get Jennifer on the phone, so we left it up to Sam to get our team together with Jennifer to talk through the approach that CSMPro would recommend. He had to get with her on the contract as well, so he took point. As it turned out, Jennifer had very strong ideas on how she wanted to proceed, with a variety of steps mapped out, templated documents, and suggested time lines. This would become the basis for our plan, along with a somewhat stronger focus on getting code complete in defined iterations, doing demos, and integrating and testing as we went along. GG would have to figure out how to make this look enough like The Process for us to pass our audits; I thought that with the CR signed and in the bag, GG could figure out a way forward.

Signposts	**Cremins United project**
	• The PCA reiterated that all interfaces needed to go through CSF and CDM; no debate was tolerated.
	• The Sales team reluctantly accepted that boundary, and at Sam Baker's urging, resolved to "stick to its own knitting" and not worry about things outside its control.
	• Mary guided the Sales team into respecting the methods that its vendor, CSMPro, brought to the table, instead of insisting on her own Lean and Agile preferences.
Guides from Beth	• Think carefully about what you want from your team. Is it compliance or engagement? You can stop the swirl, but are you headed in the right direction?
	• Methods should be tailored to the situation at hand. Repetitive, repeatable problems should have standardized approaches that undergo continual improvement; new problems need approaches that build knowledge quickly by creating and testing ideas and assumptions.
Coming up next	Six weeks have passed, and Beth takes us to TRIM's demonstration at the end of the group's first sprint.

15

The TRIM Project's First Sprint Demo: A Bit behind Schedule, but Catching Up

DECEMBER 2005

Beth:

The mid-December morning dawned clear and cold, in Southern California terms. I'd talked with my parents in Topeka last night, where they were enjoying some early snow that promised a white Christmas. No hint of that here, just a bit of extra dew in my garden.

As the holiday season approached, the TRIM project was wrapping up its first sprint with the sprint-end demonstrations. This would be the last major event of the year, after which the project would still progress to the start of the new year, but with a slower and uneven cadence as team members took time off to celebrate their holidays.

Neville Roberts, chief engineer for TRIM, had organized the event for the Shelter Island Hotel, on the waterfront near downtown. Neville and I shared a love of Shelter Island, right on the path of ships coming into the harbor, where the seals barking on the rocks provided entertainment on walks along the shore. We both loved the water—I because I'd grown up in Kansas without it and Neville because he'd grown up in England along-side it. The hotel provided larger conference rooms than our headquarters building and could more easily handle a group this big (35 people today, more tomorrow). While it was growing slightly seedy, its location was a treat, especially for the out-of-towners, adding to the "specialness" of the event without adding a lot of cost.

Alex Fuegos, on Neville's team, was the overall "scrum-of-scrums master," and he was serving, along with Neville, as master of ceremonies today. I'd run into some unexpectedly heavy traffic—I rarely drive downtown in rush hour—so I arrived just as Alex was introducing Qin Tsen (pronounced *Chin Sen*), the scrum master of the Information Management team, to begin her part of the demo.

"Our team's goal for the first sprint was to establish the first iteration of the system database and populate it from four sources for two markets," said Qin. "The sources are public records of property information, such as taxes and liens; address data with geocodes for mapping; multiple listing system data to give us for-sale and recent comparable sales information; and mortgage loan status information from two major lenders. We had a stretch goal of figuring out the consolidation or matching of the data from the different sources into one set of unified keys, and a further stretch goal of doing some basic reports for viewing."

"We took these goals, broke out the tasks, and estimated them to 8-hour or less increments. Our estimate, including the stretch goals, was for about 3,000 hours. We had only about 2,500 hours projected to be available, and we had some imbalances and missing skills—plus we had some tasks that had to be done by developers at the lender and MLS agencies. So our first set of tasks was to balance out the team and get some commitments from our partners, which we were able to do in the first week. We had some team members coming on after a couple of weeks, and the tasks for the partners were initially planned mostly for weeks 3 and 4, so the planned burn-down chart looked like this."

At that, Qin flashed a burn-down chart up on the screen (Figure 17).

"Qin, I'm sorry to interrupt, and we can take this offline if everyone else already understands, but could you explain just what this chart shows?" I asked. I was self-conscious asking it, but I figured if it wasn't worth explaining now Qin, Alex, or Neville would say so. Also, as a human resources professional in a room full of techies, I felt compelled to help ensure understanding; that's just what I do!

"No problem, Beth; it's worth explaining again, especially because we have a lot of people here new to this type of management. It shows the projected number of hours of work remaining at the beginning of each day of the sprint to complete the work we set out to do. If our plan were

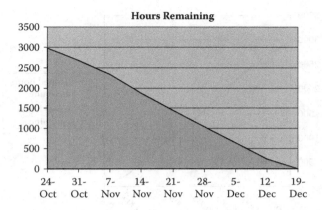

FIGURE 17
Planned burn-down chart.

perfect, we'd see the tasks knocked down right on target, and our actual burn-down would look just like the line in this chart. Of course, we've never seen that happen, especially in the first sprint of a project with a team with a bunch of new members. It usually takes quite a while to settle into a predictable velocity—meaning that we can estimate our tasks with some accuracy and match up total projected tasks to available hours with some consistency."

"Thanks, Qin. That helps," I said.

Qin continued. "Here is what actually happened." Qin put up the next chart, showing actual versus plan (Figure 18).

Gina Sebastian, Greg Allenby's boss, was sitting in the front of the room with Greg. Greg was the head of our Real Estate Division, so I wasn't surprised to see him here. However, I was pleasantly surprised to see Gina involved at this level of detail in the TRIM project. Later, Greg explained to me that because of the importance and cost of the project, Gina was invited to all of the demos. She usually couldn't attend due to conflicts, but things had worked out today and she was able to attend. Gina was the one who asked the obvious question for Qin.

"What happened? Looks like you underestimated something and weren't able to finish what you had hoped to."

"That's right in this case, although the burn-down chart could also have been explained by not getting the resources we'd planned or adding scope in the middle of the sprint—which we almost never do. We ran into a tough

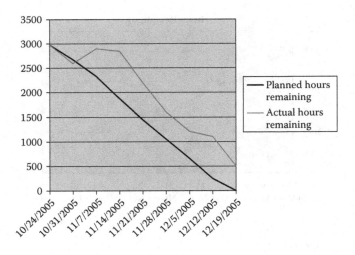

FIGURE 18
Actual versus planned burn-down chart.

problem that we still haven't completely solved. As we did the data model, built the database, got the sample files, and started to do the code to match and align the data from the several sources, we got stumped for a while. We'd expected to be able to match effectively on address and property ID number from public records, but we found that the data aren't very high quality. Not all the loan information has property ID on it, especially where the loan isn't escrowed; when we do have the ID, there is a material percentage of them that is wrong. We have some loan property addresses that aren't in the mapping data at all; we believe that's because of new construction. We spent a couple weeks exploring the data in more depth and coming up with a new approach to managing the information and doing reporting. Instead of relying on data matches, we now assume the data are somewhat dirty and incomplete, and when we do reports we have to begin the query with a specific data set depending on the kind of question asked."

Could We Stay on Track?

Greg followed up. "Neville, what do you think this means for the project? Is it okay?"

Neville spoke up. "I knew when we began this project that we'd have some data issues, but I hadn't expected it to be quite this bad. So good thing we found out now, before we went too far! We'll still do the matching, which remains critical to the solution. However, we need to be extremely careful how we describe and write each query. For example, if someone wants to know what percentage of the properties in a specific area have loans that are delinquent, we need to be sure we first query on the addresses and then match as best we can to the loans. If someone wants to know what percentage of loans in an area is delinquent, we need to query first on the loans. We just need to be cognizant that we have different data sources with incomplete matches to other sources. It'll be better than any other set of data available, but it won't be perfect."

Gina laughed quietly and smiled at the group. "My guess is that this finding is actually good for us. It makes it harder for others to compete in putting together this kind of data set. Qin, what does this mean for the next sprint and for our release plan overall?"

"We are definitely behind where we wanted to be. We didn't get the matching software complete in its first iteration, although we know what we need to do now and are confident we can finish it in a few weeks. We don't want to fall behind on getting the database stable, so Neville authorized me to bring in another developer for a couple of months to help with some of the more routine tasks so that Brian can wrap up the matching, and then the new developer can help us catch up. It'll put us a little over budget at the end of January, but we should have time to catch up; if we can't, we'll eat into the contingency somewhat."

Greg turned to his boss and reassured her and the rest of the room that the project was OK; there was nothing too unusual in this finding in sprint 1. Then he invited Qin to continue on with the demo.

Qin introduced Brian Bannion, the lead developer, and the lead developers from one of the MLS partners, both the servicers, and a contractor from Mapomatic, our partner that specialized in address management and mapping. They proceeded to spend half an hour showing the group, via the projector, files from the source systems, the database design, the loading programs, and some error management code. The climax of the demo happened in less than a minute at the end, when Brian clicked on a button and the files were grabbed by his software and loaded into the database. Brian then clicked on an icon on his PC, and a map of several blocks nearby in San Diego appeared on his screen; the houses were color-coded green for loan current, yellow for delinquent 30 days, and red for delinquent 90 days or more. Most of the houses remained gray because they only had data from the two lenders or because the homeowners didn't have mortgages. The assorted multitudes variously oohed, ahed, and asked questions.

It became clear from the questions that one big thing the Information Management team hadn't dealt with yet was that a home could have more than one loan on it. They also missed the whole set of complexities around condominiums, with multiple units that might have essentially the same address. These seemed like pretty obvious things to have overlooked. Alex was apologetic and promised to add this to the backlog—probably in the next sprint because it needed to be done fairly early. Qin showed the planned burn-down chart for the next sprint, along with the goals and the tasks, and then we took a break. I had to run back to my office to catch the regular meeting of the CU Human Resource team so I missed the rest of the day, but I was sure that I wasn't going to miss the next morning. Mary had told me that I absolutely needed to attend, to see visual management and integrating events in action: the architecture simulation.

Simulating TRIM's System Architecture

I was up early Thursday morning, and I drove back down to Shelter Island early to avoid the traffic and get in a walk on the beach before the meeting began. I didn't want to risk being late like I had been yesterday! Today was architecture simulation day, and it had proven to be so popular that Neville had to rent a larger room at the hotel. Neville and others had also invited a deeper layer of teams than usually attended leadership meetings, including all of the developers and testers assigned to work on the project. This was one of the benefits we had of holding the demonstrations in San Diego: It made it easy for more of our team members to attend. Neville had explained to me that he usually let whoever wanted to go to simulations go; he'd rarely had a problem with controlling too large a crowd.

Over my years in tech, I'd heard engineers grumbling about long, dense design documents and the ineffectiveness of doing design reviews from such documents, so I was curious about a different way. Neville had described simulations as a mechanism of visual management, one of the key integrating events that helped teams collaborate effectively.

The meeting was held in the ballroom. It was showing signs of wear and tear, but remained a light and airy space. About 60 people drifted in, milling around the props at the front of the room. The chairs were arranged in a tight series of semicircles, without tables, and they didn't invite sitting until absolutely necessary.

At the front of the room, right in the center, was Brian Bannion, our lead developer, dressed in a toga! He was taping some large charts on the wall. I wondered what he was up to, so I walked over to him.

"Good morning, Brian. That is quite an outfit you have on. I really like the leaves on your head, and the flip-flops."

"Morning, Beth. Those aren't leaves; they are laurels—sorry about the flip-flops, but I don't have any other sandals."

"What are you supposed to be? Why are you dressed up?"

"Neville asked us to try to have some fun with this, and he really loves costumes. The first time he did this, one of the cast playing the message bus actually dressed up like a bus! He still has the bus in his office."

"I've seen that and wondered what it was there for. But what are you supposed to be?"

"I couldn't think of anything; then I thought that the database is Oracle. So I'm dressed up as the oracle, like that woman at Delphi in ancient Greece. Check out this sign."

With that, Brian unfurled his sign, which proudly stated, "The Oracle Is In."

Neville had walked up to the center of the room and began dinging a small chime he held in his hand. "Places, actors, please. Audience, please take your seats, and let's get going."

The room gradually settled in, and Neville continued.

"Today is going to be both fun and productive. Some of you here have seen this type of simulation before; for others, it'll be a new experience. The goal is to walk through as many scenarios as we can, watching how our new system will work and trying to find holes in the design. We expect to show what we have planned so far, improve it, and have all of you learn in more detail how this will all fit together. The actors," he said, pointing toward Brian, "all know their roles. Yours is to be sure you understand what you are seeing and to find any holes in our thinking."

"Let's jump right in. The first scenario is the initial population of the database and then the regular updating as data changes. Introductions, please!"

Starting on the left of the room, the players introduced themselves. Sybil Gutierrez, the technology manager from the local San Diego multiple listing service, was dressed in a cardboard "For Sale" sign and represented the two MLS systems involved in this first sprint. Next to her was Basim

Chandrasekharan, from Mapomatic, which is providing the address data and mapping components. Basim hadn't quite taken up the costume challenge like Brian had; his only concession to the fun was a baseball cap that said "Mapomatic" on it. In the middle, of course, was the oracle of Brian, the production database. Brian was joined in the middle by Kamau Kahero, the lead developer of our record-matching routines, and James Pasternak, who manages the Real Estate Division's file transfer exchange. James was sitting on a two-drawer file cabinet, with a stack of file folders on top. To Brian's right was Martin Fowler, from National Servicing Group, one of our mortgage servicers, and Melissa Brown, from Public Records Aggregators, our primary provider of public records such as tax and lien information. Each had taken his or her own approach to Neville's urging to dress up and provide props; none approached Brian's enthusiasm and creativity.

Behind Brian were several large posters showing the major tables and keys in the database. James had a similar poster on an easel next to the file cabinet and an easel was set up next to each player. The basic arrangement was as shown in Figure 19.

"OK, Brian," Neville began, "tell us about yourself, and how you want to start off."

Brian asked Alex, who was helping to conduct the simulation, to pass out copies of the high-level database diagram and the initial population flow. It was a single piece of paper, with print on both sides. "I'm TRIM's central database, and I'll be conducting the simulation. To remind you, our task is

Basim–Maps

Brian–Database

Martin–Loan Servicer

Sybil–MLS

Kamau– Matching

James– FileXchange

Melissa–Public Records Data

FIGURE 19
Arrangement of simulation participants.

to populate me with data for the first time from my various data-providing partners. The diagram should help you follow the flow. You'll see that I have separate tables for the records from each source and a large junction table that ties together the various sources. For example, take a look at the 'sales record' table, which is pretty similar to other source data tables. It is fed directly from the MLS,"—nodding to Sybil—"and has a unique key that we assign, and then has the natural keys of the MLS source system identifier and the MLS ID from that system."

"Kamau here," he went on, pointing to Kamau in front of him, "is in charge of populating my matching table. He's got the hardest job. He has to read the data my friends provide and figure out how it all fits together. He writes the results here, which becomes the hub of all our reporting and online queries."

"The other major tables are all about process control—the management of the updates—and access and billing control. We're not going to go into those tables in this particular scenario; hopefully we'll have time to touch on them if we get to the system administration scenario later today, or maybe next month. Any questions before I get my first feed?"

Neville waited a moment to be sure no one else was asking a question, and, as he often did, then posed a question to which he already knew the answer, trying to be helpful to the group by elucidating a key point. "Brian, were there alternative basic designs that you considered and rejected? What kind of trade-offs did you make?" Neville was huge on considering and discussing alternatives. I'd seen similar obsession with design alternatives when I worked in the network equipment company, although there they sometimes actually began development of several alternatives. Neville hadn't gone that far yet in this project, preferring to do the development in thought first, but I wouldn't be surprised if he were to try more than one way of accomplishing something in order to accelerate learning.

"I think we talked about this a bit in the review of the sprint and the demo yesterday. I initially thought that we'd have essentially one big data table, with a single common key, and just sort of fill in the specific types of data from the various sources as they came in. Think about how great that would be: I get the address from Basim over here and create the key. Then Sybil gives me the MLS data, Kamau matches it for me, and I insert it back into the same row. Then Melissa gives me some tax data, and I do the same thing. Report development would be very easy; performance would really zip because of so few joins required—I was in love with the design. Unfortunately, the unevenness and complexity of the actual data forced us to do it this way. There are too many holes in the data, as well as too many complex relationships, to solve the problem as simply as I'd hoped."

Neville followed up. "Can you give us another example of that complexity?"

"Sure. Hey, Sybil, do MLSs ever compete for listings? Might I get the same 'for sale' record more than once and get conflicting data on status?" Brian asked.

Sybil nodded and replied, "Sure. Some cities have more than one MLS, some areas are covered by more than one service, and data exchange among MLSs is common. Depending on time of day, update frequencies, and administration procedures in the local MLSs, you'll get some duplicate and conflicting records."

Neville thanked Sybil and summarized that the only way to deal with the complexity was to store the native data and have Kamau deal with the data issues in the matching routines. We still wanted the report writing to be simple, so it wouldn't require a very high level of expertise and knowledge of the data, but that remained to be seen.

Alex had one more follow-up question on data formats. Brian replied that he had examined the various industry data standards and was going to design the database to be as consistent with the mortgage industry data standards as he could. That seemed to be the standard that best fit the need, although he'd need to do some integration of other standards-based data such as the Public Records Industry Association and the National Association of Realtors. The feeding systems supported these standards to a greater or lesser extent; they varied all over the board.

Let the Data Flow

"OK, let's start populating," Brian conducted the ceremony. "Sybil, would you please start feeding me?"

Sybil explained that her MLS system had two existing extracts that would nearly meet our requirements: a full data dump and an incremental update file. She said that she would have to postprocess the files to strip out confidential and unneeded information, such as the broker compensation arrangements and buyer and seller information that wasn't available in the local public records. She planned on doing the postprocessing instead of creating new extracts for the sake of efficiency and impact on the production MLS system. Someone in the audience asked what the format of the file would be, and she elaborated on the nature of MLS data:

"Each MLS has somewhat different data structures. For example, the same feature is called a deck in Wisconsin and a lanai in Hawaii. Because real estate is such a local business and the MLSs were developed locally for local needs, even features such as bathrooms are represented in a dizzying variety of ways: Your half-bath might be a bathroom without tub or shower somewhere else. Fortunately, over the last 15 years, the National Association of Realtors has helped us standardize to some extent, and most MLS systems now have a standard metadata description of its data that enables third-party software products to work with multiple MLS systems whose data differ."

Sybil took out six pieces of 8½ by 11 cardboard and began showing them to the audience.

"For the initial population, I take a full file extract, postprocess to clean it up, and put it into a directory on a server in our shop. The postprocess also creates a control file that contains the creation date/time, the number of records, and some check-sum information." Sybil held up two of the cardboard sheets labeled as "initial load file" and "initial control file."

From the audience—it sounded like Janani, the test manager—came a question: "Can you explain about the check sums?"

Brian answered; he had designed this control. "I'm not exactly sure what this will be yet, Janani. We didn't get that far in this sprint. It will depend on looking a little more deeply at the data. An example might be simply to sum up all the MLS IDs or maybe the current offering prices. If Sybil does a few of those totals, I do the same from the database after it's updated, and we compare, I can be sure that we have a good transfer and database update."

"Got it. That should help us test also," Janani approved.

Melissa, representing the public records system, pitched in. "We've got some mechanisms we use in our work that we can share with you, Brian. We have to get data files from hundreds of governmental units and it has to be updated reliably. What sprint is the control management planned for?"

"I think it's sprint 5," said Brian. "But it sounds like we might want to address at least some thinking about it sooner."

Neville tried to keep things moving along by asking Sybil to continue; he was better at keeping things moving than Brian, our formal conductor, who welcomed his help.

Sybil said, "OK, so here are the two files I mentioned, and here is one more: the metadata file." She held up a third sheet of cardboard, labeled "Initial Metadata File." "This contains the field names, mapped to the standards. It will allow Brian to have one table for data from all the MLSs, instead of one table per MLS. Brian and I talked this over extensively, and we think that using the single table will give enough information for the purposes of TRIM. Users can always go back to the local MLS; if they aren't realtors, they can go to public Web sites or to a realtor, if they need more information. I zip up the three files [taking a zipper out of her pocket and wrapping it around the three pieces of cardboard], put the zipped files into this folder, and securely FTP it over the public Internet to James."

"Privacy?" queried Neville.

"Oh, yeah, I forgot," replied Sybil, "I'm going to do something to ensure privacy and security, but we haven't determined what yet; that comes in sprint 3, I think. We can encrypt the whole file—I think that's what we'll do—or we can just do some of the fields, which would be better for performance. Brian is worried about how much processing he needs to do once he gets the files because our goal is to get extracts nightly and be ready to run the next morning. Given the national scope, the time zones put us in a squeeze for an available update window."

I watched Sybil walk over to James, representing our file transfer subsystem, and heard a question from the audience: "How about the other files you left at your desk? What are those?"

"Those are the incremental change files that I'll send every day." She looked at Neville and asked, "Should we go through that now also, or should we get the database populated initially and then do the incrementals?"

Neville turned to the group and asked what they would like to do. Brian answered, "I'd prefer to do the initial population first. That will show all the basic pieces, and then we can concentrate on updates. The issues in updates will then be focused on a smaller set of related issues, such as frequency, how to do deltas if the sending system can't, metadata changes, and so on."

No one argued with this, so it was back to James. James seemed uncomfortable in front of this large audience, but his technical expertise shone through his nervousness.

"First, I thank Sybil for the files—actually, the secure FTP protocol does that, ensuring that I receive everything she sends. Then I'll deal with any encryption so that I can read the files. I'll unzip them, read the control file, check the files in, and write the totals here in my database." With that, James took the cardboard sheets out of the file folder, unwrapped the zipper, walked over to his file cabinet, logged the file receipt, and copied some figures from one of the cardboard sheets onto the big chart. Then he put the folder into the first drawer.

Another question came from the audience: "How does Brian know the files are there now? Does he get notified somehow or poll your table to see what's there?"

Brian answered again, "For initial population, it will be completely manual. It's a one-time load from each source, so it'll be driven by a project-management process, and our database administrators will kick off the matching and database population programs once the needed files are here. For the updates, we haven't decided yet. That's in a later sprint. We have some options but don't see a need to decide yet."

Looking relieved to be finished, James asked if anyone had any questions and, hearing no further questions, turned it over to Brian.

The simulation continued the rest of the day. They only made it through the database population scenario, including the incremental updates and the data matching; we didn't get to reporting or user administration as we had hoped. Afterward, on the bar's deck overlooking the marina during the evening reception, I had a chance to ask Neville about the failure to complete the work. He said that he usually overestimates how many scenarios can be done in a simulation. "There is never enough time to do the simulations in the depth and breadth we'd really like," he said, "but, nevertheless, they are usually looked back upon as some of the most valuable activities in a project." From the buzz in the crowd, I was sure that would be the case in this project as well.

Signposts	**TRIM project**
	• At the end of sprint 1, the demonstration revealed that although some good progress had been made, the team was behind where it wanted to be. This was due to finding more complex data than expected. Management approved added staff to catch up.
	• The system design was vetted through a highly visual simulation. A couple more new issues were found that would need to be added to later sprint plans.
	• The extended team was forming nicely through participation in the sprint demo and simulation, as well as having been given informal time together in connection with those events.
Guides from Beth	• Sprint-end demos will regularly show leaders where the project really is while there is still time to adjust.
	• Simulations are another technique of Lean's "visual management" principle, highly valuable in early stages of system design when there isn't yet much code to show but you need to get many participants learning and critiquing quickly. Make them fun!
	• It's hard to overestimate the value of informal time together for our teams. Establish a routine of snacks and refreshments following a long day of learning to give your team a chance to explore and consolidate learning with each other and to continue informal planning.
Coming up next	Wes takes over as we enter the new year. All is "green" with the Cremins United project as it transitions from the requirements into the design phase.

16

The CU Project Requirements Handoff: An Uneasy Transition

Wes:

As 2006 got under way, the Cremins United project seemed to be in excellent shape. Requirements were scheduled to be complete at the end of January, and all teams, with the exception of Sales, reported "green" on status reports. The Sales team had received permission to miss the end-January requirements complete milestone. They were following the CSMPro development methodology instead of The Process, so they had laid out their own schedule, to which they seemed to be sticking. Nevertheless, Sales was reporting "yellow," meaning they felt there were material risks remaining in their ability to meet the September code complete date.

The project management office, led by Trevor McDonald from GRI, was still requiring Sales to do some of the specified Process deliverables aimed at ensuring what Trevor called "traceability." I'd talked this over with Mary a month ago and was struck by her subdued but unremitting hostility to Trevor, The Process, traceability, and the whole idea of even having a requirements phase.

"Wes," she'd said, "I've never seen or heard of a project actually finding something they'd forgotten via traceability. Imagine the scene," she'd gone on. "I'm a developer, and I look at the traceability matrix and find that, damn, I forgot to develop software to meeting requirement 208.b.2! If it ever comes to having that much distance between the developers and the requirements analysts, the project is so screwed that it just doesn't matter."

"How about testing, though, Mary? Wouldn't it help the testers make sure they have coverage?"

"You're just thinking about this all wrong, Wes. You are thinking batch and handoffs. If you do development that way, with big handoffs of batches of requirements to designers and then from designers to developers, and developers build code rigidly to specification, and then testers test directly to the requirements documents—well, yeah, you'd have to have traceability to try to manage all the handoffs. But if you have a team of analysts, developers, and testers who specify, build, and test some features quickly and together, there is no need at all for traceability. In fact, there often is no need at all for requirements documents separate from designs and test cases. The best way to ensure traceability is to eliminate having to trace anything."

I'd developed a fair amount of admiration for Mary, and I was excited about the possibilities we were tentatively exploring to move our relationship into a more romantic direction. By the end of January, we had developed enough trust that she'd tell me what she really thought, even though in other CU forums she remained reserved and careful not to offend. Her arguments certainly sounded logical and confirmed other bits of evidence that came trickling across my desk, so I was getting a little scared. It was hard for me to understand the official status reporting that had everyone else but Mary "green," while she was the only one in cautionary status. I planned to do some more observation to try to understand better for myself how the non-Sales groups, supposedly right on track, were doing. This brought me to the requirements handoff session for the Production Management team.

The Handoff from Requirements to Design

Right on target, on January 31, Ken Fong, the "business" lead for Production Management, had handed over to Joe Karras, the "technical" lead, the requirements for the first release of Cremins United regarding production management. The "handoff" was not quite that literal; in fact, the requirements comprised about 40 documents, with 2 documents for each major area. The documents were all stored on the project Web site, and an e-mail had been sent out to all reviewers of the documents seeking their formal approval. "James Wesleyan, representing the PCA" was displayed as an approver on each of the documents, alongside 20–30 other additional approvers. Due to the time line of the project, the approval period was 1 week from receipt of e-mail request to sign-off, and there were people tracking all the sign-offs and following up with more e-mails and phone calls. I'd started to read some of the documents and was having a very hard time understanding what it all meant. I hoped that today's session would clarify things for me.

Today was official turnover day. We were going to run through all the documents at a high level for the Technology team, marking the official end of the requirements phase and beginning of design. The meeting was surprisingly small: Ken Fong; his counterpart from BCG, Phyllis Gould; a couple of business analysts working with them; Trevor; several consultants from GRI who had actually written most of the documents; Joe Karras, the Production technical manager; Tabitha Albertson, Joe's architect; and two design engineers on Joe's team. I represented the PCA, and two quality assurance officers from the project management office were there to ensure that the documents met the requirements of The Process and would give us traceability. It was the responsibility of the design engineers and the architect to turn the requirements into designs from which the developers could work.

Ken began by explaining how the documents had been created. He referred to some PowerPoint slides he was projecting on the wall, but mostly he just talked. He really seemed to know his stuff.

"We had the challenge of meeting the January 31 date to get all our production management requirements complete. This is my first big project like this, and I questioned the need to get all the requirements done up front, given how much we don't know yet and how short a period we had to complete them. Trevor, the lead project manager, pointed out why this is so necessary, and it should be familiar to the production people in this room: the cost of change."

An Unrealistic Goal

With that, Ken flashed a slide up on the wall (Figure 20).

"Software development is a lot like manufacturing. If a customer tells us the right specifications for a job, there is no cost of change. If he tells us early, before we select the equipment to print it on or begin print layout,

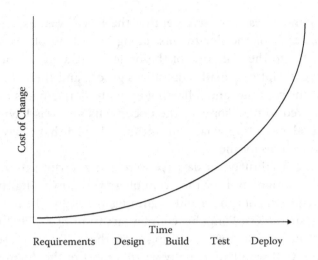

FIGURE 20
Cost of change by development phase.

there is some cost, but it's modest. If he doesn't tell us until after we have everything laid and are running the first test job, the costs really escalate. Finally, if we've already started large-scale production, the costs can become prohibitive. So we need to get ALL the requirements done up front so that the Technology team can get the design right, the developers can build the right thing, and so on. If we think of this project as just like a factory job, it all comes together."

Phyllis Gould was Ken's counterpart from the Business Communications Group. She was sitting next to Ken and supported his explanation: "This makes a lot of sense. I've been in sales support, and we constantly struggle to get the customer and the sales people to specify the job correctly. The biggest problem we have is that handoff from the customer through sales to the sales support group. We've tried a lot of things, and we plan on getting a long way toward solving it now, in this project. As Ken says, as the business, we need to get the 'order' right, which is the requirements documents we are handing over today."

Now I could see exactly what Mary had warned me about. The development model in play for Cremins United assumed that the system could be completely specified as to needs, turned into designs, coded from the designs, and tested from the requirements—essentially a predictable flow. This would make sense if these people had done something very much like this before. In fact, most of these people, while talented and dedicated, had never done anything at all like this before. Some had experience developing systems, but not this large and sweeping. Some, like Ken, had very little experience in software at all. By definition, none had experience making this large a change in this particular business. Mary, who seemed the most expert at large-scale software development, had the least confidence in even her ability to do the CU project in this manner. By contrast, the people with the least experience, like Ken, seemed the most confident. Something was very wrong with this picture!

Ken continued, "With Trevor's guidance, and the support of several analysts and project managers from GRI, we organized a series of requirements workshops. We recruited or were delegated representatives primarily from the two businesses most involved in this first phase: the Commercial Printing Group and the Business Communications Group. We also involved representatives from other groups that would be coming onto the system at a later phase."

"Here are the major steps we completed." A new PowerPoint went up on the wall, with several bulleted items (Figure 21). "Our first task was to develop a vision for how we wanted production management to function. Once we had general agreement on that, we developed a standard workflow, which we call the production management process model. Of course,

---

Requirements Development Process

- Executives: Develop Vision for Production Management
- Create and Validate Standard Workflow to Implement Vision (Production Management Process Model – PMPM)
- Requirements Sessions for Each Workflow Step
- "Scribes" Create BRDs and Use Cases; Validation Sessions

FIGURE 21
The CU project requirements development process.

that is now called the 'PMPM,' which Phyllis has taken to calling the 'pom-pom.' We then held requirements sessions for each of the 20 major steps of the pompom and generated a business requirements document and a use case for each step."

"We are very grateful to Trevor and GRI for their assistance. GRI provided facilitators for each session and scribes to write up the results in the proper formats. That allowed our business people to focus just on what we want, rather than have to learn how to write up requirements documents."

Ken had one more point he wanted to emphasize before diving into the substance of the vision, the pompom, and the requirements for each step. He clicked on the next slide, which had just two words on it: "Technology Independent."

"The requirements team's goal was to describe our vision and needs without reference to any system capabilities or limitations. We sought to stay away from any considerations of design as to HOW the pompom would be implemented, such as what system would do what and so forth. Our mission is to specify the WHAT as best we can and then hand off that specification to the technology experts to design the HOW. This was a struggle for some of our team members," Ken said, glancing up toward the back of the room at someone, "but overall I think we did a pretty good job. It is certainly much easier to do at the vision level, but it gets more difficult as the specification gets more detailed as we move into use cases."

"Ken, can I add something to that?" It was Joe Karras, Ken's technology partner. Ken nodded, and Joe addressed the group. "While we drive the requirements to be technology independent, we don't want just to do them and throw them over the wall at the designers. So we had one technology design engineer observing in each requirements session. It's been a very strong and effective partnership so far between the business and technology."

"Thanks, Joe, it certainly has. Joe's team is ready to take the requirements now and get the designs done quickly and well."

"I'll begin by presenting the vision for Production Management, and then I'll run through the pompom. After that, our friends from GRI will give an overview of each pompom step."

Trevor interrupted, "Before we proceed, I'd like to be sure that we understand the outcome of this turnover so that you can think ahead as Ken speaks. Our goal is to get acceptance of the requirements from the technology department within 2 weeks and to be sure all ambiguity and misunderstandings are eliminated. We want to be sure we capture all questions and changes so that the designers, developers, and testers can rely on the artifacts. So we don't want to dive too deeply into substance at this meeting; instead, we would like the technology questions all to be documented in our issues log, and the requirements team will formally respond to each one."

"The issues log classifies each issue as 'open,' 'resolution proposed,' 'resolution accepted,' 'reopened,' 'closed,' and 'cancelled,'" Trevor continued. "Technology should enter issues as 'open' and be sure to enter the field that links the issue to the appropriate business requirement and use case. The business will then enter the proposed resolution and move the state appropriately, and so on, until all the issues are either cancelled or closed. As issues are closed, our GRI consultants will update the related artifacts so that we will always have current and accurate artifacts. Everyone understand how this works?"

No objections were raised, so Trevor continued. "My assistant will monitor the issues log and ensure that the required turnaround times are met. All escalations should be sent to Tabitha."

The Vision for the CU Project and "the Pompom"— the Production Management Process Model

With Trevor finished, Ken proceeded to share the vision and the pompom with the Technology group. It was a compelling vision, consistent with all the business objectives that had been identified when we kicked off the project. The vision included such goals as optimizing usage of capacity, minimizing rework, accelerating throughput, anticipating customer needs and demand, rapidly turning inventory, cultivating supplier partnerships, enabling rapid product development, and driving down overall costs. The Technology staff had no questions or quibbles about the vision.

The pompom was more interesting. It began with a series of what Ken called "foundational" items, such as "manage production capacity," "develop suppliers," and "select and develop production capabilities." These items were not specifically related to individual customer orders, but were needed in order to be able to fulfill any orders at all. In addition, these activities had to produce information that would be available via "Web services" to the customer order-to-cash cycle.

Layered on top of the foundational items was the customer-oriented cycle. The pompom was a very pretty color-coded flow, in which the Product Management items were in bright red, and the related items from Sales, Finance, Product/Service, and Management Information had their own colors as well. The basic flow showed Sales generating a request for quotation, followed by job costing, price setting, production allocation and commitment, customer agreement, materials acquisition, production setup, production, packaging, shipping, customer acceptance, billing, and payment/collections. It looked logical and general enough to meet the needs of both Commercial and Business Communications, as well as the other groups who were monitoring the CU project to ensure that it would eventually meet their needs. The receiving team (i.e., technology designers and architect) had no questions on the pompom.

The lack of questions didn't indicate a lack of interest, as became evident when we moved on to the pompom's step-level requirements. Being new to software development, I found the interchange somewhat puzzling. It seemed to me that the supposedly "technology neutral" requirements actually contained quite a bit of technology-specific ideas, especially on how much should be done and in what way. But despite Ken and Joe's well-meaning assurance to the contrary, the technologists had not participated in a meaningful way, and there was no consideration of how much this might cost to do or how much business or technical risk was being specified.

I can illustrate by relaying the conversation about "allocate jobs to facilities and equipment." This was a relatively early step in the pompom, and it had two flavors. The first happened prior to the final quotation to the customer: We had to know, to some degree of certainty, where and how we planned to fulfill an order before we quoted. This was to ensure we had capacity and capability. It happened again after the customer agreed to the quotation, including consideration of any changes the customer had requested between the first quote and the acceptance. I've included the basic flow from the requirements document in Figure 22; note steps 5.1.1 and 5.1.2 in the top row.

The assigned GRI analyst began by handing out what he called the "requirements artifacts." I hated that word; it made the development process seem like archeology or history! For each pompom step ("allocate jobs to facility"), there were two detailed documents: the business requirements document (BRD), which listed in outlined, bullet

Flow of Events: Allocate Jobs to Facility

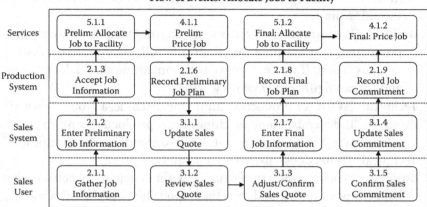

FIGURE 22
Flow of events, "allocate jobs to facilities and equipment."

format the requirements, and then a more detailed document called a use case.

The list of requirements for this pompom step was long—the BRD "artifact" listing them ran to 25 pages, although most of it was meaningless boilerplate from the template. They were organized by major requirements and elaborations, all numbered. For example, item 17 was "maintain forecast of capacity." Underneath it were listed the elaborations:

17. Maintain forecast of capacity
    a. The forecast shall be maintained real time (always up to date and accurate).
    b. The forecast shall be by production unit.
    c. Orders shall be entered against the forecast when confirmed by customers.
    d. ....

This particular requirement was needed in support of the service that would allocate work to facilities and equipment, item 5.1 from Figure 22. As the GRI analyst started down the list, Tabitha, the Product Management technical architect, and Tammy Sills and Steve Tolbert, the design engineers, began to ask clarifying questions:

Technical: "When you say 'real time,' what exactly do you mean? To the second? Minute?"

Business: "We want to avoid rework, which would happen if we allocate production to a machine that is already full. So, essentially, instantaneous is best. If we need to live with something slower, let us know and we can figure out what it's worth."

Technical: "What is a production unit? One machine, a group, or what?"

Business: "It depends. Some machines are a production unit in themselves; some combine into a unit. It also depends on the specific job."

Technical: "What does 'customer confirmation' mean?"

Business: "When the sales system updates our system to that effect, what happens prior to that update is the responsibility of the Sales team."

It seemed that this ping-pong game could go on forever. Trevor, Ken, and Phyllis tried the best they could to move the conversation along, but it was evident that the technology designers would need a lot more understanding before they could get their work done. With just half an hour left to finish all turnover discussion on "allocate jobs" (the meeting was "time boxed" to ensure it completed on schedule), Trevor shut down discussion on the requirements list. He asked the Technology team to put all their questions in writing in the issues system, as he had described, including the questions already addressed in this meeting so far. On to the use case.

Moving On—Even If We're Not Ready

The use case sought to describe how the users—in this instance, Ken and Phyllis and the group that had been in the requirements session—wanted the system to behave. It began by identifying the "actors" involved, such as the operations manager and each system involved. It then defined any preconditions that must be met before the activity started, what it meant for the activity to be completed, and main elements in the scenario. Cremins also included interaction diagrams showing how the scenario flowed— such as the one I've included in Figure 22, which is from this use case.

Ken introduced the use case, "allocation jobs to facilities," by giving us the context. "Prior to the beginning of this use case, the sales person will have configured the job, which provides the system enough information to determine how it should be produced. The sales person will have collected information such as the type of job, quantities, delivery dates required, some indications of flexibility such as whether early or late shipment would be accepted, competitive information, and so on."

Ken and Phyllis continued to walk through the use case, using a laser pointer against the document projected on the wall screen. The bulk of the explanation was of the flow shown in Figure 22. I learned some troubling things from the caveats in the document itself and the questions. These included:

- The requirements were for what GRI called the "primary" flow only; none of the exception conditions were specified. This included items such as an incomplete order (and even the specification of what exactly constituted a complete order), illogical or unforeseen customer requests, any technical exceptions such as bad data, and so on. Trevor explained that there wasn't time available to deal with the exception flows at this time; they would be added later. I wondered when that might be and how they had considered "requirements complete" without those details.
- The technical team—especially Tammy and Steve, the lead designers—repeatedly protested that the "system just doesn't work that way." I didn't know much about the technology base Production planned to use, but it appeared that system did much of what the requirements were asking, but in different ways than were required. That base system also seemed to do the tasks in a less automated way, with a different allocation of tasks to the "system" versus "services." For example, allocation of jobs to machines was done by production control supervisors, not as an automated process. The Process now demanded that Tammy and Steve take these requirements and figure out how to make them happen. That seemed like a lot of weight to put on their shoulders, and eliminated a meaningful discussion of the relative costs and benefits of accomplishing the tasks in other ways. How could we know that this way, figured out in a "technology neutral" way, was the best?

As the walk-through wound to a time-boxed conclusion, Tabitha had one more question she had to ask.

"Ken, Phyllis, can you tell us how you do this today? Seems like there is an awful lot of information and automated decision making that is required to do this task, and a lot of fuzziness on exactly how to do it."

"Today," Phyllis answered, "it is mostly a manual, person-to-person interaction, using e-mail, phones, and a variety of systems in each facility. Our sales people today mostly only sell products they know well, essentially selling for just a narrow line of business. For example, my previous job was managing sales for BCG in the Southeast. When I had a line on new business, I would call the sales support group in the plant in Atlanta, who would help me cost out the job and check on capacity. The rep would always do the job in Atlanta if he could, and if not, he'd phone the Jacksonville facility and see if they could do it. Occasionally, we'd have to go farther, but that would eat into our profits if we had to ship the output. Also, for the last several years we usually haven't had the problem of too much work, so we haven't had a lot of conflicts."

Ken added, "In the Commercial Group it works much the same way. You can see all the problems we are trying to fix; today we often don't optimize production across plants within a line of business, just hundreds of miles away from each other, much less allowing Phyllis to put business into a Commercial Group plant!"

"I see," said Tabitha. "Given where you are today, how did you decide how far to go with automation? You could just have easily specified requirements for a more people-intensive process like today's, using technology to facilitate and track the communication paths and support people-oriented decision making and communication. That would be more consistent with the base system we have and easier to accomplish in the time frame."

Joe Karras, the Production technology lead, answered on behalf of his team. "Excellent question, Tabitha. The choices were driven by a couple of things—most importantly, the vision our executive team developed and the technology architecture. The basic idea of the service-oriented architecture is to take the discrete services, many represented on the pompom itself, and build them in reusable ways. Make sense?"

Tabitha was hardly in a position to argue the point with her fellow technology group member here in front of their joint "clients," even though it seemed to me that she wasn't buying the explanation. She made a "maybe" face and then nodded.

With that, Trevor wrapped up the session by explaining how to update the plan with percent completions, how and when to enter all questions into the issues system, and deadlines for completely answering all the issues. The requirements handoff meeting for "allocate jobs to facilities and equipment" was officially over.

I walked out of the session with an uneasy feeling in my stomach. I found myself wanting to talk it over with Mary, so I called her in her office. I was disappointed she wasn't in—more because I wanted to hear her voice than for any specific questions I needed answered or advice I sought. I left her a message asking her to call me, and when she did I fished around until I'd arranged dinner together next time we were in the same city. I had become more uncertain where the Cremins United project was heading, but I was feeling pretty sure I knew where I wanted to go with my relationship with Mary O'Connell.

Signposts	**Cremins United project**
	• At the end of the requirements phase, January 31, 2006, nearly all teams reported "green," with the exception of the Sales' team's cautionary "yellow." The requirements phase was complete!
	• The Production team handed off a stack of requirements to design. The requirements were done as ideal processes, from broad vision to detailed expected interactions among people and systems, without specific technology, cost, or feasibility constraints.
	• The Design team began to absorb the requirements, wondering what each requirement really meant, how it could be operationalized in software, and why the business teams chose the degree and method of automation specified. Discussion was cut short, and they were told to document their issues in the issues log for formal tracking and resolution.
Guides from Wes	• Large-scale system development is not analogous to manufacturing a product; it's more akin to the design of a product that eventually gets manufactured. Leaders must distinguish processes that can be done with defined, repetitive prescriptions from those learning-intensive ones that must be managed empirically (do, check, adjust, plan).

- Working without constraints is a fine way to do visioning, but a troublesome way to begin systems development. While the temptation "not to be limited by the technology group" is great, the results are not; understand the constraints first and then do detailed requirements and design simultaneously.
- Having a "technology person" attend requirements sessions is not the same thing as a unified team building a system together. It's better than no partnership at all, but not much.

Coming up next

Beth moves ahead 6 weeks to March 2006, when the Cremins United PCA members, at Mary's invitation, attend a TRIM scrum. Purpose: exposure to Lean/Agile concepts. Outcome? Read on.

Section II

The Second 6 Months:
March 2006–August 2006

17

The CU Project Leaders
Visit the TRIM Team

MARCH 2006

Beth:

Mary and I had planned carefully for today's show. Frankie, Neil, Tom, and Wes were coming to San Diego for a visit. They were going to do an all-hands meeting to give an update on the CU project and host some breakfasts with team members. They had also left Mary 2 hours in the afternoon to update them on progress of the Sales work. Sam, Mary's business partner, and GG, her project manager, had voyaged out of the cold to join in. Mary seemed nervous, although I wasn't sure if it was about the PCA's visit or Wes's plan to stay the weekend. The two of them were starting to become an item!

Mary and I had conferred on whether it might be useful to expose the PCA members to Lean/Agile development concepts. Mary had become frustrated by the continual struggles she had—documents that added no value, audits that wasted her team's time, and arguments over missing milestone dates that were set arbitrarily and for large batches. She was particularly concerned about the handoffs enforced on her for data analysis and transformation development, and for testing. She knew that the PCA members were doing their best and wanted the project to succeed; perhaps, she wondered, if we could give them some more information, they would be more flexible with her team and maybe even begin to embrace some Lean/Agile concepts. We had our doubts, but why not try?

Mary had broached the idea to Frankie, who had been encouraging. Despite her stodgy, formal reputation, Frankie had an open and active mind, and although she didn't go out of her way to innovate and learn, she didn't avoid it, either. Frankie had done hands-on software development earlier in her career, and she knew that the best work was often done by small, informal teams. While she supported The Process and generally believed in it, Mary and I had observed that she was increasingly in conflict with Neil over the amount of control and documentation the CU project office was imposing on the development teams. Frankie was becoming concerned about the ability of her development teams to meet the committed dates, as code complete date drew ever closer and her teams continued to wait for the formal okay to code. In the past when she had begun to run out of time, she had occasionally thrown out process entirely and just had her best people code a solution along with whatever subject matter experts she could find. She hadn't gone so far as to think that was the right approach from the start—certainly not when trying to control an outsourced service provider like GRI. But it couldn't hurt to check this Agile thing out and to give Mary, whom she had come to respect and admire, some positive reinforcement.

We had a problem in that Mary's team wasn't doing a formal Lean/Agile process. Because of the decision to go with CSMPro and the concomitant decision to follow the vendor's development process, there weren't any sprints or scrums to see. Sam, Mary, GG, and Jennifer, the CSMPro project lead, had done some modifications to the standard CSMPro method to test earlier and more thoroughly and do more frequent software builds, interface stubs, and automated testing, but that wasn't visible. We'd talked about just presenting Lean/Agile and how it could help CU, but that felt like preaching to an audience that didn't want to be preached to. I'd fallen back on what Mary herself had been preaching to me: How do we get the PCA members to "go see" so that they could draw their own conclusions?

The answer was simple: Bring them to one of Neville's scrum meetings, as observers. We checked with Neville and Alex, and they had no objection as long as the PCA members followed the rules—no talking during the meeting. Neville had volunteered to provide the Lean/Agile context as well; he hated the idea of our new parent company wasting so much investment capital, with so many other opportunities around.

Introducing the TRIM Scrum

Immediately upon the completion of the all-employee meeting in the courtyard, where Tom had given a nice overview of the CU project, Mary led the PCA members upstairs to one of the TRIM scrum rooms. The TRIM group had set aside a couple of conference rooms for the regular scrums; this was the room used by the Information Management team. It was a medium-sized room, comfortably fitting 15 people standing up. Usually, the only furniture in the room was a round table against one of the walls and just a couple of chairs. Mary had brought in a few more chairs for this session. The walls were covered with masking tape, charts, and colored slips of paper in columns.

We'd been able to synchronize the PCA visit schedule with the regular scrum meeting time of the Information Management team, led by Brian Bannion. Brian and Kamau, the lead for record matching, were on their second project using scrum and had the zeal of recent converts. They were proud to help.

As the four PCA members—Frankie, Neil, Tom, and Wes—and Mary's team—GG, Sam, Mary, and I—entered the room, Neville and Brian greeted us, and Mary introduced everyone. The PCA members remained standing, so GG and Sam took two of the chairs. As the group settled, Mary began the session: "Thanks for taking the time to come see an Agile team in action. The purpose of the next half-hour is to let you see a recent innovation in software development process; this is strictly an educational opportunity for you that might help you in governing the CU project. Our Sales team is using a few of the concepts you'll see today, although because we're bound so tightly to the CSMPro implementation process, we haven't fully adopted it."

Mary had chosen to avoid doing the substantive explanations herself, to give the PCA members the opportunity to see Lean/Agile in action from someone not directly connected to the CU project. This way, she figured, it would be easier for them to accept because it wouldn't look like Mary was pleading for special exceptions to The Process. Who better to do the introduction than Neville? Ever the showman, he was more than happy to do the introduction.

Mary continued, "We are very lucky to have Neville Roberts, the chief engineer of the Real Estate Division's TRIM project, here to tell us about how they are using scrum to help deliver software more effectively. Neville has been doing software development for, what is it now, Neville, 25 years? He's used just about every method that's been created over that time, and he has settled, at least for now, on the scrum method." Neville nodded good-naturedly at Mary, and Mary handed the floor to him.

"I admire your openness to seeing firsthand a different way of doing software development," Neville began. "Not everyone in your positions has that kind of curiosity and desire to keep learning—which in itself is a major cause of project failures."

Tom responded, "Well, Neville, this is really all Wes's doing. He keeps assuring us that the Sales team is actually in better shape than the others, despite their not meeting the phase gates we've set up, and that coming to see this demonstration and hearing from you will give us some comfort and reassurance. With this project, I can take all the reassurance I can get!"

"Well, then, thank you Wes, and let's get going, we only have 15 minutes until the team takes over the room. I'm going to share just a few ideas and give you a few handouts to take with you." At this, I handed out the materials Neville had prepared and Mary and I had vetted. We wanted to give the PCA something to think about, without being preachy or insulting; it was a fine balance.

Applying Lean Manufacturing Principles to Software Development

Neville continued, "The problem we are trying to solve is a tough one. Software projects are notoriously prone to failure. It turns out that the ways we have been trying to reduce the likelihood of failure can actually make it more likely, and that other industries have faced and made progress on these topics. I refer primarily to automobile manufacture, especially the 'Lean' approach Toyota has pioneered, which has been adopted by many companies around the world."

"Your first page [Figure 23] illustrates some of the principles of Lean that apply to both manufacturing and to software development. As principles, these are hard to argue against—who would argue for waste? It's in how we operationalize the principles, how prominent we make their pursuit versus other goals we might have. Today you will see all these principles in play, including visual management, knowledge building, employee involvement, and flow and pull."

Some "Lean" Principles –
Applicable to Both Manufacturing and
Software Development

– Elimination of waste

– Visual management (surface problems fast)

– Build employee knowledge

– Employee involvement in problem solving

– Flow and pull

FIGURE 23
Lean principles common to manufacturing and software development.

Neil was looking a little uncomfortable; he wasn't the learning type. He did ask the only question, however. "Neville, what do you mean by 'flow and pull'?"

"In manufacturing, it means a visual, smooth progression of work in process from raw material to finished goods, with the movement of parts from one step to another governed by when the receiving step is ready to process—ideally one part at a time instead of in batches. In software development, the meaning is similar: building out pieces of functionality in small chunks, doing requirements only when developers are ready to code them, coding only when test is ready to test them, and not building any inventory of uncoded requirements or untested code. The approach is critical to reducing waste, finding problems, and employee learning—our other principles. Shall I continue?"

Wes took this opportunity to connect the concept to the PCA's experiences. "That's quite different from how we do it now, Neville. We took great care to get all the requirements done together so that we could have a complete view for the designers to estimate the full costs and to build a plan that we could reliably work. You are saying that might not be the best way to set up the project?"

"That's right, Wes. Let's continue and I hope you can see why." There were nods, so Neville continued his explanation.

"The next graph you have [Figure 24] outlines the basic differences between manufacturing and product development or, in our case, software development. In manufacturing—think of a Toyota plant, putting out a new car every few minutes—we spend 2 years or more developing the process, or specifications, for making the car, and then we build each car

Predictable Manufacturing	New Software Development
It is possible to first complete specifications, then build.	Rarely possible to create upfront unchanging and detailed specs.
Near the start, one can reliably estimate effort and cost.	Near the beginning, it is nearly impossible. As empirical data emerge, it becomes increasingly possible to plan and estimate.
It is possible to identify, define, schedule, and order all the detailed activities.	Near the beginning, it is not possible. Adaptive steps driven by build-feedback cycles are required.
Adaptation to unpredictable change is not the norm, and change-rates are relatively low.	Creative adaptation to unpredictable change is the norm. Change rates are high.

FIGURE 24
Manufacturing versus software development.

very reliably. We know its cost; we can order all the activities and expect and manage for predictability."

"However, the process of developing that car—or, in our case, software—is quite a different story," Neville went on. "We aren't making thousands of essentially identical vehicles; we are usually making one-of-a-kind systems, doing new things, using new technologies, with teams that are working together for the first time. The bigger, the more innovative, the more parties involved, the less predictable it is to get all the requirements right, and then all the design, and then to build it all. So we need to find a way to *flow* the software development, adapt to what we learn, avoid building inventory that could be full of errors, and accelerate the learning of our teams. Instead of tightly controlling and discouraging change, we need to *embrace* change and learn how to deal with it effectively."

"Neville," interjected Tom, "that's also quite different from the way we see it. We try to nail down the scope firmly, and we discourage all change so that we avoid letting the project get out of control. You should hear our change control meetings! Assuming for the moment that you are right, what happens when you try to build complex software using the manufacturing approach?"

Neville gave an ironic chuckle. "I'm not saying it can never work; with enough time and money, most things are possible. It depends on the degree of unknowns, the talent and experience of the staff, the coherence of the team, and the leadership. I had some doozies of errors earlier in my career, when we were following 'waterfall'-type approaches. One time we missed what was, in retrospect, a very obvious requirement, and we didn't find out about it until after we'd gone live; we had to pull the system out of production for 6 months while we repaired the error. That experience helped push me to embrace this leaner approach. If we'd built that piece of the system and flowed it all the way through test and into production, even mock production, we'd have found that error very quickly and not lost that whole 6 months. Sometimes we think we can specify the requirements completely, then do the whole design, then the whole build and test, and get it right enough to go live and add business value. I have to admit that neither my teams nor I am smart enough to do that on the problems we work on."

Neville finished up Tom's answer by adding, "That's not to say that there are no situations where a manufacturing-like, mechanical follow-the-steps approach isn't appropriate. We actually had a situation like that in our installation of new multiple listing systems for several years, many years ago. We'd done 20 or 30 installations and were able to develop a solid step-by-step process to do the next 20 or 30. Worked great, until we started to run into new things we hadn't accommodated in our process, like Internet access, data downloads, and PC-based programs that needed interfaces. The key, Tom, is to match the development approach to the problem at hand, and I'd argue that even where you can have a mechanical, follow-the-cookbook approach, the Lean principles can make that work better."

Neville checked out Tom's understanding and, seeing it, continued.

The Agile Development Manifesto

"One more set of ideas and I'll be done. You've probably heard of 'Agile' development?" Neville looked at the PCA members and found blank stares. "Well, perhaps not. A group of software developers got together a few years ago and agreed on a number of principles and values that summarized some of these ideas, and it has caught on.[1] Please refer to the chart in your package titled 'Agile Manifesto' [Figure 25]."

"You can see some of the Lean ideas, such as flow—here in the value of working software over documentation—and learning—here in the focus on people, interactions, and collaboration. Don't make the mistake of

Agile Manifesto		

We value.....

Individuals and interactions	*over*	processes and tools
Working software	*over*	comprehensive documentation
Customer collaboration	*over*	contract negotiation
Responding to change	*over*	following a plan

That is, while there is value in the items on the right, we value the items on the left more.

FIGURE 25
Agile Manifesto values.

thinking Agile is about throwing development process and tools, or contract and plans, onto the rubbish heap; that's not at all the case. It's more of a plea to focus more strongly on people, code, and flexibility rather than solely on a rigid development process specification."

"The final piece of theory I'll share with you is the set of principles these same people came up with. We're about out of time," Neville said, as Brian and his team began to file into the room, "but let me just point out some of the principles that might best serve you in your project [Figure 26]."

"Principle number 1 is focused on software; you can deliver requirements or other documents forever and just be accumulating waste. I've seen projects that have gone on for a year or more, building extensive libraries of 'as-is' and 'to-be' diagrams and descriptions, that have been cancelled before slinging a line of code. Pure waste," Neville declared with what almost seemed like a sneer.

"Principle number 2—to welcome changing requirements—is counterintuitive to many project managers. Often a project will construct the requirements and design documents, but then, to have a chance of making the delivery date, freeze them, regardless of changes in the business or learning as the project progresses. I had a friend who was developing a new Web site for a retailer, aimed at a holiday season launch. Development management felt they had to constrain changes or they'd never make the unmovable launch date. As it turned out, by freezing change, they made launch impossible: the old Web site had continued to evolve while requirements

---

Agile Principles

We follow these principles:

1. Our highest priority is to satisfy the customer through early and continuous delivery of valuable software.
2. Welcome changing requirements, even late in development. Agile processes harness change for the customer's competitive advantage.
3. Deliver working software frequently, from a couple of weeks to a couple of months, with a preference to the shorter timescale.
4. Business people and developers must work together daily throughout the project.
5. Build projects around motivated individuals. Give them the environment and support they need, and trust them to get the job done.
6. The most efficient and effective method of conveying information to and within a development team is face-to-face conversation.
7. Working software is the primary measure of progress.
8. Agile processes promote sustainable development. The sponsors, developers, and users should be able to maintain a constant pace indefinitely.
9. Continuous attention to technical excellence and good design enhances agility.
10. Simplicity—the art of maximizing the amount of work not done—is essential.
11. The best architectures, requirements, and designs emerge from self-organizing teams.
12. At regular intervals, the team reflects on how to become more effective, then tunes and adjusts its behavior accordingly.

FIGURE 26
Agile Manifesto principles.

were frozen, and marketing refused to migrate to the new site! We need to be able to take changes more easily than we do now because those changes are about business value we need to deliver."

I could tell Neil was uncomfortable with this principle; controlling change was one of his major mantras. But he didn't say anything, just listened with a frown on his face.

"Any questions or comments yet?" Neville checked. "Stop me if you want; otherwise, I'll just touch on a few more items so that I don't run overtime too far."

"Skip down to number 10—simplicity—if you will. Don't overcomplicate things; we find a lot of instances where we build out functions that seem needed, but in practice aren't, so we need to keep it simple until we know for sure. We also sometimes build in excessive layers of abstraction in the anticipation that we'll need them at some point in the future, but that future often never comes. If it does, we can sometimes just as easily build the abstraction layers then."

Mary chimed in on this one. "Just as an example, most of you know that I believe the universal mandate to use the common data format and central transaction switch are examples of overcomplicating things in this project." Neville paused, saw no one wanted to deal with Mary's comment, and then continued.

"The final one I'll touch on, number 11, is related: The best architectures, requirements, and designs come from development teams themselves. We have a common pattern in our business of people not directly connected with the value delivery stream 'helping out.' Try not to let that happen; get great people, build them into teams, empower them, and you will get great results. They can still use help, but let them pull it in as they are ready, rather than forcing it on them."

Neville was now waving off Mary, who was trying to get him to finish because the scrum team members were filing into the room. "OK, OK, I'm done. 'Software development according to Neville' is now ending, although you are certainly free to continue to peruse at your leisure. Perhaps tonight in your hotel rooms, you can take out the list and see how many of the values and principles you saw demonstrated in the next 15 minutes."

"Oh, one last thing, before Brian begins: Once the team meeting begins, please do not interrupt. That's one of the rules of the scrum. Brian will be too polite to tell you," Neville concluded. "Brian, go ahead and start your meeting."

Explaining How TRIM Reforecasts Its Time Estimates

"OK, I'm Brian Bannion and this is the Information Management team scrum. This is Qin, our scrum master, who will run the meeting for us. We are in the last week of a 1-month sprint. Our primary goal was to enhance our data feeds, database, and matching programs to deal with multiple loans per property. We initially thought we could also add loan application information, which was a change requested in January, but as you'll see we've had some issues with that. Qin, let's begin."

Qin spent a moment explaining what was on the wall: the team's burn-down chart and their task lists with numbers written on them in a variety of colors and columns. It was essentially their project plan—there, on the wall—that they had built and maintained together. Neil interrupted and asked if he could ask a question now, or if the meeting had already started. Qin said it was okay to ask a question because the meeting didn't begin until she asked the first team member what he or she had done yesterday.

Neil asked if this was the extent of the project plan; was there a central plan with all the tasks that did reporting for tasks that were past due? If not, how did the team know how they were doing against the plan? How did management know what was or was not getting done?

Qin confirmed that this was it—no central project plan with all the tasks on it at all, at least not for this team. She explained that there was a central "backlog" of items to do, a high-level plan for what would be in each sprint, and, of course, the burn-down chart for this sprint. Neil asked her to explain the burn-down chart; she looked at Mary for guidance. Mary asked if the team and the PCA had a few extra minutes; all agreed they did, so Mary gave Qin the go-ahead, but said that the scrum would start in 5 minutes without a doubt.

Qin asked the PCA members to gather around the burn-down chart (Figure 27). "When we planned the sprint, we estimated tasks from the back-log list that would consume our available forecast hours, balancing the work as best we could based on who was available to work. We projected 1,400 hours available time, and we forecast a straight-line burn-down. You can see that in the first week, everything went as planned, which is fairly typical.

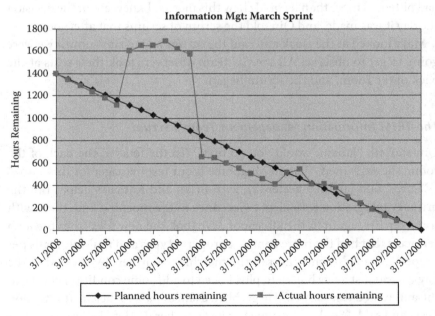

FIGURE 27
Information Management March burn-down chart.

Then, we ran into a serious problem. We found that it was going to take a lot more work and time to get the loan application data from our mortgage origination partners; you can see how the forecast time required to finish the sprint went well above our forecast line. It took a week or so to figure out what to do about the problem, and ultimately we decided to take that feature out of the sprint and put it back into the backlog. That caused our hours remaining to drop below the original forecast, and we are just about finishing up the sprint now, with somewhat less scope than planned."

Neil was troubled by this. "What happened to the feature you took out of scope? Who decided that it was okay to do that?" This was clearly not how Neil would run a project.

Neville responded, "The feature is now in the backlog and will be dealt with in planning for the next sprint, which is when, Qin? Tuesday? The team will re-estimate what it will take to do that feature now, see if it's still the next highest priority to do, make sure they have the team to get it done next month, and if it's the right thing to do next, it will get done next month. The decision to move it back into backlog was made by this team. There wasn't much to decide; it was more a recognition and communication that the team had bitten off more than it could chew this month. I knew about the decision the day it was made, and Qin told the scrum of scrums that afternoon."

Mary looked at the clock and said the scrum had to start now if we were going to get to observe. All the CU team observers took their seats at the back of the room, and the scrum began.

The TRIM Information Management Team's Scrum

Qin started, "Janani, would you go first?" To the folks at the back of the room, she explained, "Janani Mugombe is our test manager for this team."

"Sure," said Janani. "Yesterday, with Brian and Kamau's help, I ran the primary integration test script twice, once in the morning and, then, with some repairs, again in the afternoon. We took the new files from the loan servicers that had the more complex property types and multiple loans per property, loaded them, and ran the matching routines. By the end of the day we had just a few bugs left, plus I need to add some condition checks to the automated test scripts." He grabbed a slip of paper labeled "Integration Test" and said, "So this task now has just another day left. I think I can finish today, which is what I plan to do. I'll need a half-day each from Brian and Kamau, so time remaining is 16 hours." With that, he crossed off the prior estimate and penciled in "16." "I'd also like to take this task," he said, grabbing a slip of paper from the first column on the wall labeled 'prepare environment for demo.' I think the estimate is probably still okay, at 8 hours, and I'll have it done by the end of the week for sure."

"Anything in your way?" queried Qin.

"We are having a tough time with one of the lender files; they gave it to us in a format different from the one we'd agreed upon, and we had to write a format transformation in order to test. I could use some help getting them to give us what they're supposed to."

"I can take that," said Qin. "Thanks, Janani. Brian, you want to go next?"

"Sure. Janani has already spoken for my day yesterday and half my day today. The rest of the day today I'll be finishing up the demo script. I'll take the 'practice demo' task, and I'll get the team together day after tomorrow for a run-through. I don't have any barriers for which I need help at this time."

Qin continued on through the team members, and in 15 minutes the meeting was complete. Several follow-up huddles were agreed to during the meeting, and as the team left the room, a couple of clusters formed to continue discussions started during the sprint.

Neville thanked the team on their way out, and once they were gone he asked the PCA members if they had any observations or questions. Frankie said it was nice to see how the team was working together, but she didn't see that it was all that different from daily stand-up meetings that some of her teams did. Neville pointed out the tighter structure, planning, and tracking, and Frankie acknowledged that could be valuable.

Neil seemed like he'd been stewing on something, and Neville noticed and asked him for his reaction. "A couple of thoughts. First, I'm troubled by how the team just took an important feature out of scope, without any change control by senior management. I'd prefer that when a team finds something like that, they simply work overtime to get it done—that they meet their commitments. If they can't do that, as leaders we need to know about and approve changes to scope of this sort. It seems to me an abdication of our duty to just let a team do something like what we just heard about."

"Second," Neil continued describing his concerns, "it seems to me that in order for this to work, you need to have really good people who know their stuff and can work well together. It seems altogether too dependent on that, whereas The Process we use in the CU project has a lot of checks and balances and can compensate for weak people in certain roles because of the management controls and tracking. I see how this could work for a small project, but I can't see how it could scale."

At this, I had to interrupt because we'd already gone beyond our time allotment and people were waiting for the PCA members in another room. I could see that Neville was itching to respond to Neil, but it was probably better that we didn't have time for Neville and Neil to go at it. My guess is neither would learn anything.

NOTES

Signposts	**Cremins United project**
	• The PCA members visited a TRIM scrum at Mary's invitation. She had hoped that they would learn something, but it didn't appear that they had.
	TRIM project
	• The Information Management team conducted a scrum, removing an item from the sprint and putting it back into the backlog—just a routine modification.
Guides from Beth	• Don't confuse Lean manufacturing principles with Lean product development. The idea of system development standardization, while it has applicability in some instances, can be devastating to your success.
	• The Agile Manifesto and accompanying principles provide an excellent set of ideas for leaders, whether new to system development or experienced. Anyone accountable for system development should be concerned with projects that seem to be conducted in material contradiction.

1. AgileManifesto.org.

- It's a valiant effort to try to educate senior leadership on new approaches to software development, and I'd encourage you to do so. At some point, once you are sure they aren't going to get it—especially if you will still be forced to follow methods that are likely to result in failure—your only choice is to find a new employer. Don't wait too long to do so!

Coming up next   Wes takes us forward 3 months to June 2006. We see the Sales team making excellent progress within their silo, but sensing looming disaster on the boundaries. Do they report green (they are OK) or red (project is in trouble)?

18

Checking on the CU Project's Development: Green for Go or Screaming Red?

JUNE 2006

Wes:

By June, Mary and I had had a couple of dates. Mary was cautious about getting involved with someone in a distant city, given the demands of her children and work, but we were enjoying getting to know each other better. I'd checked with Beth about propriety and policy and found out that Cremins's policy didn't demand anything as long as neither of us worked directly for the other. In any case, until we were more romantically involved (wink, wink), nothing would be demanded of us. She recommended that if that were to happen, I should discreetly tell my boss, just to be safe. I hoped I'd have to do that soon.

My increasing time spent with Mary had a side benefit of enabling me to see and evaluate the CU project from a different perspective. I'd learned enough from her, from Neville, and from watching the activity in the CU project to be concerned about the prospect of CU success. I was also concerned that Tom, my boss, whom I respected as a good businessman and leader, was out of his element trying to lead this project. When I compared him to Neville, I saw the gaps in his experience and skills, which led to his inability to see beyond what he was being told by the project office and his technology partners. He had no basis by which to judge quality of people, process, or technology choices; it had taken until now, as evidence that trouble was brewing started to accumulate, for his antenna to go up. Also, his personality was one of collaboration and cooperation, which prevented him from setting up outside reviews that could have helped him gain perspective.

As for the other PCA members—well, it seemed to me that Neil's personality had become dominant. Neil was relying on his innate need for order, combined with his strong belief in tradition and structure. He had a great commitment to getting the project done as he'd promised, and as the pressure mounted, he fell back more and more on the promise that the structure that Frankie and Trevor brought, if followed faithfully, would get the job done. He was also a cheerleader, trying to ensure that everyone was working hard enough and not accepting for a moment any indication or intimation that the project might not succeed as planned. Mary had helped me see the risks in this approach, but despite Mary and Beth's attempt to expose Neil to alternative thinking, he was becoming more and more strongly committed to sticking this out according to the book that Trevor provided.

It was now June, 9 months after the CU project had kicked off, and the project was officially still all "green," for a September code complete and a November release/first use. The various implementation teams were in full swing, getting ready to acceptance test, train users, and provide help desk support. The project team meetings were starting to sound like a game of chicken, with none of the various teams ready to step forward and say they were going to miss the date. However, there was a lot of rescheduling and rescoping of various tasks and the establishment of a formal "work-around identification and approval" process to account for newly found gaps in system scope that could not be closed in the time remaining. The pattern so far had been that when a team brought forth an issue that could threaten the date, Neil would jump in to "help," and he'd supply a gang of GRI consultants to staff a "SWAT" team, have daily meetings, and generally add a lot more overhead to the people trying to get the work done. My suspicion now was that a lot of these areas were hiding out there, and no one wanted to bring them forth.

The volume of change requests and the noise around defining whether they were really "changes" or "additions to scope" was beginning to escalate. Teams were drawing sharper and sharper distinctions about what was their responsibility and what was not. It appeared that no one was focused on the system rollout as a whole succeeding except for the PCA, which was relying on effective implementation of The Process to ensure that all was well.

Tom now had enough concern that he asked me to do some informal temperature checking on how teams were actually doing as opposed to how things were being reported. I'd wanted to travel to San Diego to see Mary again anyhow, so I was able to combine a business and pleasure trip into one. Today I was going to attend the Sales group's regular team meeting and hear firsthand how that part of the project was going. The meeting kicked off at 8 a.m. San Diego time and included Mary, as tech lead; GG, project manager; Sam, business lead; Jennifer Phillips, account manager for CSMPro lead; Deb Dillingham, a test lead that Mary had brought on a few months ago and was trying to keep below the radar of the testing group (which was accountable for all testing); Dillon Flaherty, the Data team's lead assigned to Sales; and me, as an observer on behalf of the Project Control Authority. This Sales leadership team meeting was held every week, to touch base, plan, and adjust. GG typically led the meeting, and he kicked it off from his perch in St. Paul via the phone; everyone else was here in the San Diego conference room.

The Sales Subsystem Is "Green"

"I don't have much new to report from a project management perspective. I'd like to talk through how we report our status this week, whether we stay yellow or move to green or red. Jennifer will do her regular update, and I've invited Dillon to join us to talk over the data interfaces, which are our biggest issues right now. We also need to talk over our approach to testing, and Deb is prepared to help us do that. I'd propose that we start with Jennifer, then Dillon, and then Deb; based on their information, we can pick our color for the week."

Sam needed a little more context, so he asked, "GG, can you frame up the reporting question? How could we be thinking of switching from yellow to red or green?"

"That does seem strange, doesn't it? Here's the issue: As you'll hear from Jennifer, CSMPro has turned the corner and now feels quite confident that it will have a workable system for us in September, up to the point of the data interface transactions. Remember that we had to write them to the common data structure, so if that works, the sales system will work. The bad news is that the Data team now plans to deliver the transaction right at code complete, so we won't be able to start testing until then. We have some other issues with testing as well that Mary thinks threaten the project sufficiently that we should be red. So the issue is one of scope as we report status; if we report on just our pieces, we could be green, while if we report on our opinion that the sales system will actually work in November, we're probably a screaming red."

"Interesting dilemma. Let's do as you suggest with the agenda and then consider the color issue," Sam agreed. "Jennifer, you want to begin?"

"Sure, no problem. We're coming right along. We've completed setup of the integration testing environment, and as we configure CSMPro, we will do weekly migrations to it from Development. Our customizations are coming along well enough; we've done as Mary asked and are doing them in complete cycles: As we complete requirements on each, we move right into design, development, and unit testing, and move directly into the test environment. We've had to build out some testing stubs for the external transaction calls, but that's been fairly easy because we are writing to our own data formats, expecting that the Data team is going to deliver them as we have requested."

"We'll get to that in just a bit," GG concluded, handing the floor back to Jennifer. She continued, "Deb has been working with our test group; they've got a great start on an integration test data bed, and we've stepped up the integration of the Test team with the Development team to increase the coverage of automated testing. We still have some requirements to finish up on some of the customizations, but our development team is fully occupied with what's on its plate, so it's not critical path yet and looks like we should be able to finish up on time. The ongoing requirements and design clarifications are going very well; we really appreciate the four Cremins sales experts that Sam provided to us."

"I just talked to our analysts on site," Sam said. "They are very happy with how development is proceeding. Our SMEs are sitting with the CSMPRo development and testing groups, and they are able to resolve questions immediately and make changes on the fly as they understand better what CSMPro does and does not do. As development has progressed, they are now spending more and more of their time working on test plans, and last week they did their first round of testing when the integration test environment came up. Our folks think they should be able to keep up with the weekly releases and maintain a tested and working system throughout."

Jennifer continued, "Our staff is excited about the improvements we've made at Mary's suggestion about better flowing our development, doing the weekly releases to integration testing, and doing continuous automated integration testing. They just love having the Sales groups right on site, although sometimes they need to 'shut the door' for a while so that they can get their work done!"

"Next week we begin building out the production environment, and in a few weeks we can start testing there as well. Our plan is to use the new production environment as our stress testing and security testing base; we have the luxury of a new system not already in production, and we intend to capitalize on it."

"The biggest remaining risk I see," Jennifer concluded, "is the data interface. We have an awful lot of assumptions going on as we build the transactions stubs, and I'm worrried that we won't have the actual transactions to test with until formal integration testing begins in September. If the Data team isn't populated by a bunch of wizards, I can't see how we can possibly be ready."

GG turned to Mary and asked her if she had any comments on development status. Mary summarized her views: "I agree with Jennifer's assessment. I have half a dozen of my team members full-time at CSMPro's offices, learning the technology and helping with development and testing, and assisting in the improved development flows. I'm confident that we'll have a sales system in September; whether we have anything to connect it to is a different story."

"Let's turn to that," Sam responded. "Dillon, thanks for calling in. Can you explain to us how the data transactions are coming along? If you could do it in a nontechnical way, I'd really appreciate it."

The Integration Software Is "Screaming Red"

"No problem," said Dillon. "Let me first give a little context. Design was supposedly complete in April, and, in fact, we did have definitions of all of the services. We didn't have time to write all the specific transaction specifications, but we didn't think we needed to do that because we are using the CSF—the common service facility—and its common data model. Each transaction simply specified the control characteristics, and the data sections were specified by the name of the segments of the CDM."

"Can you give an example of that, Dillon?" asked Sam. "Maybe use the beginning of our sales cycle, when the sales system submits a prospective job to the production system so that we can get pricing on it."

"It's actually not very complicated in concept," Dillon responded. "I'm not familiar specifically with that transaction, but in general it would work like this. In design, we would have seen that transaction specified in the use-case flow and created a service for it. The service would have action codes—in this case, maybe 'submit job'—and associated data. The data would be something like 'customer information' and 'job information.' These would refer to the segments of the CDM that each transaction would use identically. Every system sending or receiving data would do so to the CSF, in CDM format."

"Sounds logical," said Sam.

Mary interjected to explain how the Sales team interacted with this design work. "If we continue with this example, Sam, it should help us all understand. The CDM is not complete for our needs; it was developed for the BCG and for just a subset of the needs we are exercising in CU. So the Data team has a group that owns the management of the data model and creating all the transformations into and out of the model for each interfacing system. Our responsibility was to take the business requirements documents, ensure we had the proper data elements in CSMPro to support them, and then submit to the Data team the transactions we intended to use, substituting in the data section the fields as we knew them, with our field names and data definitions. The Data team would then map our fields to the CDM, identify any missing fields, and add them in a way that aligned with all the other users of all the services."

"We were fortunate we could submit our data needs in that way," Jennifer noted. "We have good data definitions for all our fields because we need to implement for quite a variety of customers."

"From our perspective," continued Mary, "we simply write the transaction in our own data formats, with the exception of the control information. We call the common service facility, which does the translation of the data into the standard format, and then translates back into the format of the system to which we are connecting. Theoretically, it means that each system needs only speak its own data language, and the CSF needs just to maintain one map for each connecting system, into the standard data language. It's as if everyone at the UN could speak just his or her own language, and the translation department translated everything into English. Then, messages were translated from English to whatever language was needed by the message recipient. There would be no need ever to translate from, say, French to German."

"From a development perspective, this made things easy for us," said Jennifer. "We just mocked up transactions in our integration layer and are writing to those. The issue will be when we get to integration testing: How similar are the real transactions to the mocked-up ones, and how faithfully did the data translations get done? Do the other systems, especially the production management system, process the data and return us results as we expect?"

Dillon, our team representative from the Data department, re-entered the conversation at this point. "Excellent examples, thanks. Jennifer, you are right about the issue of the quality of the translations. We're finding that in translating from French to German by going through English, it's easy to lose meaning—as if there are concepts in French or German that aren't well represented in English. It's actually a little worse than that because English has plenty of words, but our CDM is immature and is missing much of the basic vocabularies. We're having to add new data elements to CDM in large quantities, and we are finding conflicts and subtleties in how various systems use data that are making CDM increasingly complex. Our tools don't support this large-scale simultaneous effort very well, and our analysts are increasingly turning to spreadsheets to try to get the mapping done on time."

Easy to Architect, but Hard to Build

Mary asked, "Dillon, the original schedule had you delivering our transactions to us by the beginning of August, at least with some functionality. What's causing the delay to September? How confident are you that you can meet the September delivery?"

"I think I can answer the first question, Mary, but I can't answer the confidence question. My job is just to do your mappings to the CDM; I don't do the mappings on the other side, and I don't have anything to do with coding. So far, the date on the project plan is still September; no one has moved off that yet."

"As to why it has been moved from August—that has to do with the commonality of the data structures. In order to stay common, any change to the

CDM has to be proposed to the CDM control group. The change has to be documented, analyzed by a CDM analyst, and then reviewed at the weekly change control meeting. Whenever a change in an object we are using is made by anyone, we have to modify our transaction definition and map. There is still extensive change going on as development is under way, so we decided not to release the actual transactions until CDM stabilizes."

"What kind of work would it be every time CDM changes? Let's say the 'job information' segment needs change due to changes in something that doesn't affect us—say, factory scheduling? Would we have to react?" Mary queried.

"Yes, we'd have to change our affected maps. All the CSF services that used the 'job information' data would have to be updated. I'd have to remap all of our transactions that use that information, and we'd have to change our code and retest. So we want to avoid making changes to the transactions as much as we can, which is why we are delaying the release."

I'd been quietly listening to this exchange and becoming more and more concerned. The CSF and CDM had sounded like such great ideas, and only now was I understanding any downside. I wanted some clarification of the impacts, so I asked, "Mary, this will affect even the direct interfaces, like the Sales to the Production Management system, won't it?"

"Yes, it will; all interfaces go through CSF and CDM, Wes. We had this argument with Janice early in the project, and the PCA issued an edict enforcing this decision. It's not just an issue with change management, Wes. There are possible implications to testing complexity, data mapping integrity—the French/German problem—and, of course, performance. We are required always to send the complete data segment, even if the transaction only needs a few fields. We'll be doing a lot more data access, transmission, and transformation than we really need to do. We also risk getting the maps wrong because the Sales and Production team members don't talk directly on how the fields map. The maps to and from the CDM take some judgment and can be done more than one way, so it's possible we can get this very wrong. The benefit is supposed to be standardization, interoperability, and modularity—like we can snap out one sales system and snap in another easily."

I followed up, "Does anyone have any suggestions on how to deal with this risk? Sounds to me like we are finding a lot more complexity here than we'd bargained for. What do we do in August or September when we find we can't finish on time? Do we continue slogging down this path, or should we be considering abandoning the CSF and CDM, at least in parts, to make this easier to get done?"

"Do you want to talk that over now, Wes, or wait until after we hear the testing report?" asked Deb. "My news isn't so good either."

"Great," I replied, thinking forward to what kinds of options I might relay to Tom. "For the sake of discussion, let's just assume that we have testing problems that will make CSF and CDM even more of an issue. What can we do now to be ready for possibly hearing bad news in the next few months?"

Mary knew that while I was posing the question to the whole group, it was her opinion I wanted most, and she answered accordingly. "Wes, I have to admit that I don't know where to go with this problem. I could never imagine trying a risky strategy like CSF and CDM, given the short schedule and what's at stake. Why put the company's success in jeopardy for benefits that seem nebulous at best? I prefer getting business benefits as quickly as we can and then dealing with speculative needs like having to swap out the sales systems at a later date, if necessary. From what I can tell, Janice and her team brought this; perhaps they saw something like it at a conference or in a book or bought the standard 'spaghetti chart' vendors sell hook, line, and sinker. I just don't know enough to have a reasonable judgment on whether we can make it work with some modifications, or if it's a good-sounding idea that is impractical."

"So what would you suggest?" I wasn't going to give up so easily.

"We find someone who has done this type of thing before and get some advice."

"Do you think you could do that?" I asked.

Mary thought for a moment, and while she pondered, Jennifer from our CSMPro partner spoke up. "I think I know someone," she said. "We had an engagement last year with a large company that had made some progress implementing an enterprise service bus—something like what you are trying to do with the CSF. They had a consulting firm helping them, and there was a consultant there who specialized in data integration. How about I check with him?"

"Thanks, Jenn. That would be great. I have some ideas I can pursue also; I can make calls this afternoon. Wes, what would you like out of this? Maybe a brief engagement, confined to our team, get some ideas on what might and might not work, just in case?"

"That's probably all we can do now. Neil or Frankie wouldn't go for a suggestion to bring in any help now: Frankie because it would imply that she hasn't done a good job so far and Neil because we have no 'facts' that there is a problem with the basic approach. Let me know what you find out, Mary, okay?"

"Sure enough, Wes, I will. Ready to talk about testing?" asked Mary.

"Indeed we are," said GG. "Deb, what do you have for us?"

Lots of Testing Groups and Phases, but Gaps Still Remain

Deb was blunt in her assessment. "I've been digging into the test planning, with Mary's help, and what we've found is quite concerning. It seems there is no overall coherent approach to testing. There seem to be three levels or stages involved: *unit testing,* for which we are responsible within our own team; *integration testing,* which the technical testing team owns; and *acceptance testing,* which the 'businesses' own. I can go through each stage quickly and assess how it affects us."

Deb went on, "First off, *unit testing* is pretty straightforward. It's considered part of development, and no formality or standards are around it that I can tell. It includes whatever the developers want to do to be sure their code works, up to ensuring that the software technically connects with interfaces. I've talked to several of the other development teams, and it's clear that what our team has done is far beyond what any other team is undertaking. We're completely testing our code, up to the interfaces, so in September, when we enter formal testing, we expect our system to work completely. None of the other teams is doing anything like this."

Jennifer added, "We're basically doing our standard test protocols, which we always do prior to beginning customer testing; we've just added more automation and are doing it more incrementally as we complete features. Our software should be good to go by the time testing begins; as we said, it will all depend on the quality of the interfaces the Data team provides us."

"The other groups don't have any testers on their development teams," Deb said, "so it's up to the developers to do unit testing. Some of the developers are writing automated unit tests as they go, but they aren't sharing those tests with the 'official' test teams. Basically, when the developer is sure his piece works, it's called 'unit tested.'"

"That puts most of the burden on the technical test team, in the *integration testing* phase, and on acceptance testing. The technical test team begins testing once the development teams put unit-tested code into the integration test environment. They view their accountability as to ensure that the system connectivity is present; for example, they'll ensure that the production management system calls the pricing service, but not that the prices returned are correct. They view that 'correctness' testing to be the responsibility of the business acceptance testers. They have thousands of test scripts, each based on the use cases; they have a tool that converts the requirements statements into test cases and test conditions, and a management system that will report how many of these test cases have been run and how many have passed or failed. Mary and I looked to see how well this covered our interfaces, and we were stunned that, although there are hundreds of test cases, none of them has completely specified input or expected results."

GG asked, "Then how can they tell if the tests pass?"

"They have a test data generator that provides the basic information about a customer or a job, so they can load data. For results, they check a few fields to see if they look reasonable. They leave the detailed testing to the acceptance group. They seem to have a philosophy that the testers shouldn't have to know anything about the system they are testing; in fact, they are configuring it so that the testing group in India can run any tests, just from the scripts. There doesn't seem to be any functional alignment of testers to code or business area at all. They have no automation other than the input generator and the pass/fail tracking."

Mary added, "The quality of the testing will be completely dependent on the completeness and accuracy of the scripts, which in turn are completely dependent on the quality and completeness of the requirements documents. It gives a theoretical complete traceability, and if all the artifacts were complete and accurate and the transformations into test scripts perfect, it will theoretically work. It scares me, though, especially with our software; we didn't do complete requirements because we were starting with a complete system that we were just modifying. I'd think that other groups have the same issue. Especially in this situation, we need to have people who intimately know the software doing the testing."

"That brings us to the *acceptance testers*," said Deb. "Acceptance testing begins after the technical team finishes integration testing. There are formal 'exit criteria' that have to be met before the code moves from the integration test system to the user acceptance test system—such as all tier 1 problems cleared, no tier 2 problems without workarounds, and so on. If integration testing doesn't get done quickly, the acceptance testers might not even get the code until the 2-month test period ends!"

"On the plus side, the acceptance testers have constructed, completely independently of any knowledge of the software, a hundred or so end-to-end test scenarios. To their credit, they do have specified data inputs and expected results, and they will run the tests end to end. They'll also do some targeted testing at some specific services, like pricing and the accounting linkages. But because they explicitly chose not to ensure that that all parts of the system were being tested—just the scenarios they had constructed—we have no assurance of test coverage."

"It's handoff from the unit testers to the integration testers to the acceptance testers, with no overall coherent view of test completeness, no common test bed of data or scenarios, and no sharing of data or automation from stage to stage," Mary summarized. "Just what I was afraid of."

Mary pensively chewed her pen for a moment before asking Deb to summarize. "How would you assess our biggest risk right now, our linkage via the CSF to the production system? Are there good tests for that?"

Deb replied, "It was hard to tell. We don't have requirements that cover that linkage directly; it's included in a lot of processes and use cases. I'd bet that there are 200 or more test scripts in integration testing that touch on it, as well as almost every scenario in acceptance testing. It's certainly not how I'd be testing this; I'd want to have a focused set of tests that load known data into the sales system, specify where they land and how they look in the production system, and automate the entry and checking. We should test the integration of major systems explicitly, with people who know both systems, instead of relying solely on functional integration and acceptance testing."

"I'm with you on that, Deb," said GG. "That's our biggest risk, and we should go after it. How about I get a meeting with Joe Karras, the tech lead for Production, and we see if we can put together a team to build out and execute sales to production data integration testing? We won't be able to start it until September, but we should be able to fit it in."

"I think he'll go for it," said Mary. "I know he is privately skeptical of the integration through CSF. As long as we call it 'unit testing,' the test groups won't have any problem with it, unless it interferes with their test schedules. But we should be able to work around that."

"Is it okay if I get a few more contractors to help?" asked Deb. "We don't have the horsepower to get this added task done." Jennifer added, "The CSMPro team hasn't planned on this either, so it'd have to be an addition to our existing statement of work to do this. Our contract ended at the transactions in our own data formats."

"Well, we're being told that time is more important than money and to pull out all the stops. Go ahead and plan for it pending the meeting with Joe; just add it into your forecasts next week, and I'll put it into my status report," said Mary. "It's extending our accountability out a bit, along with Joe's, but it's our best hope to get this integrated effectively. It's how we should have done this to begin with—having a cross-system team configuring, coding, and testing the interface. Better late than never!"

Reporting the Silo's Status, Rather Than That of the Project

"With that," GG interjected, "we have just one topic to deal with: What color are we? I can give you my view, based on the instructions I'm getting from the PMO. There has been quite a debate, going back months, on what exactly the colors mean." Sounding as though he were ticking each color off on his fingers, GG said, "It's pretty standard. *Green* means nothing major threatens completion on approved scope and time; *yellow* means we have some threats but think we can deal with them; and *red,* of course, means threats and no current plan to get back on track. Our issue is the scope of the coloration: Is it just our own defined responsibilities or our judgment on whether our system, in combination with all the others, will be ready to go live in November?"

Sam, who had been listening quietly most of the meeting, was very interested in this topic. As the business lead, he was in some sense the overall owner of this team, although, in practice, his role was limited to providing people to help with requirements, testing, and deployment, and making some trade-off decisions on system functionality. "I don't think we can be yellow anymore; we've made it through the issues that threatened our own delivery, so we have to be either green or red because we see threats to delivery in November and don't have a plan that we think adequately deals with them. Does everyone agree with that?"

Everyone did, so Sam continued. "Hey, Wes, do you have any guidance on this? What would PCA expect?"

I thought for a moment and then said, "I'd think the PCA wants each team to answer for its own responsibilities. In this case, the assessment of the integration risks would be coming from the Data team and the Test teams. While you have concerns about other areas, your status report color probably isn't the right way to report them. From what I've heard today, you are green. But let me ask GG: You are in the Project Management office, what are the official rules on this?"

"My understanding is as you said. I checked with Trevor this morning on the interpretation, and he was perfectly clear: We report on our part only, we don't make what he called 'speculative assessments' on others' work or on how our work will integrate with others. For example, it doesn't matter if we don't think testing is prepared to test our code adequately or there isn't enough time to test our transactions because delivery was moved out a month. Those issues are outside our accountability. My interpretation is that we are a nice clear green as well, but I don't feel very good about it."

"The only reason, then," Sam commented, "for us to go red would be to raise to the PCA a bright warning flag that we think the other groups are not prepared and that the schedule has probably already been breached, even though the groups responsible will be reporting all is well. I don't want to fight that battle; does anyone else?"

No one had a taste for that conversation, so it was unanimous: The Sales team was green to go, even though none of them believed there was a meaningful chance that in November their system would be working as part of the larger CU deployment.

* * *

That night, I joined Mary and her kids at her house. Mary and I were making pizza for dinner—what better way to get them to like me? While we were making the dough, the kids were in the backyard playing, and we had a chance to debrief on the day at work.

"There's no chance this thing is going to work in November, is there, Mary?" I asked.

"We're off duty now, Wes, and off the record?" she replied.

"Of course."

"I can't see any possibility of it working in November. I'd be surprised if it was working a year from now."

"Wow, that's really pessimistic. That would be horrible! The project certainly does seem to have violated an awful lot of your Lean and Agile principles. Just today, in the discussion on the data interfaces, we must have seen half a dozen principles blown through. Let's see—certainly the 'towering technical competence' idea; Janice and her team seem to have brought us into this CSF/CDM approach with little other than some vague architectural beliefs. Also, there are the 'Agile' principles of the best architectures coming from the teams doing the work, instead of a high priesthood of architects, and the principle on simplicity and avoiding work if you can. We've no concurrent engineering on this; we just went ahead, assuming it would work; we also have no continuous integration. We don't have one-piece flow in development; everything is in a big batch, supposedly coming together in a big bang in September. And handoffs—wow, we seem to have made an art of handing things off from one group to another! Our focus has been on document artifacts, rather than code, and on process over teams and interactions."

"Why, Jim Wesleyan, you are really beginning to get it! We're going to make a software development manager out of you yet!" Mary beamed at me and gave me a little kiss.

"Maybe, maybe, but what can we do about it? It's June, just a few months to code that is supposedly complete and it looks like a disaster looming to you and me, but officially the project is green and we're getting ready to deploy it in November. Why, just today, your own team decided to report 'all's well' even though none of you believe the system will be ready in November."

"I don't know, Wes, I've more or less given up on influencing the broader project and am just trying to get my piece done. You're the management consultant; you must have some ideas."

"Right now, I'm about stumped, Mary. I guess I'll just crack another beer and drag you out back to play with the kids while the dough rises."

"Now that I can agree to!" It was off to the sandbox, as Mary and I left the CU dilemma simmering in her kitchen.

Signposts	**Cremins United project**
	• All was well with the Sales team; code, up to the point of integration with other systems, looked to be on track.
	• Investigation of integration and testing scared the team about the Sales–Production interface through CSF. The team decided to reach out to the Production team and arrange more intrateam focus, outside the formal project structure, on their critical interface.
	• The Sales team changed its status color from "yellow" to "green" after getting guidance that they should comment just on their own area and should avoid speculating on what will happen once integration testing began.
Guides from Wes	• Only now, a few months before code complete, are the flaws in the project beginning to come to light. They were there all along, buried in the mounds of inventory (undesigned requirements, uncoded designs, untested code).
	• The PCA had earlier convinced the teams that it did not want to hear their opinions, just reports on what they had been told to do. So problems are not being surfaced. Leaders need to work hard to keep the channels of communication open, including exercising the "go see" commandment.

- Handoffs in testing are as pernicious as any. There should be one testing plan that covers from beginning of requirements through introduction to production. Of course, there will still be multiple phases; a unified plan ensures there are no unknown gaps, that test data can be reused, and that the proper kind of testing is done early enough that results can be accommodated. For example, user interface testing that might reveal needed changes should be done very early, rather than waiting for "user acceptance testing" at the end.
- Testing should proceed as follows: test each component; put components together into assemblies of units and then test those; put multiple assemblies together and then test their interfaces; put the whole system together and then test it end to end. In addition, each sprint should have testable code and, as the project proceeds, end-to-end testing of whatever is ready should be done. Final assembly should be of tested subassemblies and tested interfaces, much as would be done in a car, where the engine is tested, the transmission is tested, the engine and transmission are tested together, and so.

Coming up next

Beth resumes narration in July 2006, following a month's passage. We learn that TRIM is doing well and how the TRIM and CU projects are seen from the perspective of Cremins's senior management.

19

A Status Check:
TRIM Is OK, but CU May Be in Trouble

JULY 2006

Beth:

Walt was finishing up his financial overview of the Real Estate Division and Cremins overall when I entered Greg's staff meeting, about half an hour late. Before he had finished, I was able to pick up from Walt that our division was doing quite well, but the company as a whole was suffering continued revenue losses as customers moved increasingly to the Internet. There was a lot of pressure to keep costs low and to find new electronic-based sources of revenue—essentially, to hurry our strategy of needs-based customer sales and fulfillment. That set a compelling framework for our next two topics: a review of the TRIM project and a discussion of Cremins United.

TRIM's Visual Status Report

Neville went first and reported that TRIM looked to be mostly on track, still looking at a mid-November release with two large lenders and the MLS and public records systems in Atlanta and San Diego. He reported on the status of the development project by handing out a one-page chart, another in his series of simple, strikingly visual communication and monitoring devices (Figure 28).

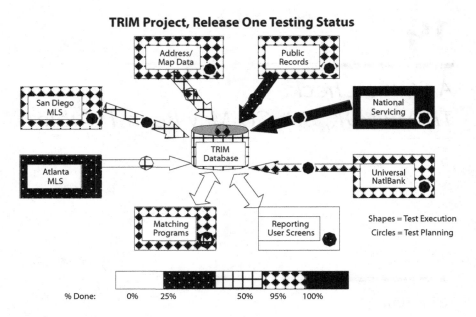

FIGURE 28
TRIM test status chart.

"Oh no, Neville, not the 'psychedelic chart' again!" Walt complained. Apparently, Walt had seen this device before. I hadn't, and I was struck by how much information it communicated and how clearly it did so. I saw Walt's point, though: There were a lot of shades and patterns!

"Sorry about the patterns, Walt. They've now become something of a tradition—the graphics our team loves to hate. We do it this way to avoid the cost of color printing. Bear with me and I'll show you how the project is coming along."

I found the comparison of Neville's chart to the Cremins United status reporting approach striking. CU had endless lists of detail, but little evaluative information, while Neville's chart conveyed both an overall evaluative look and enough diagnostic detail to back it up.

"I'll take you through some of the highlights," Neville began. "The interfaces to the servicers are going very well. Our first few sprints were focused on getting the data loaded, and we had good success, especially with National Servicing. You can see from the diagram that the national interface is done and totally tested. Our second partner is having a few issues, and we have some lingering bugs we are driving to finish up. The loads from the MLS partners are coming along; they are the focus of our current sprint, and we expect to finish up San Diego this week and Atlanta next month. The Atlanta group hasn't been able to give us a decent test file yet; I think they are farther along than just the 25% indicated, but our testers are a skeptical lot."

"As they should be," said Greg, "especially with the listing agencies. Their data vary so much from place to place that it's always harder than you might think to get it lined up."

"We are certainly learning that," replied Neville. He continued, "Our interfaces to map, address, and public records services are coming along. The public records data have some of the same variability characteristics as the listing data, which accounts for our slow movement there. We are a little behind where we should be, but we have the feed for San Diego mostly done; that is enabling us to test the matching programs effectively. I'll know more about whether this is a serious concern by our next staff meeting."

"Can you let me know as soon as you do, Neville?" asked Greg. "You know I trust you to deal with this, but I worry nevertheless."

"Of course," Neville responded. "The final two parts of the system for the first release are the matching programs and the reporting user interface. The matching is in excellent shape, fully tested for what we know using real and mocked-up data; we just can't mark it complete until we have production-like test files from Atlanta and the public records service. The user interface development is only beginning now, so the test plan is in active development."

I studied the chart, and I just had to ask a question. "Neville, can you explain the '% doneness' levels? What does it mean to be, say, 50% done test planning? How do you know it's 50% and not, say, 55%? Why does 'doneness' go from 50 to 95 to 100%? That seems like strange increments."

"Wow, Beth, a lot of questions. Is this different from how CU reports status? Let me first answer what the percentages mean, then your very interesting question of how we know the percentages."

Neville explained, "There is actually a decoding table I can get for you that has more detail on each of the levels. For example, 50% test planning complete means that the test plan and test scripts have been written and reviewed, but haven't been approved yet; 50% tested means that testing is under way and we believe we've found and fixed 75% of the bugs we expect to find. That's a tough status to call because it's hard to know when you reach this point; it's more of a feeling at that point that we're on the home stretch than something scientific. As for the 95% done level, we've found that test planning and testing tends to get to 95% and stay there for very long periods, so we want to make that stage, as well as the progression to truly done, highly visible for our teams."

Finished with what the percentages meant, Neville turned to where they came from. "The overall accountability for the chart lies with Janani Mugombe, our test manager. Ultimately, these are his judgments. He gets his input from testers and developers. Each component has test plans and test owners. We hold these people accountable to tell us the status accurately, with Janani's supervision. I've found it's too hard to tell status from a bunch of details, such as number of bugs found, number remaining, or the like. Instead, I have people interpret that information and just cough up their opinions. If they are wrong or lying, Janani will catch that pretty quickly, or else I will eventually."

"Value individuals and interactions over process and tools, eh, Neville?" I was proud that I could quote the first of the Agile Manifesto values.

"Very good, Beth!" Neville responded. "Next thing we know you'll be inventing Agile human resource management!"

Greg resumed his interrogation. "Neville, looks like your team is cooking! What's happening in the market? Any change in expectations on how the product will be received? Any new partners?"

Neville reported that nothing significant had changed in the real estate markets other than some growing nervousness about home prices having outraced their true values and the beginnings of some downward price movements in the most inflated markets—California, Florida, and Las Vegas. As the year had progressed, additional lenders and MLS areas had been reviewing the project, and a couple more had signed on; several others were in a wait-and-see mode on the project progress and the market evolution. The development sprints were going fairly well, and each month brought added functions that our sales staff could show to potential new customers and partners. All seemed well in Neville-land.

Concerns about CU: On Track or about to Derail?

Mary went next, reporting on CU. The official project status remains positive, she reported, even though her opinion was that it was poised for a blowup. Code complete and the beginning of integration testing remained scheduled for September, just 2 months away, but there seemed like an awful lot of work left to do. Also, she reported, only 2 months had been set aside for integration and acceptance testing, and it was hard to imagine that was enough time. Her own team's work was in good shape, and they were taking on some additional integration testing that the test teams had not undertaken that she thought necessary.

No real news here, but it was interesting to hear Greg's take on the situation. Gina, his boss, was on the senior steering group for CU, and they were still being told the project was on track. The senior leadership, starting with Evan, the CEO, was becoming increasingly concerned about the pace of spending on the project. They had given the direction that time to market was more important than spending control this year; however, the rate of spending increase and the recent projection for end of year had given them pause. Most of the company's discretionary systems development expenditure was going for CU, freezing initiatives in other areas that were needed for revenue growth and cost controls; therefore, results were needed sooner rather than later. The secular decline of print revenues seemed to be accelerating. CU was the primary investment aimed at helping our company do a better job of understanding customer needs, matching them to our capabilities; helping us speed our migration into electronic products; and enabling us to manage our capacity down gracefully in line with the secular demand trends. There wasn't a good backup plan; we needed CU to succeed.

Accordingly, Cremins's senior management was standing behind the CU project and giving the PCA complete support. They'd approved the spending projection, but they also made it clear to the PCA that they expected delivery. Budgets for 2007 were being drawn up, and the lines of business were putting in benefits from the system, based on the schedules for extension into additional lines of business and added functionality. The benefits were not very specific—for example, a 1% increase in gross margin, a 2% increase in sales, or a 1.5% increase in capacity utilization. Greg didn't understand precisely where these benefits were coming from; no one seemed to, but through faith or wishful thinking, everyone was assuming that CU would deliver on its promised business benefits.

Our division was one of the few bright lights in the company. We'd already made the transition from paper dependence to electronic products; we had pioneered that movement, profitably, which was why Cremins bought us.

The projections for next year, boosted by but not entirely dependent on TRIM revenues and profits, looked good. Gina was pleased with TRIM's progress, although she was very clear that there would be no additional investment capital if we had cost overruns. TRIM, Greg said, had to be run as a fixed-cost project; any investment beyond our initial stake had to come from ongoing profits or through bringing in up-front cash payments from customers or partners. Neville said he was fine with that: We looked OK on costs, and there was plenty of interest by industry participants if we needed more investment before cash flow turned strongly positive.

Mary asked Greg if Gina and Evan had any idea how much risk was in the CU project right now and how inefficiently money was being spent. Greg said he thought Gina had some inkling, but didn't feel able to do much about it. Greg had counseled her to ask to see the code, to get a demo for the steering group. The PCA had responded with a series of screen mock-ups in a design-simulation tool, and it had been received well by the senior team. We all had a sense of quiet before the storm.

Signposts	**Cremins United project**
	• July's official status was still positive for September code complete and November go-live.
	• Cremins's senior leadership was feeling pressure on revenue and profits from printing's secular decline, and it was counting on the Cremins United project delivering value soon.
	• The CU team had recently demonstrated mock-ups of the new systems to the steering group; they had been very well received.
	TRIM project
	• Neville showed TRIM's testing status on a powerful visual chart. There were some bumps, but progress in July had continued on pace for the planned November release.

- Market conditions were looking more favorable for TRIM as house prices began to decline in some of the most inflated markets, and more industry participants were interested in signing on.
- Due to Cremins Corporation's growing travails, TRIM would not receive any more capital investment beyond what had been already committed. Neville believed he could get to cash flow positive with what he already had in pocket.

Guides from Beth

- A highly visual status report showing each major system component and its state, coded by pattern or color, can be a primary communication device. Customize it for your particular project! Be sure to include status of each interface because that's where a lot of the risk lies.
- Getting the team members to give you their summary opinions on status, rather than just a bunch of facts that you have to interpret, is a superior approach. By all means, "go see" the details as well; don't just trust—verify as well. This is all the better if you can have someone on point, like Janani is in this chapter, to consolidate and do quality assurance of the views.
- Seeing a demonstration of a mock-up is not the same as seeing the real software. Focus on the code because that's what best tells the story.

Coming up next

Wes brings us 2 months ahead—to September 2006, when the CU project is supposed to be code complete. It's not, so the Project Control Authority imposes some more controls.

Section III

Year 2:
September 2006–
February 2007

20

A Dismal Reality Check for the CU Team

SEPTEMBER 2006

Wes:

Every Tuesday, we had two morning meetings: the weekly CU senior project team meeting, followed by one of two weekly PCA meetings. Today promised to be momentous: an assessment of where the project was and, hopefully, decisions on what to do about it. Everyone involved now knew that we were in trouble; the question was how bad it was and how far it would set the project back. I'd spent some serious time over the weekend thinking about how to orchestrate this morning and, after some soul searching, had resolved to take some risks to try to highlight for everyone the true state of affairs. I'd talked over my plan with Tom, and he was supportive of it. I hoped it would give the PCA the jolt they needed to make some changes, although I wasn't sure what they should be.

The Dreaded Weekly Meeting of the Senior Project Team

The senior project team was supposed to begin at 10 a.m. central time, to allow the West Coast participants to join in at a reasonable time; in practice it never began before 10:15 or so. As participants filtered into the room, roll call was taken, and we dealt with teleconferencing issues. The meeting had grown to what seemed to me a ridiculous size. It included all the PCA members, plus the business, technical, and project leads for each development team, plus the leads for testing, deployment, training, and support, plus miscellaneous others like human resources, finance, and data. All in all, upwards of 50 people participated, probably half in St. Paul, and the rest on the phone. As the project had progressed, this meeting had continued to grow in size, even as it reduced in usefulness.

The meetings were typically run by Neil; Tom usually didn't attend, or if he did, he mostly sat silently, except to inject cheerleading-type comments periodically or reject any suggestion that we needed to reduce scope. Neil wasn't a strategist when it came to meetings of this type; he mostly saw them as a way for him to examine how the teams were doing in meeting their schedules—public examinations of whether people were working hard enough. He seemed to rejoice in finding obstacles that he could help with; to him, 'help' meant putting in more structure, resources, and reviews around specific problems, usually by starting up another SWAT team staffed by GRI consultants accountable to him. As you might expect from this description, the meetings were dreaded by most of the participants.

Neil started the meeting off by reiterating how important the project was to Cremins, how the CEO was trusting this team with the responsibility to bring it to production, and how serious failure would be for the company and this group. He seemed to have a continuing need to remind people of their duty, to try to make everyone feel the same sense of commitment and dedication he felt himself. He seemed to have no ability to read how his lectures alienated the group, or maybe he really didn't care; he may have been the least people-oriented leader I'd seen. Neil very rarely patted people on the back, and when he did, it usually sounded insincere.

The next item of Neil's agenda was to hear from our testing managers. At this stage of the project, Dave Prentiss and Angie Lockhart, the managers of integration and acceptance testing, respectively, were moving to the forefront of the project. They were now the gates between the code and production; their ability to test the software and drive bug resolution was now the critical path. The pressure on them to find ways to test incomplete software quickly was relentless, and the finger-pointing among them, the development teams, and the PCA was escalating. They had responded by trying to stick completely to the facts, encouraged by Neil and Frankie's almost reverent respect for facts. To an extent that was quite remarkable, their reports avoided any interpretation of the facts or any judgment as to the quality of the software or its readiness for production. Their job was to test and report, no more.

Dave gave his report first. He had an extensive PowerPoint deck that showed, by area, the number of scripts, the number that had been run, and the number that had passed. It was followed by the bug report, which showed the number of bugs by status, split among system areas, and a chart showing open bugs over time. It was very professional looking, and, in fact, Dave seemed quite capable in a structured sort of way.

"Integration testing was scheduled to begin 2 weeks ago, when all code was scheduled to be migrated to the testing region. Unfortunately, only 87% of the modules represented on the integrated project plan were available at that time, and as of yesterday, only 93% of the modules were checked in. Of the missing modules, half are services in the CSF, making it impossible to test much of the system connectivity. You can see that only 3% of the scripts have been run; we don't run scripts where components are missing, and none of them have passed. To date we have logged 127 incidents, of which 59 remain open. The average turn time to close an issue, of the issues closed, is 4 days, which is 2 days more than our assumption that would have permitted us to complete testing in the forecast time. The actual turn time is much longer, of course, because we have many incidents that remain open."

"Of the 127 incidents, over half were classified as data issues—missing data, mistranslated data, and various other data-related issues. Many of the rest were what I'd call one-time issues related to the migration of the software from the development to the test environment, and we expect to find many more of those. The test team is spending most of its time working with the development groups to get the system running well enough to begin testing."

Tom Stillman had come to this meeting, although he didn't often attend. He could see the jeopardy into which his project had fallen and was struggling to understand. "Dave, I take it the status you reported is not exactly what we'd planned. How do you account for what sounds like the poor shape our new system is in?"

"All I can speak to, Mr. Stillman, is what I've seen in testing. The most obvious explanation is that we waived the entrance criteria to begin integration testing. Our master test plan said that testing would not begin until 100% of the software components were complete, including unit and connectivity testing. When it became clear a few weeks ago that not every component would be done, the criteria were waived, and we were instructed to begin testing with the components we did receive. That is what we have done."

Neil then asked Angie to report on acceptance testing. She had nothing to report other than that her team was continuing to prepare. The entrance criteria for acceptance testing were that all severity 1 integration testing incidents were resolved, and there were business work-arounds for all severity 2 and 3 incidents. That now seemed some time away.

Neil then led the interrogation of each development team—Sales, Production, Services, Management Information, Data, Infrastructure, and Deployment. Sales was in excellent shape, ready to begin testing. Production had several significant components still in development, as did Services. Data was in the worst shape; several SWAT teams were under way, and a swirl was going on with regard to how the mapping was being managed. As the meeting continued, Neil got more and more frustrated, becoming visibly upset at times.

I knew the next step would have to be to come to grips with where the project really was, to acknowledge that we'd missed the September code complete date and therefore we'd missed the November release date. Tom knew that also, and he now took the reins of the meeting. That was unusual in itself and got the rapt attention of the participants.

How to Get the Project Back on Track?

"It's evident to me now," he said, "that we've missed the September code complete date, and we don't have a realistic chance of making the November release now. We all find this terribly frustrating, especially because you were all reporting that everything was 'green' right up until the middle of August. We're going to have to investigate why the status reporting was so wrong and how we can improve our planning and reporting. However, we need first to figure out what our new plan is. When can we finish our code? When can we begin integration and acceptance testing? When can we go live?"

"A friend shared a couple pearls of wisdom with me when I took this job. One of them was 'don't trade a bad date for another bad date.'[1] So, I want to get your collective opinion on where we stand and what you think might be a good date. Wes and I have talked over how to approach this, and we think we have an interesting exercise that can help. Wes, can you take it from here?"

"Sure, Tom. In the past few days, since we realized we weren't going to make our deadline, I've talked to several of you about what might be a reasonable date for us to complete the code and begin integration testing. I've received several opinions, ranging from a month to 6 months or more. I've also sensed that some of you may be reluctant to speak openly. So, we've designed this approach to structure a way to get in front of the whole team what you think, while allowing you to remain anonymous."

While I explained this, I avoided making eye contact with Neil, but could see that he was agitated.

Tom had sprung this exercise on him, and Neil understood that it showed lack of faith in him. Tom wanted to know what everyone thought—a very different approach than Neil's. Neil's approach to the project, as he had explained at last week's PCA meeting, would be to set a new date himself, force the teams to put a plan together to meet it, and then fiercely inspect the plan progress to ensure the task dates were met. Neil figured that if you made people work weekends to catch up on any missed tasks, people would work hard enough during the week to get done; if they didn't— well, weekends were essentially infinite. In Neil's view, Tom's somewhat more participative approach (well, actually mine) was wrong, but given that Tom was his boss and had introduced the exercise, there wasn't much he could do about it, but fume.

I continued, "I'm handing out slips of paper to each of you [see Figure 29]. You can see that there are two possible new code complete dates: January 15, 2007, and April 15, 2007, and two columns: your percentage estimate that your team's work will be ready to begin integration testing and your percentage estimate that the entire system will be ready to begin integration testing. By 'ready to test,' we mean code complete, unit and connectivity tested. This is entirely anonymous; don't identify either yourself or your team. Take a few minutes and think about it, and then I'll collect the ballots. Please don't talk among yourselves because we want your individual honest opinions."

"For those of you on the phone, please send an e-mail to my assistant. She will compile the information and just give me the totals; you will remain anonymous. If you are not at a computer, you can phone her." I gave out her number and e-mail address. "After you complete your ballot, you are free to take a break. We'll reassemble in 20 minutes to see what you all think."

My Estimate of Code Completion

Date	My Team	Whole Team
Jan 15	_____ %	_____ %
April 15	_____ %	_____ %

FIGURE 29
CU delivery confidence ballot.

New Time Estimates for Project Completion: 4 Months? 7 Months? More?

There was a nice buzz in the room as people muttered and chatted with each other, despite my admonishments, as heads went down and pencils came out. I watched and started to collect the results, pushing people who hadn't finished in 5 minutes to do so to enable me to compile the results. I took the collected ballots back to my cube, and my assistant and I compiled the results. Mary had copied me on her e-mail to my assistant. It was consistent with what she'd been telling me in person:

> Wes, here is my vote. See explanation re: April 15. If we don't change more than the date, our challenge next summer will be how much whoever is left can salvage and redeploy. That'll include the sales system—it's good.
>
> Jan 15. My team, 100%. Already done. Whole team, 10%.
> April 15: My team, 100%. Whole team, 50%. This means they will say they are done, not that it will actually work and meet business needs.

Reading this, I felt a bit chastised about how I'd defined "done." I could have made that clearer—after all, fuzziness around that definition was perceived to be one of the problems with our status reporting. I'd picked a goal of "ready to integration test," rather than "ready to add business value." I guess that was consistent with where we'd come from, and now with our goals; it was about going live and showing we could do that, rather than about providing any immediate business lift.

My assistant took the results and put them into a PowerPoint for me, and 30 minutes after we'd started I reassembled the meeting and presented the results.

"Let's take a quick look at what we think about getting this project done [see Figure 30]. It seems that most of you are confident that your own work can be completed by mid-January; on average, you are 90% confident, and the lowest team is over 50% confident. However, you aren't as confident that your teammates will be ready. On average, you are 60% confident the overall system will be done, and some believe the chance of being complete is as low as 10%."

"If we look 3 more months out, to April, you believe it's almost certain that you will be done with your own work and quite confident that the entire team will be complete as well."

"Any comments?"

Joe Karras, the tech lead for Production Management, was the first to speak. "Looks like January might be a good target, as long as we manage very tightly and keep our team committed."

Amit Banerjee, the tech lead for the Management Information team, spoke up from across the room. "I'm not so sure about that, Joe. Remember that most of the teams were 'green' until just a month ago; best case is that in 1 month our overall team lost at least 3 months. We seem to seriously underestimate our work. If we set the date to January and miss again, we'll have created waste in all the groups working to support the rollout, plus the teams that will be done and waiting for the other groups to finish. It might be better to bite the bullet now and move it to April."

Date	My Team	Whole Team
January 15	Average: 90% Minimum: 60% Maximum: 100%	Average: 60% Minimum: 10% Maximum: 95%
April 15	Average: 95% Minimum: 85% Maximum: 100%	Average: 80% Minimum: 50% Maximum: 100%

FIGURE 30
CU delivery confidence.

Trevor, the GRI project leader, supported Joe. "I think we can do it in January," he said, "if we tighten up the plan and manage to it. We can redeploy resources to any tasks falling behind, if we know exactly where we are at all times."

Neil responded to Trevor, reinforcing his last thought. "We have to find a way to make this project more controlled and predictable. We can't go another quarter or more and not do what we say we are going to do. Trevor is absolutely right; we need to batten the hatches, ensure we are working on solely the things we need to be working on, have a tight plan, and work it rigorously. We need to make this predictable."

I saw Amit, sitting right across from me, rolling his eyes and whispering to the person next to him. My guess was he was saying that we were already quite predictable—predictably failing.

At this point Tom stepped back in, thanked the group for their input, and said that the PCA would consider the situation in its upcoming meeting and communicate its decisions on where we go next as soon as they were available. The large team meeting broke up, and the PCA members wandered out for a 15-minute break before their meeting began.

The PCA Meeting: How Did We Get So Far behind Schedule?

Tom opened the PCA meeting by simply asking the others what they were thinking and feeling. The frustration was palpable, and Neil immediately gave it vent. "How," he began, "could we have gotten to this point and only now be hearing that we have risk of even making an April date? Trevor, you've been leading the project tracking and status reporting; why didn't we see this earlier? Frankie, your people are doing the development; didn't they tell you we were in trouble?"

"I'm afraid," replied Frankie, "that our insistence that we would be ready now was taken as a firm deadline, and there was a lot of wishful thinking going on. As the developers got to the tasks they had slated for July and August, they found that some of the requirements were not clear, and then they found some of the designs to be confusing and incomplete. They also found that some entire pieces needed to connect up the systems had simply been missed and that some of the estimates to complete important components were underestimated. We also found that some of the technical infrastructure wasn't ready on time, and we had problems with build processes. We've learned a lot now, which positions us better going forward."

"I hope we get a chance to use that learning," said Tom. "I need to get with Evan and give him a coherent story about this. We are spending a lot of money, and his confidence in us will be in doubt. The company isn't doing well and this project is consuming most of our discretionary resources. My guess is he'll support us in one delay, but if we don't deliver on our next commitment we're all going to be in real trouble."

Tom looked at his team and said, "We need to answer two questions: When can we now deliver what we've promised, and what are we going to do to ensure our success?"

Frankie responded first. "We need to balance scope, time, and resources. Tom, which do you think are the most important elements to Evan? Could we cut some scope, maybe try just to support one of the lines of business to start? Maybe we could drop the capacity management functions until a later release? I think scope reduction would give us the best chance to deliver something; the complexity we've undertaken is challenging our teams."

"We can't cut scope back any more, Frankie," said Neil. "The cost/benefit analysis is based on benefits in revenue generation and cost reductions, and now that we are adding costs and delaying benefits, the project won't work financially if we can't deliver the benefits. I'm afraid that if we don't get this thing up and running soon, Evan and his team will lose confidence and could kill the whole thing. We need to deliver the scope we promised, as soon as possible, even if it costs us somewhat more over the next few months."

Tom nodded his head and said he agreed with Neil. Getting the promised scope done quickly was the priority, even if it cost a bit more over the short term. Given these goals, he asked what date should now be set and how we could be sure to hit that date.

Neil had his answer: We had to go for January. Most of the teams felt confident they could deliver, according to our balloting, even if they felt less confident in their peers. "We just need to be sure that all the teams have plans to which they commit and then hold them to those plans. Our problem was that teams reported that they were done with tasks, such as the requirements that Frankie reported as requiring rework, when they weren't really done. If we can better define 'done,' be sure we have all the tasks clearly identified, and enforce overtime when tasks are missed, we can hit January."

Trevor spoke up now. "We have been somewhat lax in our commitment to The Process," he said. "Teams have been modifying the standard formats, skipping some of the defined sign-off processes, failing to log all issues, not following up on due dates, and inaccurately reporting on task and project status. We need to tighten up on this, be sure we get things right the first time, and know precisely where we are as we move toward January."

Mary and I had, of course, talked about the likely response of the PCA to the date slippage. Her view was that the slip was due to many factors, including a bad date (too soon); too much scope; weak leadership; lack of expertise; architectural issues; team issues, such as the separation of testing from development; and process issues, such as the formality of requirements and designs and the serial handoffs. She saw no simple way to change the project to deliver more effectively; if it was up to her, most of the leadership would be replaced and the whole nature of the project changed. I saw her points, but knew there was no way that would happen. Instead, I expected what I was seeing now: Rather than any realization of what had put us into this situation, the PCA was going to fall back even more strongly on what it believed—that strict process control and enforcement were the answer, rather than part of the problem. In Trevor, they had just the means to do that.

Tom wasn't naturally as drawn to rules and planning as were Neil, Trevor, and Frankie, but he was searching for a way forward and had now been offered one that seemed to offer some potential for success. He wasn't one to dally in decision making. I could almost see the wheels turning in his head and his resolve firming around this revised approach.

We spent the rest of the hour putting together the plan forward, guided by Trevor and Neil. The key elements included:

- Stronger control over scope needed to be established. While the broad strokes had not changed, Neil, Frankie, and Trevor felt that as the development progressed, teams continually found what they thought were functional gaps and filled them, which caused delays. From here on, staff would be instructed to work only on approved items. A process would be established to link all project plan tasks to business needs, and a committee led by Jamie Kawalski, business liaison, would deal with all new requests.
- Teams that were complete, or nearly complete, with the approved scope would have their budgets cut to just what was needed for inte-

gration testing, bug repairs, and any new long-lead-time items for the following release.

- A tight focus on the January release would be maintained, which meant that follow-on releases would be slower. We wouldn't publicize this fact, but had little choice, given our need to contain spending.

- The existing project plan would be closely audited to ensure it was limited to existing approved scope and contained all the necessary steps in The Process to ensure success. Trevor would bring in a dozen or so additional project management consultants from GRI—funded by cuts in the teams that were near completion and reduction in effort on future releases—to do the audits and maintain control of the plans.

- Each type of task on the plan would have a clear definition of "done" to prevent the rampant misreporting of status that had plagued the project so far. Each task, or group of tasks, would have a document called the "exit criteria confirmation" required on its scheduled due date, with a checklist showing that it had met the definition of "done." If not done, a plan to complete was required, including an explanation of how completing it late would not affect other scheduled tasks.

- As a backup plan, we agreed that any task that could not be completed as planned would go through a "necessity review," in which a SWAT team would determine if there would be a work-around to not having that task complete. If there was no work-around, they would look at other tasks on that team's plan to find a substitute that could be worked around.

- Eliminate the "swirl" and "noise" over decision making. There was a tendency to make and unmake decisions, continually revisiting choices. Roles would be more rigidly enforced: The business would be accountable for deciding what was needed, and the Technology group would be accountable for deciding how to deliver that.

- Overtime, whether longer days or working weekends, would be required from now through the week of Thanksgiving. Everyone would be expected to work at least 8 hours overtime per week. We would do a checkpoint in mid-November, and if we were back on track, this requirement would be relaxed.

By the end of the meeting we had agreement on the plan, and we felt good about our chances of success. I've always believed there is more than one way to skin a cat, so to speak, and I thought this approach might well work, even if Mary would give it little to no possibility of success. Mary's approach required talented, committed team members, a coherent and aligned management team, and a culture that supported the Lean/Agile approach. Perhaps that type of project would be more efficient and effective than what we were trying to do, but that didn't mean that we couldn't succeed with an alternative approach. I was starting to think of the comparison between our current approach and Mary's Lean/Agile approach as akin to the Soviet Union's command/control 5-year plans versus the freedom and chaos of capitalist development. Over time, the Soviet Union's approach was doomed, but it was able to put a man into orbit, develop nuclear submarines and missiles, and dominate Eastern Europe for a generation. Surely we could get this project done.

A New Commitment to Meet the New Target Date

It was a crazy couple of days after the PCA meeting. We had to get in front of Evan and convince him we knew what we were doing and could deliver, revise our contract with GRI, put together new procedures and decision-control forums, realign budgets and forecasts, and communicate all of this to our teams and get them on the path. Tom was a great help in this; he was seen by most as a straight shooter—focused on getting results and practical. He held an impromptu "all hands meeting" for all the CU participants, and in his usual dramatic way painted a picture for the team that was both dire and hopeful. I could see the skills that had brought him to this point in his career: real salesmanship, ability to read his audience, and a drive to succeed. Tom admitted that rules and controls weren't his thing, but, given how we'd blown our commitments so far and the need to deliver benefits quickly while limiting our costs, we had no choice now but to be very sure we did just the things we needed to do in the right way.

The reaction of CU team members was, predictably, quite varied. There was a sense of relief that the project would continue and that no significant people or organizational changes were made in response to the date miss. Some welcomed the more stringent scope control, especially the more "traditional" IT managers like Joe Karras. Other, more entrepreneurial managers like Mary and Amit chafed under the new enforcement procedures, bemoaning the added layers of project managers and waste. Tom's explanation of the need to work overtime was probably the most talked about issue, with many embracing it (many were already working that much) and some simply vowing to ignore it. (I knew that included Mary because she would not abandon her kids in that way.) There was a storm of e-mails mocking Tom's concession that working overtime wouldn't be enforced the week of Thanksgiving, pending the progress checkpoint.

In any case, the die was cast for the next several months. All was now focused on getting something "done" by January 15 and getting into integration testing. The project was back to green because we had a new approved plan. Mary thought we'd be green right up until February 1, when testing had progressed enough to show how bad the software and solution were. I desperately hoped she was wrong.

Signposts	Cremins United project
	• It was September—code complete date. Code was not complete.
	• The PCA polled the team on expected delivery date. The anonymous feedback indicated January was possible, but April likely.
	• The PCA responded by setting a new code complete/integration testing entry date of January 15.
	• To ensure success, the PCA doubled down on control measures: more consultant project managers, more detailed task tracking, enforced overtime, and more.
Guides from Wes	• When problems are hidden and suppressed intensively, their emergence can be overwhelming. It's better to ensure that they emerge one by one in flow.
	• There is more than one way to do a project. Certainly, even the most poorly run project can succeed, whether through exceptionally talented and committed individuals or the brute force of money and time. Doing things badly does not always equate to failure. But why not give yourself every chance to succeed?

- The analogy between Cremins United and the Soviet Union's 5-year planning is an apt one. Neither unleashed the full creativity of its subject, neither was efficient, and neither was much fun.

Coming up next

Would Cremins United succeed, as the Soviets did in getting to the moon, despite the manifest weaknesses of its methods? We'll find out, but first Beth brings us back to TRIM at year end 2006 as it deals with problems and changes after it successfully launches.

NOTES

1. From Jim McCarthy, *Dynamics of Software Development,* Pap/Cdr ed., Redmond, WA: Microsoft Press, August 9, 2006. This is one of the finest, most accessible books of simple, straightforward software development principles.

21

The TRIM System Goes Live: Managing Problems and Growth

DECEMBER 2006

Beth:

Neville had left me a standing invitation to attend his monthly TRIM project leadership review meetings. Unfortunately, I hadn't been able to fit one into my schedule for several months, until this cool mid-December California day. I had become somewhat out of touch with the TRIM project, hearing only that it was going well via Greg's staff meetings and some work I was doing with Neville and his team.

The TRIM project had established a headquarters room, which Neville called simply the TRIM team room. Others called it his war room, or command center, but neither analogy sat well with Mr. Roberts—a gentle soul and a stickler for language that built culture. At Toyota and other manufacturers who were adopting Lean product development, Neville had seen team rooms called *obeya* rooms after the Japanese term for "big room."[1] As usual, he had adopted and adapted the idea, and during the TRIM project, he had adapted it once again.

Neville's challenge with TRIM was how to deploy the team room, which is dependent on physical proximity (it works best when participants are co-located), when several of his key leaders worked in different cities and states, and many worked for other companies. He had struggled to get the right balance between scrum-of-scrum daily leadership meetings of the

15-minute variety, with longer, more in-depth decision-making meetings of a more senior level of leadership. He also needed to balance the use of the team room and its in-depth discussions with the formal end-of-sprint demonstrations happening every month for every team.

Neville had settled upon a management meeting regime about 6 months ago, and it had been fairly stable since then:

- daily scrum meetings for each team;
- monthly sprint planning meetings for each team;
- other meetings for each team as it saw fit, with bias not to meet too much;
- monthly demos for each team, usually done in San Diego, all at same time over 1 day, if possible—typically open to all comers on the project;
- daily scrum-of-scrum meetings, scrum-masters only, led by Alex (although observers were allowed);
- an in-depth, in-person management meeting done in the team room twice a month: once the day after the demos and once offset by 2 weeks. The offset meeting was typically shorter and accessible via phone and video conference for those who could not travel; the demo-aligned meeting was in-person only. Typically, the scrum-masters or team leads (e.g., Brian came for Info Management instead of Qin; it depended on how the roles evolved), lead developers, lead testers, plus functional leads such as Marketing/Sales, Finance, and Legal were included. No observers or other outsiders were at this meeting or the one described next; and
- a steering committee meeting every 6 weeks, aimed at the most senior people in each of the partner organizations, plus Neville and Alex representing the larger team.

The TRIM team room was used not only for Neville's every-2-week reviews, but also by a couple of the teams for their scrums, for the daily scrum-of-scrum meetings, and for ad-hoc and informal get-togethers. It could only be scheduled for the scrums and reviews; other than that, it was open for team use.

Upon walking into the team room, I was first struck by what seemed like clutter. There were several movable walls—really just tall cubicle walls—that were mostly covered with charts, graphs, and reports of various sorts.

The walls themselves were similarly covered, and there were a couple of movable white boards. There were several plain folding tables set up end to end and a mishmash of chairs seemingly rounded up randomly from all over the company. Laid out around the tables were microphones for the speaker phone, plus a few portable microphones; a video conferencing camera was mounted on a rolling tripod—no doubt for the off-cycle Neville reviews. A coffee machine, a refrigerator full of soda, and, today, a large plate of bagels completed the scene.

This meeting was the on-cycle session; the demos had all been held yesterday, and a new round of sprints was just about to begin. The demos had been tightly focused on the results of the latest sprint; there had been little talk of how the overall project was going or what was ahead much beyond the next sprint. These were topics for today.

Reviewing the First Two Live Launches

As I entered the room, Neville was standing against the far wall, chatting with Alex, the lead project manager for TRIM, and getting ready to begin the meeting. I recognized most of the attendees: Qin and Brian from the Info Management team; Janani, the test lead; June, Alex's assistant; Sybil Gutierrez, from the local MLS and lead of the Property team; Jack Spence, lead of the Buyer team; Jeff Zambrow and Martin Fowler from our two lead lending partners; Walt, our CFO and lead for Finance for TRIM; Nancy Mills, our national sales manager for TRIM, redeployed from our MLS sales team; and Kamau, our lead developer for matching data records. There were also two people I didn't recognize, but I later met them: Nanette was our legal/compliance lead from an outside firm and Quincy was the new lead from the Watcher team, from the Federal Mortgage Finance Agency.

Neville called the meeting to order, and everyone settled in around the tables in the center of the room. "Don't get too comfortable," Neville warned. "We're going to take just a few minutes here, and then we'll start our rounds. Good day yesterday, looks like the last month was very productive, and we are in good shape for release coming up in February. Today, I'd like first to review production status; we've been live in San Diego and Atlanta for a month now, with our first two lenders. Let's talk over how things are running and any issues we have in production. Then we'll get an update on the sales and financial results and outlook, and we'll end with our usual cruise through the team boards. Brian, can you start us off?"

"Love to, Neville. Could I ask you all to get up and come over to the Info Management board so that we can see how things are going?" Brian pointed to his area of the wall, where he had his team's burn-down charts, statistics and graphs on production, and several large issue and problem sheets. Each team had a section of the wall or one of the movable partitions to use to show its status, plans, issues and problems. Some of the attendees rolled chairs over to Brian's area, some sauntered over and stood; all gathered within easy sight distance.

"Production is going very well, with just a few problems." Pointing to a chart not reproduced here, Brian went on, "Simultaneous usage has grown from just a few a month ago to about 30 maximum today. The other lines on the chart show various measures of performance, such as response times and memory usage—no real problems to report yet. The chart next to it [also not reproduced here] shows batch load performance, and here is where we are developing an issue. You can see how the load completion time for daily updates is creeping up. Whereas we finished loading by 2 a.m. Pacific time the first week, as our database grew we kept slipping until now we are at about 4 a.m. Pacific time—almost cutting into the beginning of the workday on the East Coast. This is our major concern now."

Neville asked, "Do you have a plan to address this yet?"

"We are getting close," said Brian. "Right below the chart is the A3 [see Figure 31][2] about the problem, and I have handouts for all of you. I'd like to spend a few minutes on this because you should all be aware of this, and maybe some of you will have some ideas to help. I've already talked to many of you about this, but for some of you this is probably new."[3]

"I've covered the problem and goal statements. The causes are also well known: We do this in batch once we've received all the files, so we can't start until the last file is in. Also, unencryption is slow, and the matching software can use some tuning. Er, sorry Kamau."

"No offense, man," Kamau responded. "It'll get better."

Brian winked at Kamau and moved on. "We have a temporary solution. We will take the unencryption out of the batch process and unencrypt upon receipt on a separate, very fast server. The longer term solution is to move to what Kamau is calling 'flow-match'—dealing with each record on its own as it comes in. This is going to take some time. Kamau thinks he'll have version 1 up in February, at which time we'll test it and see if we replace the current batch processing. We believe we should be able to meet our deadlines indefinitely, but will keep this group informed of our

<table>
<tr><td colspan="2" align="center">Improving TRIM Batch Load Performance</td></tr>
</table>

Problem Situation	Counter Measures

Problem Situation

- Batch should complete by 3 a.m. Pacific
- We are now at 4 a.m. and expect more volume soon
- This is critical to our users; they need data at beginning of day

Counter Measures

- Temporary: move unencryption to faster server(s)
- Long-term: Flow-match, not batch-match; tune SQL and matching algorithms

Goal

Complete by beginning of workday, for continental US, for any volume

Cause Analysis

- Cannot begin matching until 1 a.m. Pacific due to batch schedules of partners
- Unencrypting data consumes ½ of batch cycle now
- Matching software is early-stage, needs tuning

Implementation

What	Who	When
Fix unencryption	Juko	January 2
Tune SQL	Brian B	Dec 27
Design Flowmatch	Juko	January 15
Validate	S o S	By end of January
R1 of Flowmatch	Juko	Feb 15
Improvements	Juko	Ongoing

Follow-up

Every two weeks in leadership meeting

Author: Juko Wambukawo, Dec. 10, 2006

FIGURE 31
TRIM batch load performance A3.

progress. We are going to need more servers, but that was expected in the financial plan as we grew."

Brian, Kamau, and the others proceeded to talk through the problem and potential solutions; I heard some discussion about getting partners to get their data to us more quickly, whether flow-match would really be possible, whether it would give the same business results, how much tuning could help, and more. After a few minutes of discussion, the plan was agreed to, with a slight modification, and Brian was done. The entire meeting moved across the room to the Marketing/Sales board, which had recently been joined in a small corner by Finance.

Another Problem, Another "A3"

Nancy Mills, the sales lead, was new to this kind of visual management, so her charts and graphs were few and simple. Her biggest chart showed the number of markets signed up, the number of lenders signed up, and projections for these and other users. Her report on the market was encouraging for the TRIM project, but sobering for the economy and homeowners. Delinquencies were escalating faster than expected, and some lenders who specialized in nonprime loans were showing signs of stress; a couple had actually failed. She had recently added two more sales people to her team to deal with growing interest, and prices had been raised from our initial entry levels. Walt pitched in with a financial report, showing us ahead on revenue and profits, even though we had picked up spending beyond initial projections due to market conditions demanding that we get more coverage more quickly than planned.

Nancy, like Brian, had major issues she wanted to bring up. She had one "problem" A3 about the demo system. She had also partnered with the Lender team, Jeff and Martin, on a proposal to change priorities in the upcoming two sprints and wanted to understand the process by which customer or sales requests were taken, prioritized, and executed. Neville asked to take the latter issue offline; he'd asked Alex to get a plan together to make the transition from a pure development project to an ongoing system/product maintenance and enhancement process, and Alex had scheduled a half-day session later in the month to align the team around the necessary changes, mostly drawing on existing processes in other parts of the Real Estate Division. Alex was also planning on doing some value stream mapping of the function/feature request process, from the request all the way through prioritization, planning, development, and release.[4] Nancy was fine with that; in fact, that's what she wanted because she was used to those processes, which worked well enough.

Nancy presented the demo system issue, which in format looked much like the batch processing problem A3 Kamau had presented. The problem was that the sales staff was selling furiously to a wide variety of potential users, but the demo system was primitive: It didn't have future functionality, it wasn't stable or fast enough, and we couldn't give out passwords and let prospects play with it. Neville pressed on how much that was actually hurting sales and, given our limited capability to deliver new markets, lenders, and functions, whether that mattered or not. After a heated 5-minute debate, the team agreed that this appeared to be important enough to consider in our next sprint planning. We debated who should take ownership of the demo system. Part of our discussion was around why we had these issues, and at the bottom of our informal "5 Why's" review was the fact that no one owned the demo system, so it didn't get the focus it now seemed to deserve. Neville said he wanted to think through how we should handle this because it didn't have a logical home, so we moved on.

Understanding the Problem by Using the "5 Why's" Approach

I need to take a short detour to explain the "5 Why's."[5] This is an important concept in Toyota's product development process. It works very simply: Once a problem is identified, you ask "why?" five times to get to the root source of the problem. There is nothing magic about five times versus four or six, and there is no "right" way to do it. Rather, the technique simply reinforces a quest to find, understand, and fix problems, at their systemic root cause instead of just dealing with symptoms. Typically, the answer to each "why" reveals a larger and more systemic problem that the team dealing with the problem often has little leverage to fix. It takes experience and leadership to know when to use this technique, how far to go, and what to do with the results.

In the discussion of the demo system, the inquiry to root cause was done, but it was a messier discussion than straightforwardly asking "why" five times. I'm repeating the discussion in Figure 32 in an idealized format; the team that had the discussion would recognize the content and wish they had been so organized.

You can see how the deeper dive into the problem resulted in a richer understanding of the issues and a solution that wasn't aimed directly at the problem (e.g., we could have said OK, we'll move the demo system to larger hardware and add some functionality) but rather was aimed at underlying issues, the solution to which would result in solving a larger set of issues (in this case, integration with Sales and some roles/ responsibility issues with development). By way of contrast, this type of discussion was almost never heard in the Cremins United project; it would be interesting to do the "5 Whys" on that, but it's off topic for this chapter!

Responding to User Requests for Changes

Finished with Sales, Marketing, and Finance, Neville led the team to the next station, Lenders. Martin, the group lead from one of our lead lender partners, summarized the schedule, plans, and a few problems and issues. Then he got to the meat of his update:

What is the problem?	The demo system lacks functionality, is slow, and unstable
Why ?	It's on minimal hardware and is just a copy of the most recent (mostly) tested release
Why is it on minimal hardware and not a special system?	We took the shortest possible path to get a demo system completed
Why didn't we devote more resources to it?	Devoting more resources to the demo system would pull from our development efforts, which was more important at the time; this now seems to be changing, as we now seem to need demo system to make needed sales
Why didn't we notice the changing need and deal with it effectively?	Sales and Marketing's voice in project priorities has been too low, and none of our project leadership has been focused on meeting their needs. Neville cares, but he's pulled in too many directions.
Result:	We need to continue to better integrate Nancy Mills, our sales lead, into priority discussions, and we need to have one of our senior development leaders be accountable to ensuring our demo system meets our sales needs.

FIGURE 32
TRIM demo system: "5 Whys."

"I've been asked by my management to request a change in project priority; we would prefer that our next major functional priority be the creation of public access to the data. We are beginning to get a lot of heat from some communities about foreclosed homes clustered in certain neighborhoods or even blocks, as well as complaints about foreclosed or abandoned homes that are not being properly maintained. There isn't a good source of information today that reveals the servicer for a particular property; the public records just show who formally holds the liens, but it's often not the current servicer. Sometimes the servicing rights to the loan have been transferred without recording, and often the lien is held by a trustee for the bondholders or an industry consortium to enable lower cost book transfer of the liens. We'd like to remedy this as quickly as we can."

Neville suggested that Martin hand out his proposal A3, which he proceeded to do (Figure 33). Martin explained, "Nancy was nice enough to prepare the document for Jeff and me. We think this is a compelling business case; the servicers need this and are willing to do some funding, and it creates more compelling reasons for additional geographies and services to sign on, which is good for Cremins. You can see our proposal—that Cremins creates a public access site funded by subscribers to the extent we can do that, with any shortcoming made up by participating servicers if

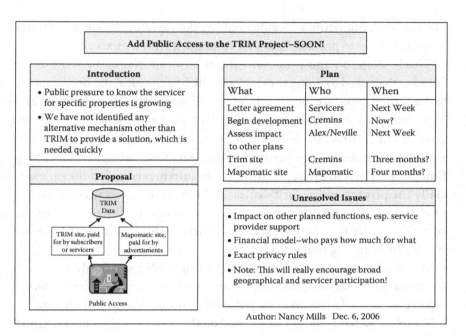

FIGURE 33
Add public access to TRIM A3.

we have to. Also, Mapomatic would like to do a for-profit site funded by advertisements, and we would like to do both approaches. See, Neville, we are learning about concurrent engineering!"

Martin continued to explain: "The plan we show is mostly wishful thinking; we need help to figure this out. We would like to start soon, and at least a couple of us servicers are willing to pony up now to get going. We're putting a letter agreement together to get things formally moving forward. You can see the unresolved issues regarding what putting this feature ahead of others might mean, as well as the details of financial and privacy arrangements."

As Martin wrapped up his pitch, he turned to Neville for a response to the proposal. It was remarkable how in many situations Neville took a back seat to other team members, giving them opportunities to lead and shine, while still clearly being the one everyone looked to when we had this type of priority or approach conflict. It wasn't just his positional power, although that was not insignificant; he was trusted to be able to make a call on how to proceed, integrating all the various factors pulling on a situation like this one. Sometimes Neville could make rapid decisions; sometimes he needed time to ponder. Today he responded with a mixture.

"Nicely done on the proposal—smart to draft Nancy to write it up because she's used to doing these. I basically like the idea; the need appears to be strong, you are putting money and commitment behind it, and Mapomatic's desire to do a for-profit site is a good endorsement as well. My guess is the technology development is small—a simple Web site, which would use dumbed-down versions of the search, reporting, and mapping functions we already have. Getting the requirements nailed down, especially the privacy and security rules, and the financial arrangements will likely take the longest time. I am not fully current on the urgency of the service provider functionality. Is anyone here familiar with that? What do we lose by bumping that out a bit?"

Martin responded: "I don't think we'll lose a whole lot, if the delay is just a few months. The service providers are very fragmented, and we are still working to get a critical mass lined up. Jeff, Nancy, would you agree with that?"

"Absolutely," said Jeff. "As we worked on the A3 I did some checking, and that's my conclusion as well. We would like to do a more formal check-in to be sure and give them a chance to speak for themselves. We didn't want to do that before we ran it up the flagpole here."

Neville now had enough information to make his decision. "OK, this is approved. Alex, can you communicate this tomorrow in the scrum of scrums, and ask the teams to include this in the planning for their next sprints? Let's try to get it done in two sprints—would be about 3 months from now—I don't want to interrupt the sprint just starting, other than to do enough work to plan the next two sprints. We'll need to do the user stories and the estimates. Alex, do you know if there is enough service provider work for us to bump out to squeeze in the beginnings of public access?"

"I think so," said Alex, "but let me check. I'll e-mail this group tomorrow."

Identifying "Reflection Topics": Looking Back on How the System Was Developed

Now done with the Lender team, Neville moved on to the Administration team, dragging the group along behind him. The meeting continued for 2 more hours this way: getting status, dealing with issues, setting next steps, exploring problems and solutions. I won't relate much more of it because it's mostly details that don't illustrate much about how the project was being run. I will, however, relate how the meeting ended: the reflection period.

Neville had reserved the final hour of the meeting to kick off a reflection event that was going to culminate 3 weeks from now in a daylong session. Today he wanted to get the big issues out on the table, to lay out the agenda for the session to come, and to ensure proper preparation.

Neville and his team were known for the tightly organized, participative meetings they held. Neville had explained the importance of these meetings to me and how the meetings themselves demonstrated and implemented some of the leadership principles he sought to teach his group. These principles were simple and included ensuring that all the members of the team felt they had contributed to and owned solutions and directions; that problem solving was at all times rigorous, that sloppy thinking did not seep into our work through lack of willingness to confront each other, that people didn't "go along to get along"; and that, at all times, management demonstrated respect for the ideas and time of its people by ensuring that meetings were efficient.

Today Neville was facilitating a brief session with a goal of identifying reflection topics. He had chosen to use the nominal group technique,[6] which sounds more formal and complex than it is. He believed that in many instances a well-planned and facilitated session would produce far better results than the usual meeting (i.e., asking the group for what topics they wanted to discuss). No argument from me there!

Neville had the 15 people in the room sit at three tables in groups of five. He opened up his "tackle box" full of meeting props and handed out 5 × 7 cards and fine-tipped markers. He taped up a large sign that said "Topics for Reflection" to be sure that what we were seeking was clear.

"In the next hour," he started, "our mission is to come up with the topics we want to cover at our reflection meeting in 3 weeks. I'm primarily going to facilitate this meeting, although I will probably add a few items if you don't."

"Here's the plan. We're going to start by taking 10 minutes in silence, working alone, thinking about what things each of us thinks that he or she needs to improve. Each of you will fill out cards, one per item, like this."

With that, Neville fetched a blown-up card, filled in for us (Figure 34). He later told me he called this a "tool advertisement," which he usually included in all of the sessions that he facilitated. It's critical, he said, that the participants in a meeting understand what is happening, what's going to happen, and how best to participate effectively.

Reflection Topic: <u>End of Sprint Demo</u>
<u>Scheduling</u>

Rationale: <u>Doing all the demos in one day</u>
<u>is too hard to absorb; spreading over two</u>
<u>or three days might be more effective</u>

Suggestion for Discussion Approach:
<u>Group pro/con listing and consensus on</u>
<u>go-forward approach</u>

FIGURE 34
Reflection sample card.

"Simply fill in as many as you need to; if you don't have a good idea for how to approach, leave it blank, and you can complete that section as a group. Once you finish your cards individually, we will reconvene at our tables. You will appoint a team spokesperson, and that person will facilitate your table and report out. You will share your cards with each other, consolidate to eliminate duplicates and, if you can, improve the clarity of the topics, their rationales, and the suggestions for how to approach. When the tables are done, we will convene as a large group and do the same. Any questions?"

Sybil, our active participant from the local MLS, asked about boundaries. "How open shall we be? Anything off limits?" she asked.

"Just use your good judgment," said Neville. "For example, I'd rather not see a card suggesting that I need to bathe more often or that Brian needs to get some more help because he doesn't know what he's doing. We deal with those types of issues, which can hurt feelings and are more personal, in more private settings. But other than that, I want you to identify the most important things we need to deal with to be successful. I'll ultimately be accountable for sorting this out, but you've already seen, I hope, that I use my ultimate accountability power sparingly. This is a team, and we need to reflect on what has worked and hasn't and what we need to change going forward, openly and honestly, but respectfully of each other."

We took 15 minutes, mostly silent, writing up our cards. I hadn't been very involved in the project and had tried to beg off, but Neville thought as long as I was here I might as well contribute. In fact, I had a few ideas. When time was up, Neville handed out instruction sheets to each table lead. We elected Alex to manage our table. He read the instructions and explained that we should each read a card, eliminate duplicates we held, and edit the card to reflect our whole table's concerns. Then we would put our consolidated cards on the wall and consolidate with the other teams. Alex asked Sybil to begin.

Sybil began with her first card. "My topic is our team structure. I think it worked well while we were figuring out our requirements and doing our primary development and testing, but now that we are in production I suggest we should re-examine it. Maybe something more like a product/requirements team, a development team, a reporting team, and an administration team?"

Alex chipped in, "I had a similar item. What is your suggestion for how we deal with it?"

"I was thinking we might want first to identify what is working with the structure and what is not, and then put up some alternative structures. I've become convinced the backlog management, sprints, and scrums are the right ways for us to work, so I'd rather not put that on the table. Just the composition and mission of each of our teams and how they interrelate," Sybil finished.

By the end of the hour, we had first expanded the topics of concern and then consolidated and narrowed them to six: our team structure, our meeting schedules, our process for going from request to acceptance into specific sprints, our cost management and budgeting, the formality and consistency of our requirements documents (whether user stories plus whatever the teams chose was still acceptable), and user support management. Neville solicited volunteers to lead the discussion of each area, and he promised to set up time with each volunteer to talk through the approach. Neville thanked the group for their openness and willingness to get problems on the table, and with that, the biweekly on-cycle meeting of the senior leadership of the TRIM project concluded.

Signposts

TRIM project

- By year end 2006, TRIM was successfully live in production.
- Being live revealed several problems and opportunities. They were formalized using a one-page problem-solving format called an "A3" and further analyzed using the "5 Why's."
- The TRIM team conducted its monthly management review in its dedicated team room, rich in visual displays and set up to support rigorous collaboration.
- TRIM team members requested a change in priority due to recent changes in the marketplace; the request was welcomed, analyzed, and accepted, bumping less critical elements out a sprint or two.
- The TRIM team held a reflection event and established workgroups to improve team structure, meeting regimen, process from request to commitment to specific sprint, cost management, format and consistency of requirements documents, and user support management. Even though success appeared to be assured, continuous improvement remained the highest focus.

Guides from Beth

- The "big room" has proven to be an effective technique at Toyota and others practicing LPD.
- Problem solving is not an inherent skill. Establishing a common language and mechanism, such as the Toyota-derived "A3," can improve your company's ability to identify and resolve problems, address opportunities, and align around strategies.
- Remember that it's not the format of the problem-solving document that matters; rather, it's the rigor and collaboration around its creation and discussion that matter.

- Welcome change into your projects. To enable this, you have to establish a shorter time sequence from expression of need to delivery than most projects can handle today.
- Build reflection into each major milestone of your system development projects. Use techniques such as nominal group, shown in this chapter, to help team members participate effectively. Facilitative leadership matters and it also is not an inherent skill; teach it!

Coming up next

We move to February 2007 and hear from Wes that the Cremins United project is now back in green status; the higher degree of control and focus seems to have worked and entrance criteria to integration testing been met. What will testing show, as CU moves toward its committed go-live date in March?

NOTES

1. James M. Morgan and Jeffrey K. Liker, *The Toyota Product Development System,* p. 152, New York: Productivity Press, 2006.
2. See, for example, p. 269 and following pages in Morgan and Liker, 2006.
3. In Toyota's implementation of Lean product development, A3 reports are rarely sprung completed onto a team. Instead, they are developed incrementally, with the owner consulting with peers and partners in its development, ensuring they have consensus on the definition of the problem, and building agreement on solutions. The A3, then, can be less about a format to document problems, but rather about the standard information format for discussion and consensus building. In Japanese, the consensus-building process that surrounds A3s is called *nemawashi* (Morgan and Liker, 2006, p. 264).
4. There are several good references for value stream mapping, although as far as I know, all are concerned with manufacturing processes rather than product development processes. The pioneer and still the classic is Mike Rother and John Shook, *Learning to See: Value Stream Mapping to Add Value and Eliminate MUDA,* Cambridge, MA: Lean Enterprise Institute, 1999. Doing value stream maps for product development requires some modifications, most notably adding a time line on the top because time frames tend to be more elongated compared to manufacturing flows.
5. See, for example, Jeffrey Liker, *The Toyota Way,* p. 252, New York: McGraw–Hill, 2003.
6. NGT is a common technique in quality approaches; it is documented on the Web site http://syque.com/quality_tools/toolbook/NGT/ngt.htm

22

The CU Project Is Finally Officially Code Complete

Wes:

It had been an unusually stressful holiday season for me at work, compensated partially by my growing relationship with Mary O'Connell. The CU project changed to a new phase, probably best characterized by a single word: *control.* My idea was to have more control and less risk at work and less control and more risk in my personal life. I spent Christmas away from my parents for only the second time in my life, joining Mary's family in an initially awkward but ultimately promising adventure. Now, in the depths of the misery of the St. Paul winter, I wasn't sure where either my work or my personal life was going; although one seemed promising, the other seemed ominous.

A New Set of Controls to Get the Project Back on Track

In October, while development teams were working frantically to try to finish up the software originally scheduled for a month earlier, the project managers, business leads, and development managers were involved in long meetings with GRI consultants scrubbing the project plan. We had established a new set of controls in late September in response to the missed date, and Neil made it clear that nothing was to get in the way of establishing the controls. There was to be no brooking dissent or, as he stated it, "noncompliance."

The primary control was the project plan. No one, Neil declared, should be working on anything that wasn't on the plan. Every hour of every team member now had to be accounted for. This was done by assigning people to the tasks on the project plan and requiring that, at the end of each week, each person submit time sheets to the GRI project management team. Simultaneously, the GRI team and our project managers were integrating the various pieces of the plan, estimating time to complete, matching lists of resources to tasks, and putting the procedures to gather information and maintain the plan into practice.

There were a variety of reactions and assessments to the greater degree of control. Frankie and Trevor claimed that the "noise" had been taken out of the project. The development teams, according to Frankie and echoed by Joe Karras, were now protected from distractions and scope creep, and they were able to finish their jobs. The formal project reporting bore this out; by mid-January, our revised code-complete date, only a very few development or unit testing tasks remained open. The intense focus that we brought to bear in October and continued through the end of the year appeared to have paid off. Development tasks were completed on time, formally delayed to a later release and supplemented with formal "work-arounds," or, as soon as the plan indicated slipping end dates, attracted extra project managers and "expeditors" from our project office and GRI. The formal project reporting continued "green," with entrance criteria to integration testing completed by January 15 and all signs "go" for March go-live.

The alternate view, for me at least, came from my informal and personal discussions with Mary. Her view was that the project was being completed in form only. True value delivery, she contended, was now so hidden behind the completion of plans and process-specified deliverables that very little was actually getting done. Her team was spending the bulk of their time and effort on project planning, time accounting, the request process to add or modify project plan items, change control, work-around planning, and other activities that she classified as "waste."

Integration and acceptance testing had both just begun. Dave Prentiss, the integration test lead, had reported to the PCA this week that his group had been able to begin testing; they had encountered some stability issues, but had been able to make some good progress. Angela Lockhart, in acceptance testing, explained how her group was doing targeted testing of some critical elements, such as pricing, while waiting for availability of the integration-tested end-to-end flows. Angela had asked for, and received, a special exception to the acceptance test entrance criteria that allowed her to do this type of testing. However, she said, she needed the entire integrated code base, running well, by the third week in February in order to ensure they could run all their critical tests by the end of March, when we planned on going live. Angela explained how they would test in two shifts and expect bug fixes on a 48-hour turnaround. There were still some risks, but Neil, Trevor, and Frankie were feeling fairly confident. I didn't share my trepidations, but went to see for myself.

Checking the Project's Status by Sitting In on Unit Testing

I asked Mary for a suggestion for what I could "go see" to give me a better feeling for how the project stood than the charts and reports Dave and Angela shared. She suggested the daily meeting of the team that the Sales and Production Management groups had formed last October to "unit test" their interface. The meeting was held in Production Management's temporary team room in an office in one of our printing plants in a suburb just outside St. Paul. I drove out there a little early to meet Joe Karras, the technical lead for production, for coffee before the meeting started. Mary tolerated Joe, describing him as a "journeyman" development manager. Joe wasn't flashy, curious, or innovative; didn't go outside his box as it was defined for him; and wouldn't say "crap" if his mouth was full of it. However, he was well intentioned and reliable. Joe came and met me at the security desk and brought me over to the cafeteria. We got our coffee and sat down at a window overlooking the parking lot and the lightly blowing snow. Mary and I had begun talking about a future together and, on days like this, California beckoned.

I asked Joe to tell me about this Sales–Production interface team, and he was glad to do so. I got the feeling that he didn't get asked for his opinion very often.

"Last September, I believe," he started, "GG, the project manager for Sales, called me and wanted to talk about testing the Sales–Production interface. It took me a while to understand what he was talking about; I had assumed that the integration testing was all going to be done by Dave Prentiss's team and hadn't looked in any detail at what Dave had planned. My team had been fully occupied building out our system functionality.

We had a lot to do: a lot of new functionality, plus building out interfaces to Web services, which were new for us. By September we were moving along fairly well, so I had time to think about what GG had said and, to tell you the truth, he kind of scared me."

"What did he say?" I asked.

"He said that the Sales team had investigated the test plans and scripts in both integration and acceptance testing, and they didn't believe that there was a complete set of tests. They also were concerned with the data mapping through the common service facility and the common data model because they hadn't seen it and, by then, delivery of the code was late. He proposed that we—Sales and Production—put together an ad hoc team of our own staff, along with whomever we could muster from Data, CSF/CDM, and Testing, to test and debug our interface. GG positioned this as extended unit testing and asked that I talk about it that way so as not to raise territorial concerns from the test teams or the process police."

"I did some checking around with our test, data, and CSF contacts, and everyone thought this was a good idea: to do better unit testing, as I described it. No one felt confident that GG's concerns were overblown or that the processes in place dealt with them sufficiently. So I agreed with GG to put some folks together, assess the position, and do what needed to be done to make this work. I never dreamed that the result would be what we've now seen!"

Curious, I asked what that might be.

"Well, we had our first meeting in late September. Since that time, I'd guess we've had a dozen or more full-time people engaged on it—think of that: maybe four full person-years so far just testing and debugging this one interface! I couldn't have imagined it. The worst of it is that we aren't done yet, and I don't know when we will be done."

I was puzzled by that statement. How, I asked, was this represented in the project plan? Why didn't this issue show up in the PCA reports?

"All the code itself is complete; GG's team wrote their interface to their own data specification, we wrote to ours, and each of us unit tested to our native interfaces. The CSF team did the mapping, at the data team's direction, to our interfaces and did the conversions in and of the common data model. They unit tested the conversions, so all of us are reporting 100% code complete. Dave's integration test team is just starting to run their tests. The Process doesn't have a deliverable or phase for this type of intensive testing of a single interface; it more or less falls between the development and the testing phases. We are all charging our time to the 'testing support' bucket on the plan. The only way someone looking at just the reports would know there might be an issue would be to see a lot of hours being charged there, although because we aren't doing much on the next release, it would make sense that most of our hours are there."

"I guess the reports can't show everything," I said. "Sounds like a reader of the reports would have to be able to read between the lines to get what is really going on. That's why I wanted to come see this meeting."

"Why don't I tell you what we've found so far," Joe said, "so that you can have some context to understand the meeting. We've got another half-hour and that should be enough."

Finding the Problems: A Tangled Testing Mess

"The first thing we did," Joe said, "was to be sure there weren't tests in place, and that was quick—Deb, Mary's test lead, showed us what she'd found, and it was obvious. By the way, Mary was sneaky getting her own test lead; I was told that Testing would be responsible for testing and just relied on that. So I had no one to pair up with Deb because all I have is developers and a few designers. On our team, we get the requirements from our business partners and the high-level design from the architects; we just do our part in the middle. Mary manages differently, looking at the whole solution. I don't know how she gets away with that! I was able to peel off one of my lead designers to work with Deb because he didn't have much new in development; his name is Sai and he's a pretty good guy."

Joe paused, took a few sips of coffee, and then continued. "Deb drove a quick drafting of a test plan for the interface. We have about 25 distinct transactions. She proposed leveraging the test data from the test team and using those data as a base to construct data to input to the sales system, execute each transaction, and specify what we expected to see as a result in the production system. Sai and a couple of other developers worked with Deb; we began with our first logical transaction: loading customer information and then maintaining it. It was quite an eye-opener! We found we had to create a map from the sales database to the sales service call through the central data model to the production system service call to the production system database and back. No one had done that; all we had were pieces. We had no tools to manage these maps; we had to use Excel, which was hard to create, maintain, and share."

"Then we put together the first set of tests, putting actual data into the maps, first logically to specify input to the sales system and where it should land in the production database, and then in code, with input files and test code to check on its landing spot. This was time consuming and error prone also. Finally, we starting running the tests while we frantically worked to create more. I can't remember a more confusing testing process. We found problem after problem!"

It sounded like a tangled mess. "What kinds of problems did you find?" I followed up.

Joe stopped for a moment to catch his breath. He sipped his coffee, shook his head, and continued. "You name it. We found problems in the logical maps from the native system data structures to their own Web services, problems in the logical maps to and from the CDM, and problems in code to implement the maps—all made worse and more confusing by problems with our own test cases and test data. Our team members were more or less making this all up as they went along, under time pressure and already tired from the project, while the CDM, Data, and CSF staff who had done much of the critical work suffered turnover and some of the contractors involved left. The problems were really hard to figure out as well because debugging might involve five or more groups."

"Other than that, Joe, how'd it go?" I tried to make a joke, but Joe didn't laugh.

"It gets worse. This testing was just about the 'happy path,' where everything technically works and all the transactions and data are correct. We're making good progress on happy path now, although it's hard to tell when we'll be done. Now we're working on the exception scenarios, and we don't have good answers. What happens when the sales system calls the CSF service, which turns around and calls production, but production returns a partial error? Where should we enforce data integrity and field requirements, especially cross-field validations? We've found that the CSF services and the CDM schema have rules of their own that neither the sales nor the production system enforces or requires. They came from other systems supported or out of the thin air their architects and designers breathe. Do we add those to our systems or get them to relax a bit? I just don't know."

I didn't know what to say, so I just sipped my coffee. Joe sounded like a defeated man, but after a moment he looked back up at me and said, "Well, we'll find a way to make it work. Our team is very committed and we are making progress."

Not exactly a ringing confirmation of the "green" ratings the PCA continued to receive.

Signposts	**Cremins United project** • As of February 2007, the project was again green as the teams, through intense work and tight control, made their code complete date and delivered to integration test. • Wes heard doubts on the reliability of that status from Mary, so he did a "go see" of the informal collaboration to test the Sales–Production interface. Hidden behind the statistics of the project plan was a tremendous effort to test and fix the interface, with indeterminate projections as to finish date.
Guides from Wes	• Leaders must "go see," rather than just believing statistics and reports. • Enforcement of very tight controls can ensure compliance—at the risk of snuffing out creativity, initiative, and honest feedback. Leaders can't afford this in systems development; we need all team members taking initiative to drive results, rather than woodenly following rules and tracking compliance.
Coming up next	Still on the same day in February 2007, Beth relays a conversation among Mary, Wes, and her, following up on earlier inquiries as to the suitability of the common service facility and common data model for their part of the Cremins United project.

23

CU Project Retrospective: Slip Charts and Some Towering Expertise (Too Late)

FEBRUARY 2007

Beth:

I walked into Mary's cube for our monthly one-on-one meeting just as she was getting off the phone with Wes. She looked up and smiled at the daisies I'd brought her. Mary explained that Wes had just attended the Sales–Production interface testing team meeting and was in full-fledged panic mode. Mary said she tried to calm him down, saying that even though the technology design was wasteful and poor, they'd probably be able to make it work, at least for pilot.

"My hope," Mary said, "is that we learn from this and make the changes we need going forward."

"How about we cover a couple of items we need to touch base on, Mary, and then you explain the problem to me? Just curious," I replied.

"Sure, I can do that in just a few minutes now. Remember when we tried to figure out the data interface problem a few months ago, and Jenn, from CSMPro, mentioned she knew someone who had a lot of experience in this area and might be able to help? We pitched in and hired him for a couple of weeks, and we now have a good model and understanding. I can show it to you."

I did remember and wanted to see it. But first I had to go over Mary's resource lists, task assignments, and staffing model projections. As the controls had strengthened in the CU project to ensure focus on the right things, more and more people had been drafted to gather, collate, review, and interpret status and plan information; HR had drawn the short stick on people management. Mary and I worked to put together an acceptable summary sheet, showing a declining staff level and cost as focus shifted simply to supporting testing. Because the other teams were all too busy finishing code and fixing bugs, almost no work was aimed toward future releases, and resources were forbidden to do more than token work in that direction.

As we finished up the report, I wanted to turn the topic of conversation to Mary herself. I started with an open-ended, "So how are you doing, Mary? Not the project—you."

"Actually, Beth, personally I'm doing okay, although I don't think it can last. I am enjoying the work within our team, with CSMPro, and now even with Joe Karras and the Production team as we work together on our interface. I think we've built a solid sales system for the future and a team that can support it. On the other hand, the larger project is extraordinarily frustrating: The amount of overhead keeps escalating, wasting so much time! They keep putting more project managers and consultants and architects in between our teams. And the meetings—It seems like every meeting has 50 people in it, going over long lists of things that project managers assemble, which they barely understand! We never seem to talk about the substance of what is actually going on; all we focus on is process, plans, and statuses, as if we are trying desperately to convince ourselves that all is well."

"How are you dealing with it, Mary? You seem to be somewhat withdrawn," I said.

"That's why I think I'm doing okay," she replied. "I've given up on trying to influence the project as a whole; I've become an interested bystander. I tried so hard for so long to contribute to the process, team structure, technology architecture—you name it—but I have been so unsuccessful. For now, I'm focused on getting our part done and influencing others only to the extent it affects our own code—like our newfound partnership with Joe and his team. If they can make the rest of the project work, I'll be very surprised, but pleasantly so."

"What a shame, Mary. It sounds so sad," I said.

"It's not so bad. I'm still learning. I think we're doing something that will be valuable eventually somehow, and I can't think of what else to do. I can't leave my team now. It's sort of a calm before the storm right now. Our team is in good shape, slowing down, and I'm spending more time with my kids and on myself than I have for quite a while."

"How are things with Wes?"

Mary smiled at me, and stared at the daisies for a moment. "Good, good," she replied. "I'm not sure where we're going, but we like being with each other when we can find time. I've never had a relationship with someone at work; that's confusing sometimes, but kind of nice too."

"He's told Tom and you've told Greg and Frankie?" I wanted to be sure.

"Yup, and no one is too concerned at the moment. I don't report to him, so it's not against policy, and we don't routinely work so closely together that there's been a problem. Living several thousand miles apart lowers the risks also."

Using a Slip Chart to Track a Project's Progress

"Tell me more about this 'being a bystander' thing," I queried. "How does that work for you?"

"I can actually show you," Mary brightened. "You know Alex, the project lead for TRIM, don't you?" I nodded. "He has been following the CU project from a distance and has created what he calls a 'slip chart.'[1] Take a look [see Figure 35]."

Mary handed me the chart shown here in Figure 35 and explained it to me. It seemed to me that she was avoiding my question and using the chart as a diversion, but if she didn't want to talk more about how she was dealing with the CU project, I could respect her wishes. So I turned my attention to the slip chart.

The chart displayed the announced go-live date on the horizontal axis, against the date of that announcement on the vertical axis. So far it showed the initial go-live date of November 2006, announced in October 2005, and the slip in September 2006 to the current goal of March 2007.

"I guess that counts as observing," I said, letting Mary off the hook gently. "What do you think the chart shows about the project?"

"That wouldn't be fair for me to interpret it, would it? I'm too closely involved. Alex is enjoying the observation, though, and he has a theory, although there aren't many points on the slip chart yet. He thinks it shows a bad initial date, to which management clung as long as possible, shown by the slip date coming so close to the initial target date. A lot of people

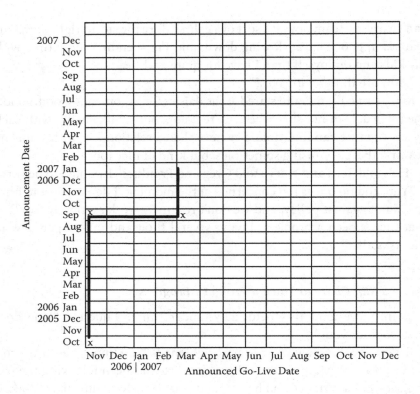

FIGURE 35
CU slip chart, February 2007.

had to know the project was in trouble for quite some time, he figures, as shown by the long initial slip: 6 months—more than half as long as the initial development period. He likes the long slip because 'death by a thousand slips' is such a painful and wasteful way to watch a project die. Now he's waiting for the next point to plot, being the pessimist he is."

"I like it," I said. "I wonder if he might make the chart a bit easier to interpret by putting the official reason for the slip on the chart so that it could tell the story more completely, yet still with no bias whatsoever." Mary liked the idea and promised to get Alex to add that to future versions.

Just then the phone rang, and Mary saw from the caller ID that it was Wes again. She indicated to me that she was going to take the call, but gestured for me to stay. "I'll be quick," she whispered.

Mary picked up the phone, listened for a moment, and then told Wes she was going to put him on speaker.

"Wes, Beth is in my office, and I promised her that I'd explain what Jenn and her consultant explained to us about the data interface. I'm e-mailing you summary slides right now." While the e-mail was en route, Mary printed out the slides and handed them to me.

"Hi, Beth," Wes said. "OK, Mary, I've got it. Beth, I'm trying to figure out what to do about the data connections issue. I saw the Sales–Production interface team yesterday, and while it was impressive to see their progress, it got me scared about how difficult the testing and debugging is going to be. What really worries me is what's going on in our other interfaces, where we don't have the newfound Mary–Joe direct partnerships. Mary thinks she's got some insights into how serious the problem is, and she promised to share them with me when I had a moment."

"Thanks for letting me listen in, Wes. I've been wondering about this, too, and hoping that it would be all right," I said.

"Glad to have you, Beth. I'll need to be able to explain this to Tom, who understands less about technology than you do. So, you'll be a good test of whether this makes sense," Wes replied.

Mary was ready to go. "Let's start on the first slide, which shows systems A and B and some lines in between [see Figure 36]. Got it, Wes? OK. The basic question," she started, "is the advisability of inserting an abstract data structure between two systems—in essence, converting the data from the native format of system A to an intermediate format, call it format C, and then converting from format C to the native format of system B. The first diagram shows this: Do you go direct, as in the first arrow, or go through the intermediate format, as in the second?"

"Theoretically, using an intermediary can have great benefits, especially when there are many systems interconnecting. For example, let's say

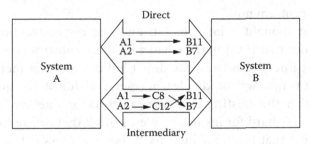

FIGURE 36
Direct or intermediary connections between two systems.

system A now needs to connect to system D; if system D already 'speaks' format C, there are no problems! So it can be a valuable option to put an abstract layer in the middle—even kind of seductive."

"Now, Wes, turn to the next page [Figure 37]."

"Jenn's consultant friend has been involved in real-time system data integration for more than a decade. He's worked with two different consulting firms concentrating in this area, and he has used most of the major integration tools and approaches. He has also consulted for a couple of standards organizations and business-to-business exchanges. His take on the issue is that the advisability of using a facility like CSF and a model like CDM depends on a number of factors. The factors that he thought relevant in our case and his take on how that would argue that we should have designed our Sales–Production interface, is in the table. Note that Joe's analysis is only for this one interface, and does not imply anything else about CRF and CDM."

"You can read it yourself, Wes. Suffice it to say that Joe thought we were taking major risks in doing the interface as we have and strongly recommended that we revisit the decision—sooner rather than later. None of the factors argues strongly to do it the way we have, and almost all argue for a more direct connection. Joe emphasized that this is not to argue that such a design is never appropriate; far from it, this pattern has fairly broad applicability. It might even apply to other areas of the CU project. Just not in this case."

Wes was silent for a few moments as he read and absorbed the material. Then he asked, "One more CU example of not bringing the right level of expertise to the table, eh, Mary? I suppose it's also about doing things we didn't need to do, imposing architectures on teams, and I'd bet a list of several other of your danged principles. Not much we can do about all that, but we do need to address whether we can do anything about the immediate problem now."

Mary had thought a lot about it, and she responded quickly. "I'd also point out that this interface had a lot of unknowns—it might have worked just fine. But because we didn't build it and test incrementally in coherent teams, we couldn't learn, react, and adjust. the question for me is whether the existing interface can work or whether we need to junk it now. It's hard for me to say, Wes. I think that before we scale up, if we ever get that far, we should fix it, but my guess is that spending the money to fix it now might be a waste because the rest of the system probably won't work anyhow. Also, I can't imagine how we get the PCA

Factor	Argues for Use of Intermediate Reference Model at Runtime	Cremins United Project – Sales / Production Interface: Argues for Use of Intermediate Model at Runtime?
Maturity of Reference Model	A model is available that well-represents the business functions on both sides of the interface; it is proven in similar implementations; it represents a wide range of users of similar systems; additions/extensions to model to support this linkage are low compared to support provided.	NO. The model is immature, untested, and proprietary.
Maturity of Supporting Infrastructure	The governance of change, available expertise, and (if a physical environment is provided) technical infrastructure is mature.	NO. The CSF is immature, there is little to no experience with governance, and expertise is low.
Number of Systems to Interconnect	There are many systems with common data needing connection, and each system on each end needs to connect to multiples for each type of transaction on the other end.	PARTLY. Most CU systems need to connect to just a few others; each specific transaction is essentially confined between two systems only.
Likelihood of Future Swapout of One Side of Transaction	Swapping out or adding another system to one or both sides of the transaction is likely, AND mapping and transforming data from the new system participant is likely to be easier to do to the common model than direct system interconnections.	NO. Systems in this environment tend to last for many years (e.g, predecessor systems are over 20 years old); and because the CDM model is proprietary, there is no advantage of mapping to it versus more direct mappings.
Affiliation between owners of systems	Loose affiliation (e.g. mortgage companies and insurance providers).	NO. All systems are managed by the Cremins technology group.
Time, cost, & risk to market; ongoing maintainability	Depends on other factors — if others argue for use of intermediate, this will be faster.	NO. Other factors argue for a direct connection; this factor emphasizes the criticality of going direct.

FIGURE 37
CU evaluation of direct versus intermediary connections.

and the architecture team to let us rewrite this based on this analysis. They are so committed to enforcing their architectures and designs—even though they are not strongly grounded in experience, expertise, or a business case—that I can't see them opening up their minds to this type of expertise."

258 • A Tale of Two Systems

"Unfortunately, neither can I, Mary. I guess we just hold this information in our back pockets, see how testing goes, and use it if the time comes. It doesn't give me much confidence that we'll get this thing working, though."

"That makes all of us, Wes," I said.

"Thanks for the info, Mary," Wes replied. "I won't share it without first letting you know. Gotta run; talk to you later." With that, Wes clicked off.

Mary and I were silent for a moment, until I said, "The project is screwed, isn't it, Mary? Do we have any chance?"

"I doubt it, Beth. We've made a lot of mistakes, and it's going to be tough to recover. Look at just this issue: We had an architecture set from outside the teams, based on inadequate experience and expertise. We so totally split the technical decision from the business choices that no consideration of the suitability of the design was made at all. We didn't do any study phase on it, no testing, and no trade-off analysis. Even though it was highly risky, we didn't do any concurrent engineering, like trying to do the connection through the CSF/CDM and writing it directly, so we'd be more likely to have something that actually worked. We did handoff after handoff and didn't continuously integrate and test. We had no chief engineer type of leadership, just committees and process enforcement. Take this problem and multiply it by 10 or more, and the chances for success look pretty slim."

Depressed and concerned about Mary and the company's future, I made a sad face for Mary. "On that cheery note, I have to run to my next meeting," I told her, and I retreated to the more productive land of TRIM and the Real Estate Division.

Signposts	Cremins United project
	• Mary introduced Alex Fuegos's "slip chart" diagramming how the project's target date had moved. His interpretation: the initial date was set too aggressively, but he liked the long slip (6 months on an initial 11-month development period) as a way to avoid "death by a thousand slips."

- An expert consultant gave Mary and Wes feedback on the CSF and CDM design for their primary interface. Conclusion: inappropriate and, perhaps, unrecoverable.

Guides from Beth

- Towering technical expertise is one of my favorite LPD principles. In doing commercial software development, there are few problems that you will be the first in the world to face. Find the best expertise, get alternative views, use external experts, and outsource to specialists. Identify the risky technical choices and be sure you understand the business reasons for making them.
- Business leaders may be tempted to "leave the technology to the Technology department." If the technology leaders are, in fact, business leaders who understand the technology trade-offs in business terms, are able to articulate them for their peers, and are completely aware of the need to apply towering technical competence even if it's not in their shops, the business leaders may well be safe doing so. If not, Technology's failure will be theirs as well.
- The "waterfall" nature of CU prevented learning of the data connectivity issues until it was too late. If the project had done continuous build, integrate, and test, the difficulties of the sales production interface would have been exposed much earlier, perhaps early enough to change course.

Coming up next

We move ahead 3 months to May 2007, by which time CU is supposed to be live. Beth brings us to Greg's staff meeting, where we learn how both TRIM and CU are doing.

NOTES

1. Gerald M. Weinberg, *Quality Software Management. Volume 2: First Order Measurement*, pp. 73–88, New York: Dorset House Publishing, 1993.

Section IV

The Beginning of the End: The Last 6 Months of 2 Years of Work

24

18 Months In:
Status Updates for Both Projects

MAY 2007

Beth:

Greg's usual weekly staff meeting had become a ritual by now, 20 months into my tenure with Cremins Corporation. Greg had missed the two prior weeks; he'd been out on vacation, tooling around Tuscany visiting vineyards and cathedrals. He had just returned yesterday and didn't have any particular agenda for today, so we used the time to catch up with each other.

Greg started with a quick update on the company as a whole. Evan was under a lot of pressure to show that his strategy of tying the various divisions more strongly together was going to work and that there really was synergy in the various acquisitions that he had championed. Our financial results weren't showing the benefits yet; indeed, even anecdotes illustrating crossover benefits were scarce. The implementation of the strategy had been invested primarily in the Cremins United project, which had taken a technology/systems approach to the problem; so far, that project seemed stuck. The senior leadership was divided on what direction to take. Gina, Greg's boss, had lost confidence in the CU approach and was increasingly skeptical that the strategy itself was valid; she thought, and Greg agreed, that the various divisions might do better on their own without the financial and process overhead that Cremins was imposing. Evan, on the other hand, remained committed to the strategy, and he continued to support the CU project strongly, doubling-down on his bet.

"I share this with you just by way of giving you the flavor for what is happening around us. My expectation is that as the year progresses, we will see increasing debates around this basic theme. Hopefully, having an understanding of the strategic debates under way will help you navigate some of the shoals we'll come upon."

"I'd like to pass on Gina's thanks to you all for the great performance you are delivering. Our revenue is up 20% so far this year, and our profits are up a little more than that. TRIM is delivering both revenue and profits, and its success is giving us a lot of momentum in the market. Our other businesses are almost all doing well also. Our challenge now is more about picking and choosing from the opportunities ahead of us than struggling to find opportunities—and, of course, to execute what we choose to do carefully and find ways to move ahead without additional capital infusions from the parent. Cash flow is tight at Corporate, and there will be continued emphasis on conserving cash while we feed the Cremins United project appetite."

"Let's spend our time today getting an update from Neville on TRIM and then from Mary on CU. We'll wrap up with Walt's financial review, and Beth wants to talk about our people development program changes. Neville, can you start?"

Update on the TRIM Project: Looking Good!

I'm only going to convey Neville's and Mary's updates because this is a book about those two projects. The financial news was mostly good; Walt covered the basics and began to set the stage for 2008 budgeting. I had been working on extending our training approaches, delivering on our commitments to continue to build expertise in our team members. Nothing was controversial or revelatory about either of our discussions.

Neville had bad news about the economy and the housing markets, but continued good news about TRIM. In March, revenue from TRIM had begun to surpass costs, and that trend was continuing and accelerating. Public access to the data had been delivered last month, and the first elements of service provider functionality were due in July. A lot of work was going on to streamline the addition of lenders, multiple listing service providers, and other sources of data; Neville was driving continual improvement efforts using Lean manufacturing techniques to find and eliminate waste. User administration, scalability, disaster recovery, and other "back office" functions were the focus of the current sprints, and the project organization continued to morph in response to feedback from the team and the evolution away from a systems development project into an ongoing system maintenance and enhancement establishment. While there remained much to do, the project was a clear success and much promise remained ahead.

Update on the CU Project: Looking Bleak

Unfortunately, there wasn't as much promise with the CU project. Mary had brought two handouts for Greg and his team: the updated slip chart and the bug trending chart. She started with the slip chart (Figure 38).

"I think I've shared this with most of you before. I got the format from Alex. You can see we've had three slips so far. The first was last September, when basically the code just wasn't done on time. At that point we were supposed to go live in November, so the delay came just a few months before we were supposed to go live."

"There was never any chance you were going to make November, was there Mary?" asked Neville.

"I never thought so. Even if we'd had a crack team that had worked together for years, the project was too big to get done that fast. The PCA bit the bullet on having to move the date out, but wound up trading a bad date for another bad date. This wasn't obvious at the time, given the length of the initial slip—6 months compared to the initial development period of 11 months. We were supposed to be code complete in January and go live in March, which turned out not to be enough time to test and fix bugs, given how we had done the project."

Greg commented, "Sad, isn't it? We have so much riding on this project, yet can't seem to get it on a good path."

"Indeed," agreed Mary, "especially because my team worked so hard, and so well, to meet the unreasonable deadlines. Anyhow, by the end of February, it was clear that we needed more time to test. Code was declared complete; that was quite an effort and people worked intensively through the holidays. Anything that couldn't be finished had to be reported to the PMO, and work-arounds were created and documented. By Valentine's Day, we had 150 or so work-arounds, all nicely on a work-

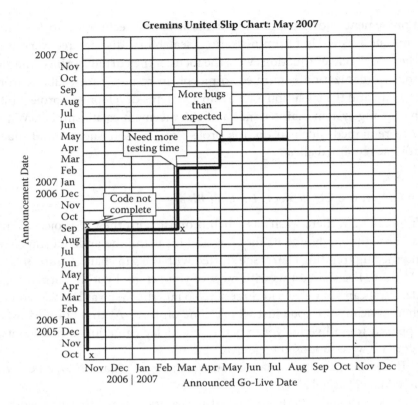

FIGURE 38
CU slip chart, May 2007.

around Web site. Teams were prohibited from working on any new functionality, repairing work-arounds, or even fixing bugs until they were prioritized by the PMO. The idea was to control scope rigidly and ensure that the 'business' had control over what was done. The goal seemed to be to have the 'business' define the minimum needed to go live and for the project team to take as little accountability for what we were delivering as we could get away with."

"See, Mary?" Walt, our chief financial officer, winked, "another benefit of clearly separating technology from business. If the Technology team can arrange things so that they deliver the set of trade-offs the business has chosen, regardless of how well or poorly business needs are met, the Technology team can succeed! You could learn from that and maybe build yourself an easier job."

"Very funny, Walt," said Greg. "Seriously, though, it seems like we have a dramatic demonstration of the lack of a 'chief engineer' as we use the role. If there were someone who took true accountability for the business benefits, I can't imagine so much effort going into figuring out just how bad the system could be and still go live. The focus would be on what had to be done to get business benefits and how soon we could get them."

Mary said, "That's my take on it too, Greg: a lot of posturing and a tremendous amount of inefficiency as a result. Anyhow, at the end of February the testing period was extended to May, and just last week it was extended again, to August. The explanation of this move was that we are seeing more defects than we had expected, and the turn time to solve them is longer than our plan. We now have a model that shows the expected bugs by system and type, as well as expected fix times; it shows us completing bug-fixes in mid-July. The go-live date was set a month after that to give us some slack."

"Here is the bug situation," Mary said, as she handed out the summary bug chart. "You can see that the number of total outstanding bugs is still going up. We're finding more than we are fixing, although the slope of the chart is leveling out. The official plan is shown in the blue line, with total bug count starting to shrink next week and then fairly rapidly falling after that, until we get to a low and acceptable bug level in mid-July."

"How did they do a bug projection?" asked Neville. "Do you buy it?"

"GRI, the consulting firm, has a testing center of excellence that has experience in large projects and used their standard model to project. No, I don't buy it at all. I think we have, for practical purposes, essentially an infinite number of bugs in this system. The only way we'll be on that curve is to limit the testing we do—which, by the way, seems to be exactly what is happening. The test cases have all gone under rigorous change control, and the test cases are being prioritized for criticality so that we can do 'risk-based testing.'"

"The challenge is going to be that the lines of business have become skeptical of the status reporting and the plans, and they have asked their audit groups to give independent reports on status each month. So information is being very tightly controlled, and our meetings are less valuable than ever because Audit is sitting in on a lot of them."

Greg sighed, sat back in his chair, and crossed his arms. "Not very encouraging, is it?" He paused a moment and then turned directly to Mary. "How's your team doing, Mary? It's got to be tough on them."

"They're OK," she responded. "Our code has been done for some time, and we've been trying to keep moving forward to build out more functionality because we have time. It's tough, given the controls on what work is authorized, but we're getting some good enhancements done under the radar. We've got most of our people involved in the testing and bug-fixing, although we don't have many problems left and we are not permitted to extend the testing more deeply with our interfaces. The amount of swirl involved in the bug list management, repair prioritization, code migration, and so on is amazing. I do have some good news, though: The connection to the production system, our most important interface, is now looking pretty good, although I doubt it will scale."

I wanted to add a little color for the team, so I spoke up. "Mary is doing a truly remarkable job as a leader," I said, smiling at Mary and Greg. "It's a fine line she is walking, getting her part done and cooperating as best she can with the dysfunction of the broader team. You should all be proud of her."

"As we are," Greg said. "This is truly outstanding work you and your team are doing, Mary; keep it up and do what you can to help the project succeed. I'll update Gina on our take on the project; it seems that the continued deployment of Gina's auditors might be the best we can do. Let me ask one last question, Mary: Is the project making progress? With enough time and money, is there any chance we'll get anything out of this?"

"Great question, Greg. Much as I dislike how the project is being done, I am glad to report that we are making progress. My guess is that with enough time and money, we'll have something that barely works, won't scale, and doesn't have much momentum toward adding true business value. Perhaps once we get it running we can make the changes needed to accelerate value delivery. I guess that slim hope is why I'm still on to the project."

That wrapped up the CU discussion, and we moved to Walt's report.

Signposts	TRIM project
	• By May 2007, the housing market's slide was evident, and the need for TRIM was confirmed.
	• TRIM was now delivering growing revenue and profits and had earned the Real Estate Division a view to other new opportunities as well.

- New functionality was being delivered regularly, and administrative functions (e.g., streamlining accession of new geographies and lenders) and technical robustness (disaster recovery, user administration) were the current priorities.

Cremins United project

- Cremins Corporation financials continued to deteriorate and CEO Evan Nogelmeyer's strategy of synergy, which drove the CU project, was coming under doubt. Evan was sticking to his guns, and he needed CU to succeed to prove his judgment was correct.
- The CU project had slipped twice since February. First, testing was extended to May and then just recently extended again to August. The reason was that there were more defects than expected and fixing them took longer than anticipated. Go-live was now planned for November.
- Mary believed that some chance of success still remained. Go-live could show that the system worked—at least somewhat—and that perhaps, with enough time and money and better decisions, the investment could still be rescued.

Guides from Beth

- TRIM demonstrates how an early focus on the right priorities (in this case, business functionality) can create the success to worry about other items later. This avoids waste; if the early deliveries fail, the later ones won't be needed! Contrast with CU, where everything was anticipated up front but, ultimately, little was delivered. How much functionality in CU, even that which works (such as the sales system), will wind up being total losses?

- Multiple project date slips undermine confidence in leadership, which is the intent of "don't trade a bad date for another bad date." If you are involved in a project that is undergoing multiple slips, like the CU project, be sure to step back and ask what's wrong. It may be that nothing is wrong, but more likely there are leadership, technical expertise, or other people issues.

Coming up next   Wes brings us forward to November 2007, the go-live date set in May. Testing has revealed an astonishing array of problems; are enough of them resolved to justify keeping the go-live commitment?

25

The Decision to Go Live with the CU System

Wes:

As usual during the last several months, the PCA meeting this morning began with the bug chart. The number of outstanding bugs had started to turn down in June, at last, after 4 months of testing and repairs. The curve was much flatter downward than anyone would have guessed; it seemed we kept finding almost one new bug for each one we fixed, and some of the bugs were confounding. I had learned about bugs hiding behind other bugs, memory leaks, cross-field validations, required versus nonrequired fields, deadly embraces, optimistic versus pessimistic locking, code migration problems, and more data mismapping, syntactical confusion, and arguments about the meaning of and process for changing the various bug status codes than I care to recount.

The Final Push to Finish

By early October, Neil and Frankie thought we were at the point where a final, all-out push could bring the project home. Neil had declared September to be "production quality month," instituted a third daily

271

incident review meeting at 5 p.m. central time, and asked everyone to work at least half-days on Saturdays until we were bug free. The CU team responded in a remarkably positive way, evident from the haggard looks of our staff and the piles of coffee cups, Mountain Dew cans, and empty pizza cartons littering our conference rooms. By now the process of finding, assigning, repairing, migrating, retesting, and closing bugs had become a well-oiled machine staffed by a veritable army of Cremins soldiers. Mary remained skeptical of the whole enterprise, believing that Neil's approach resulted in what he wanted: a lower bug count. However, it didn't get to the root requirement of a quality system. The team, she contended to me privately, had stopped looking for bugs and was accepting more and more work-arounds.

Whatever the truth was with the actual code, the bug chart was now looking encouraging, and it was with that fact that the PCA meeting began. Our meetings had become much more formal in the last few months since Jacqueline Armister, a senior auditor, had been "given" to us as a new PCA member. Tom now had me do an agenda and minutes for each meeting, and he tried his best to inject some structure into our discussions despite his more free-wheeling inclinations.

Today's agenda was simple: making the go/no-go decision for bringing Cremins United up live. I had structured the discussion and, at Tom's request, I managed the flow of the meeting. First on deck was Tom, to set the stage.

"Before we go too deeply into the substance of this decision, I'd like to pass on some thoughts from Evan Nogelmeyer, our CEO, on the state of the company and how this project plays in that. I'm going to give you some of my perspective, also, to help us make this difficult decision."

"You all know that Cremins Corporation is at a critical junction. The strategy that Evan sponsored, even before he became CEO, was to transform this great but threatened company from a leader in the declining printing business into a customer-focused growth company in the business communications and data management business. Evan's predictions on the decline in our traditional businesses are proving right, unfortunately, and they are happening more quickly than we had feared. The problem is that our transformation into our new focus is lagging—much of the lag due to those of us right here in this room. Evan and the board put a lot of confidence in us, and they asked us to lead the Cremins United project, the centerpiece of the transformation."

"Evan brought together many of the pieces we needed: strong support from the top, several acquisitions to fill in pieces of the puzzle, and plenty of investment capital. As it became evident that we couldn't meet our initial commitments, he was patient with us, giving us more time and a lot more money—money that deprived some of our struggling lines of business of desperately needed investments of their own."

"Now we need to answer the question: Was this all just wasted? Have we produced anything of value? Does the company need to look in another direction, either a different way to realize the strategy we've been on for several years or a completely different strategy? I can tell you that Evan and the board are considering many options, some of which would result in a very different looking company, and most of which, if we fail, don't look very good for any of us."

"Evan is expecting that we give him and the board the information they need—soon. 'What do we have here? What can we expect?' We must give that information soon."

"Any questions or comments?" Tom asked in conclusion.

As usual it was Neil who spoke up first. "There is only one way to find out what we've got, and that's to go live. We have spent more than 2 years building this and spent a hoard of cash. The bug count is getting down, we've analyzed and documented and prepared work-arounds, and we can contain the risks. Let's go live and see what we've got."

So much for my agenda. It was off to the races!

Pushback from the Lines of Business: Worry about Risk

Jacqueline Armister, the auditor, responded. "Neil, we just can't put the business at that much risk. None of the lines of business are prepared to sign off on the system and the procedures—both because of risks in the working of the system and because the work-arounds are so severe and the functionality so limited that they don't believe they'll get any benefits."

"We've been through this a dozen times, Jacqueline. If we keep the volume low, any newly found bugs can be handled manually, or we can even do the work in both the legacy systems and the CU systems. The business units aren't seeing the big picture; their commitment to the vision is marred by their current realities. The only way to make progress and prove that we're building a revolutionary solution, is to show it now. If we have another delay, all Evan and the board can do is assume that we'll never get this done." Neil was adamant, totally determined.

Frankie was ready with an alternative. "Neil, Jacqueline, I think you are both right. The system is getting more stable and ready for production, as you say Neil, but it remains risky and limited. I'd suggest that we compromise: instead of going live and rolling out to the two business lines and a whole region to begin with, we call it a 'beta' and roll out just to a few users. We put our whole help desk and support apparatus on the job, and we make sure that no matter what happens with the systems, we don't disrupt our business. That way we can accomplish what we need to, without taking on unreasonable risks."

Jacqueline nodded her head and said, "I can agree to that, and I'm sure the lines of business would be okay with it as well. It's the prospect of a broad system-imposed disaster they cannot abide; they've seen it before on a smaller scale and just can't afford it in this business climate."

Neil turned to Tom and asked, "Tom, do you think that would be enough? If we can show it works in beta, on a small scale, could that create enough confidence to give us the time and funding we need to get it deployed?"

"No matter how good a showing we might make, Neil, we'll have less funding going forward than we've had to date. Evan thinks we've been profligate in our spending, and he's going to put us on a fiscal diet regardless. That said, Evan and the board would like nothing more than to have a reason to believe we can succeed in this. It may not be enough, but it's all we have, and I say let's do it. When could we be ready?"

Neil turned to Trevor, the project management office leader, and raised his eyebrows interrogatively. Trevor looked at the bug list, thought a moment, and said he thought we could go live the Monday after Thanksgiving, assuming we could get team members to work that Friday and through the weekend to get code migrated to production and tested out in the production regions.

"Oh, they'll do that, I'm sure," Neil said. "They know their jobs are at stake, so I don't think we'll have problems."

I turned to Tom and asked, "Tom, for the purposes of the official notes, do we have a decision now? Live beta, Monday after Thanksgiving, small number of users and transactions, intense support to limit risks, create visibility of results so that Evan and the board can have the information they need to set next steps?"

Tom looked around the room for consensus and, seeing he had it, gave me a simple, "Yes, that's it."

He continued, "I'll pass this on to Evan directly. Frankie, Neil, I suspect you have a lot of work to do to get ready; we don't have much time. It all comes down to this now, doesn't it?"

Execution now fell into Neil's and Frankie's hands. As the meeting broke up, they stood in a corner of the room with Trevor planning next steps.

I left the PCA meeting and returned to my desk. It looked like this was going to be one of those years when year end really marked significant changes; we'd know if our project was going to succeed or not, and I was going to be in for a change in job, geography, and marital status. Mary and I had decided a few weeks ago that we were committed to each other; given her family, that meant, for both of us, marriage. I wasn't quite sure what I'd do in San Diego; I was leaning toward returning to consulting—maybe building on the hard-earned lessons from CU.

I sat down, phoned Mary, and conveyed to her the results of the PCA meeting. The plan was pretty much what she'd expected, and she made her own expectations clear to me. She had seen Qin at the coffee cart yesterday, and as they talked about the likelihood of CU going live, Qin had conveyed what she said was an ancient Chinese saying: "You can't long hide fire in a paper bag."

A few minutes later, she e-mailed me what she figured would be the next Cremins United slip chart, dated a few months from now (Figure 39).

Qin's wisdom was the title of her e-mail: "You can't hide fire in a paper bag." Once the light of day shone on the actual system performance, functional gaps, work-arounds, and the long runway in front of us to get to real business value, she didn't see how Evan or the board could do anything but kill the project. I so hoped she was wrong, but, for me, the Cremins United project was over and I was on to the next stage of my life.

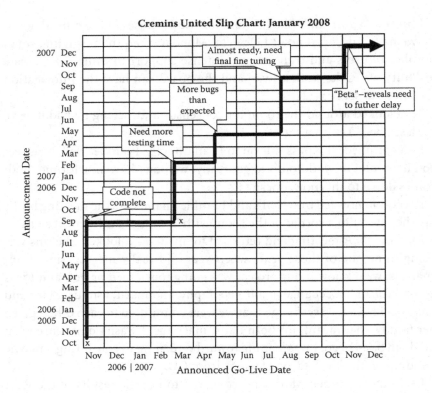

FIGURE 39

CU slip chart, January 2008.

Signposts	**Cremins United project**
	• November 2007 arrived, and although the lines of business wouldn't allow a broad system implementation, they agreed to a limited scale pilot.
	• As we saw at the inception of this tale, the pilot was a failure. While the systems ran to a minimal extent, the number of bugs, extensive work-arounds, and poor system responsiveness forced the lines of business to refuse to extend it until it was more solid and more functional.
	• The estimates to complete given by the PCA were not believable to the board, and under mounting financial pressure, the board terminated the project.
	• CEO Evan Nogelmeyer's strategy of fusing printing with information technology, thus creating a customer-centered sales and product delivery focus, was in tatters.
	• The jobs of Mary O'Connell and most of the rest of the members of the CU project teams were eliminated, and Cremins Corporation entered 2008 in a state of uneasy uncertainty. Beth Dumas assisted in the terminations and decided to write this book.
	• Wes quit his job and moved to San Diego to marry Mary, taking away from the Cremins United project a newfound appreciation for Lean and Agile software development.
Guides from Wes	• Don't put systems into production unless they actually provide a business benefit. This is simple and obvious, but sometimes leaders can overlook this in their intensity to show that their software project is succeeding.
Coming up next	Our two tales are complete, so on to "Lessons for Leaders," a summary of lessons to be learned from the two projects.

Section V

Final Lessons for Leaders

Epilogue: What We Learned from the TRIM and CU Projects

Finally, after 25 chapters and more than 2 years, in this chapter I (Michael Levine, the author) get my own voice back!

The two projects we've watched over more than 2 years are, of course, fictional, although hopefully both illustrate powerful truths. Cremins United was run according to deep beliefs that following prescribed processes, and implementing defined roles was the key to success. As it began to unravel, leadership doubled-down on its commitment and continually increased the level of control to improve fidelity to the prescription. That project failed miserably, and its failure threatened the company's primary business strategy, undermined the company's leadership, and hurt the careers of dozens of team members. The TRIM project, in sharp contrast, emphasized the creation of a "container" that spurred people to think collectively and creatively, make rigorously fact-based decisions, and explore and learn quickly. Instead of holding people accountable to follow prescribed processes and fulfill and respect specified roles, it held them accountable for observable results. TRIM created a thriving new business and helped a large sector of our economy manage through a deepening crisis.

Although the Cremins United and the TRIM projects are fiction—and, of course, as author I got to connect the positive results to the approach I believe works the best—the principles and techniques shown are not. In this chapter, I want to speak directly to business leaders involved in systems development and enhancement about those principles and techniques. I won't repeat the material covered in the story; instead, the principles embodied there will be abstracted, with the hope of providing a "true north" to help business leaders succeed at business technology.

By "business leader," I mean anyone from an operations manager sponsoring her first technology project to a development manager, project manager, systems architect, tester, or systems analyst. These are principles and ideas that can help you succeed. Absorb them and apply them to your own situation; as Mary and Neville repeatedly emphasized, there simply is no cookbook, no shortcut!

My magic number of ideas is four. I'll call them my Lean and Agile lessons for success:

1. teams of responsible experts;
2. entrepreneurial system designers/chief engineers;
3. relentless focus on business value and delivery; and
4. humility.

The number of lessons here is the same as those chosen by Allen C. Ward, the remarkable pioneer in formulating and teaching Lean product development, in his book *Lean Product and Process Development*.[1] I have chosen two of his principles, the roles of teams and leaders, as my first and second as well. My third lesson, "Focus on Business Value and Delivery," draws on Ward's central goal for product development and, in addition, synthesizes some other Agile ideas, such as focus on code. My final lesson, "Humility," is my sole contribution to Lean/Agile idea synthesis. It may well surprise people who know me well that humility is my unique contribution ... wonders never cease!

I would also refer readers wanting to learn more about Lean and Agile to go back and read Chapter 4, in which Mary explains Lean and Agile to Beth; and Chapter 17, when the PCA members visit the TRIM scrum and Neville tries fruitlessly to enlighten them. The many books and articles footnoted provide more extensive education.

I'll cover each of these areas in turn, elaborate some important points and answer some questions, and illustrate with examples from the Cremins Corporation.

LESSON 1: TEAMS OF RESPONSIBLE EXPERTS— TAKING INITIATIVE, LEARNING, TEACHING, NEGOTIATING, AND CREATING

One approach to success in business technology is to make projects "repeatable" and "predictable" by enforcing rigid process methodologies, putting

---

[1] Ward, A. C. 2007. *Lean Product and Process Development*. Cambridge, MA: Lean Enterprise Institute.

people into neat categories, and defining how tasks get handed from role to role. A goal may be to reduce the dependency on specific people, which can result in a wide variation of results. This principle contends that success comes not from trying to reduce the impact of individual people, but rather from rejoicing in and leveraging what talented, committed people can do working together toward a common goal. It also encompasses the requirement of having a single unified team, with everyone focused on the business goal, as opposed to "business" and "technical" teams trying to stay aligned.

With Cremins United, Mary's sales team became such a team, as did Neville's TRIM team. In fact, Neville worked hard to break his project into several smaller teams, each of them aligned with a specific area of the business opportunity or the technology space, and each of them with as complete a set of talents and roles as he could arrange. (See, for example, Chapter 15, when the TRIM Information Management team does its first sprint demo.) In contrast, most of the Cremins United project never formed into such teams, instead relying on process-defined handoffs. (See Chapter 16, when the budiness leader of the Production Management group drives to complete requirements with little concern for whatever comes next.)

Mary and Neville also sought out the best experience and talent. Mary went so far as to discard her own software product for that of a specialist vendor (Chapter 13) and to seek and find an expert in system integration to enlighten Wes and her about how much trouble they might be in with a critical design element (Chapter 18). On the other hand, the balance of the CU project had mediocre or inexperienced leaders who didn't realize the difference the right people can make—for example, the decision to force a single interface design on all teams (in Chapter 14).

Team structures, processes, leadership, co-location, and other factors can vary widely, depending on the people, mission, organization, and culture. Some critical ideas are listed here.

- *Teams should be complete and aligned with the business they support as much as possible:* project manager(s), systems analysts, operations experts, developers, and testers. Support intermittent needs from shared groups such as Database Administration, data analysts, Infrastructure, Network, Security, Legal, and Finance. Recall the costs of the separation of the testers from the developers with respect to Cremins data (Chapter 20) and compare that to the integration of test lead Janani Mugombe in the TRIM scrum (Chapter 15).

- *Be careful with language.* It is not unusual to hear about the "business" and the "technical" groups. Aren't technical people "business" as well? Try to eliminate the "two sides" in project teams, and use words like: operations, development, testing, marketing.
- *People can be organized in a variety of reporting relationships,* with matrix management to the team structure or to functional organizations, depending on your own situation. Toyota's Module Development teams are a great example. However your organization is structured, the team member alignment must be primarily to the business results, rather than to each individual's specific tasks or role.
- *Scale projects or development organizations by creating additional teams of this type and adding layer(s) of functional support.* The functional support could be a central testing support team that manages the test tools (bug tracking, shared test data beds, shared integration test environment) or a project office to support learning, status reporting, and financial management. It could be "communities of interest" such as a systems analyst support group responsible for sharing best practices and managing a training budget.
- *The teams should have significant independence and be encouraged to learn, teach, innovate, experiment, and create.* This requires sophisticated governance and leadership to balance this freedom and initiative with broader goals of consistency and commonality. Think of the difference between Neville's team and Mary's: Both were high performance and they shared some general principles on how to operate, but they were free to operate differently given their unique circumstances. Compare both teams to the Production team of Joe Karras et al.—that team had little freedom, other than to follow the rules (Chapter 20). If you are smart enough to specify all the rules and are sure they will work, go ahead; however, the rest of us would prefer a team of smart, expert people adjusting as needed.
- *Intrateam linkages need to be explicitly identified, structured, and managed.* In CU, the sales and production teams had no formal interconnections beyond common interfaces to the architecture, the data team, the CSF, and The Process. They didn't start to make progress on their interface until they put together a subteam focused directly on that interface, working together on it. Often teams are

aligned with individual systems; they also need to be aligned to the end-to-end business processes that cut across systems.

- *Business leaders need to be trained in how to manage technology development teams and/or be given support to help them do so.* This is a different kind of leadership from that in a traditional technology organization because it advocates pushing complete development teams as deeply into the associated business units as possible. The limiting factors are skill set to manage and ability to create governance and support for distributed teams. Business leaders must be responsible for the technology that supports their operation, and they need to be held accountable not only for the immediate business results but also for the long-term stability and suitability of their systems, including how their systems fit with and support the broader organization.

- *Leaders need to help their teams form, rearrange as needed, orient toward Lean/Agile approaches, balance the local and the more global demands, and stay on track* through inspection of results (not inspection of process, except to the minimal possible amount required for safety and balance). Stay out of the way as much as possible.

- *The "expert" in the principle cannot be overemphasized.* Leaders must hire the right level of expertise and create an environment of continued learning, codification of knowledge, and teaching. You cannot build systems without building expert people. In the CU project, Janice, the lead architect, appeared to lack the experience required for the position. As we saw in the discussion on the Sales architecture in Chapter 13, she was a bureaucratic leader rather than a substantive one, and in defense of her position, she sought to enforce control rather than earn cooperation, and to protect her turf rather than open it up to true rigor, options, and expertise.

- *"Expertise" includes skill in leadership.* The kind of leadership that Neville provided to TRIM is partly a function of his native personality and abilities, but at least as much is a learned behavior. We didn't see much about how Greg created the Real Estate Division, but suffice it to say that leaders like Neville, Mary, and Alex need to be recruited and developed. People can learn how to help others learn, demand rigorous thinking, and create environments that facilitate contribution and commitment. Here is where a leader with few "technical" skills can make a great contribution to a technically oriented group.

- *How can a nontechnical manager ensure the proper level of expertise—* or even a technical manager, for a discipline with which he or she is not familiar? Leverage outside help. Develop relationships with vendors, consultants, peers, and anyone who can help. Bring in experts for brief training periods, code reviews, design reviews, and plan reviews. Never assume someone knows what he or she is doing unless you know from experience, through a trusted referral, or through acceptance by a team you trust. Always err on the side of confirming expertise. Ignorance, arrogance, and even well-intentioned bumbling can kill your project. Consider the centralized data facility in the Cremins project—a good idea, poorly applied, played a material role in its failure. It didn't have to; once Mary and Wes reached out for expertise, it wasn't hard to find experienced and thoughtful voices. Another mechanism is to take more than one approach someway down the road before settling on a single solution.
- *Listen to your teams.* Really listen—listen to what their problems are, where they are having disagreements, what they are afraid of, what expertise they are lacking, what roles they are lacking, and what parts of your company or partners aren't supporting them as they should be. If the team's ability to deal with its issues deteriorates and it cannot identify the repairs needed, help from business leadership is required. You won't know if you aren't listening. Compare the PCA members, who seemingly willfully chose to ignore the views of their team (such as ignoring the schedule they'd proposed and cramming a much shorter one down their throats, in Chapter 9) to Neville, who worked hard to provide mechanisms and forums for productive listening (Chapter 10's sprint planning or Chapter 21's reflection session).
- *If you do not trust your team members or leaders, you cannot work around that* by requiring detailed plans and demanding detailed accounting of task achievement—at least not for long and not broadly. If you don't trust your people, then develop them, move them to positions into which they fit better, or move them out. Nothing helps a team more than getting rid of a bad fit, and nothing creates trust in leadership better than the team seeing the leader recognize the bad fit and then act on it. After his visit to the TRIM sprint in Chapter 17, Neil was right to reflect that Agile software development requires great people; the answer to dealing with mediocrity or less is not

to fall back on processes that accommodate the gap, but rather to accelerate the attraction and development of more talent and skill. Most people have excellence within if the culture is there to bring it out in them.

- *Avoid rigid allocation of project deliverables/artifacts to specific roles.* The CU project was over the top on this: The "business" did requirements, designers did designs, testers tested, and architects directed. Teams should be flexible, people should be able to do more than one thing, roles should overlap, and, by all means, everyone should test!
- *The value of face time cannot be overemphasized.* This becomes more and more difficult as our enterprises are spread across the country and around the world and travel expenses escalate. As Neville's monthly in-person demos and meetings showed, there just is no substitute—not yet. Keep this in mind as you structure your company and your projects. For example, build teams in one geography, realign team members if needed, and give assignments out on projects with geographical skills distribution in mind. Treat face time as the very precious resource it is and use it wisely.

LESSON 2: PROJECT LEADERS ACTING AS ENTREPRENEURS AND SYSTEM DESIGNERS, RATHER THAN AS BUREAUCRATIC MANAGERS

This principle flies in the face of the idea that a project manager who has project management skills can manage any kind of project—building a system, constructing a building, whatever. It also rejects the idea of project offices that get requests for projects and assigns project managers across a broad range of business and technical areas, assuming that someone new to an area could actually provide the leadership needed.

At Cremins Corporation, Neville and Mary are both entrepreneurial system designers. Trevor is not. Neville and Mary were cultivated over years by Greg and put into positions to grow their knowledge and skills. The success of the Real Estate Division's most critical projects was up to them. Success comes from this type of leader; where will your organization get them and how will it develop and sustain them?

- *Toyota calls these leaders "chief engineers."* Developing them is one of the company's critical success factors. The Real Estate Division under Greg's leadership had a sharp focus on building these people, whereas in Cremins Corporation, more broadly, the emergence of this type of leader was institutionally impossible.
- *How do you build a chief engineer?* You begin with someone with deep and strong skills in one of the central disciplines. At Toyota, this is almost always an engineer. For software development, it could be a developer, a systems analyst, a process engineer, a financial manager, an operations manager, a marketer, or a tester. Then the budding chief engineer needs to broaden his or her experience and expertise and grow by leading parts of projects and then his or her own small projects. These people need training, mentoring, and challenging. They need to understand the business. But above all else, if the software implementation is at the center of the project, the chief engineer needs to understand software development and implementation! Cremins United, run by a marketer and a financial manager, had little chance of success; only if Frankie had been a chief engineer-type herself, and had been permitted to operate as one, could it have succeeded.

  Some companies, like Cremins, are structured in ways that make building this type of person nearly impossible. "Technology" might be in a completely separate department, separated by project processes and rigid role separations. Project management may be defined in a sterile, process-control straitjacket. The required disciplines for a chief organizer may never come together in a single group of people.
- *How should chief engineers fit into your organization?* At Toyota, they typically report at a very senior level and have only a small direct staff of "assistant chief engineers" and project assistants. The technical expertise resides in the functional departments and is assigned to the various development projects. Chrysler has tried the matrix the other way, with direct reporting to the chief engineer role and functional engineering departments supporting the project engineers. I've seen the role done well with very few direct reporting relationships, as well as with complete teams in the reporting structure. Neville had a mixture; some reported to him and others to functional areas, and that configuration changed over time.

- *What do you do if you don't have any people with these skills?* Encourage the people you have with the skills and talents aligning with chief engineer to behave with more ownership and technical expertise. Help technicians gain business skills; help operations managers and marketing staff gain technical skills. Keep project managers who have only process guidance skills subordinate to team members with substantive skills and knowledge. You can get "chief engineer" work done by teams of people supporting each other, even if none of them has the whole package of skills.
- *Not every project needs a chief engineer.* If it's routine, repetitive work, a process manager can lead the work. Adding new geographies to TRIM might be this type of work. However, there were situations where what seemed like routine work changed into more creative work that needed more empirical process control, and the management didn't understand that a change had happened.
- *Manage by exception.* If you have a chief engineer, don't inspect the project plan in detail; don't look for missed tasks and ask for explanations. Make it the responsibility of the leader to communicate status to the people who need to know. Find out the status yourself by "going to see"—preferably, regularly scheduled integrating events. Go see a team meeting; go watch a demo; read the statement of work or the master test plan. Checkboxes on a list that these artifacts are complete on time can mean nothing at all. As we saw in Chapter 22, in February 2007 CU was "green" despite the massive difficulty of completing and testing the Sales–Production interface, which showed up nowhere on the plan or in status reporting. On the other hand, Greg and Gina felt confident they knew TRIM status because they trusted Neville to tell them where it was and because they regularly went and saw the results.

LESSON 3: FOCUS ON BUSINESS VALUE AND DELIVERY

Sounds so obvious, doesn't it? But think about the CU project. Although at the top level Cremins leadership defined business value, that got lost in the translation. The project was too focused on "implementing the strategy," "getting something running," "proving the viability of the project," "gaining confidence," and the "right" architecture. As the project began, there were no burning identified needs, and as the project extended out, no constituencies, other than the top leadership, clamored for its completion. There were no cost takeouts or identifiable revenue generators that were going to be accomplished upon production, just generalized beliefs about what the system would enable. On the other hand, TRIM managers knew what the benefits were and they were in a bona fide hurry to get there.

- *Know the benefit, and get there the most direct way, unless you have very good reason not to.* In the CU case, a benefit was to have been enabling sales of capacity in additional channels. If that had been understood and had driven the project, what explanation could there have been for doing anything other than connecting the sales and production systems together as quickly and effectively as possible so that sales could begin?
- *Code can be refactored.* It's not like we're building a factory; it's called *soft*ware for a reason. If we do something quickly to get business benefits and fear that it won't be flexible enough over time or support possible future needs, we can always change it. If we have to use less than "perfect" technology and the benefit is compelling, we do it, learn from the implementation, and rebuild it when we need to.
- *Subordinate architecture to development.* To reiterate, we are not constructing buildings here; we're making software. We want our development to be driven by results-oriented developers; we do not want our results to be overly constrained by noncoding architects. The real estate analog is design-build firms; they get the job done quickly and cheaply, and they keep the architect subordinate to the development leadership. We do need the tension between the global and the local, the abstract and the concrete, but we need to keep the weight on the side of delivery; that's where the benefits are. Architecture should be a cooperative enterprise of the senior developers and chief engineers, rather than a top-down academic exercise.

One example in the Cremins story is the (see also Agile Manifesto Principle" in Chapter 17) common data interface. To an architect, the idea of a single, uniform set of data interchange may be heavenly; to an engineer, who has to write and test the translations, the idea is somewhere in the other direction! (see Chapter 22 for the conflict explanation.)

- *Architecture and shared services are supposed to help, not hurt.* Be cautious about making your project teams use shared services; if they don't want to, there is probably something wrong. Shared hosting services, shared database support, shared "SOA infrastructures"—if they are valuable, project teams will use them. Resistance is a signal, so pay attention to it.
- *It's all about the code, so honor the coders.* Working code is the only meaningful measurement of project progress, and teams need to focus on that above all else. Because everything depends on the developers, get great ones, and get them business context, requirements that work for them, and the right tools. Developers are typically very smart people; don't turn them into robots turning specifications into programs.
- *Honor and develop testers.* The progression of code from requirements to production can be greatly smoothed by having outstanding test management. Agile development requires that testing be integrated to project teams in much deeper ways than other approaches require. Consider the failed approach of the Cremins United project—with fragmented testing handing code off blindly from phase to phase, whose gaps are not fully revealed until late in the integration test phase (Chapter 22)—with TRIM's unified, end-to-end testing managed from the inception of the project through code delivery that began to find bugs at the end of the first month (Chapter 15). Bringing testers into a community with requirements analysts and developers has great payback.
- *See what you don't have to do.* What tasks, steps, or modules in your project can you avoid doing altogether? In traditional "waterfall" approaches, the requirements documents sought to be completely comprehensive because if it wasn't in the requirements, you weren't going to get it. In an Agile, iterative approach, we can build the minimum we need to get business value and iteratively add the bells and whistles.
- *Continually ask this question: "What is the minimum set of functions we can put into production and get business value?"* Then do that. Then do it again.

LESSON 4: BE HUMBLE

In this context, I mean respecting the complexity of our tasks; respecting the knowledge, skills, and opinions of others; and avoiding arrogance about our own capabilities to proceed flawlessly. There is no shortage of literature on how prone to failure modern technology implementation projects are; as an industry, while we have great successes of which to be proud, we have no cause to believe we can reliably and repetitively solve complex, new business problems with software. If we approach our work with this humility, we can take steps to improve our chances of success.

The CU leadership illustrated lack of humility in many ways. They chose a scope much larger than needed for an initial release (Chapter 5); they assumed that their team, which had never done anything like this before, was capable of delivering it and they thought they knew better than their own team when setting dates (Chapter 9); they believed they could implement an exceedingly complex and abstract architecture on the critical path to business benefits (Chapter 14); and they believed they could specify process steps that would fit this project optimally, without adjustment (Chapter 5).

By way of contrast, TRIM was managed to test, see results, and adjust continually.

- *Expect change, surprises, conflict.* For a project of any size or complexity, it is impossible to create a budget, schedule, requirements, or design that will be right from the inception. We are after business benefits rather than plan compliance, so we must accelerate learning as much as we can. Welcome change—it's what aligns our projects to business benefits.
- *If we are to welcome change, how can we ever get a project done?* Do it in small pieces, harvest value, learn, and do more. If you write a 200-page requirements document that covers a 9-month development cycle, you can be sure that there are errors in it, that learning is to come, and that the business will likely change over that period. That requirements document is inventory, just as piles of work in process in a factory are inventory. If you have a smaller inventory of ideas to change, change can be positive, instead of a threat. Think of unimplemented tested code, untested code, designs not yet coded, and requirements not yet designed as inventory waste, like computer

parts when the industry moves so fast the probability of obsolescence is high.

Here is where the Lean manufacturing concepts of flow apply. A "software factory" must avoid batching, have cadence, and use visual management, just like a manufacturing plant. The trick is to marry these concepts with the concepts of Lean product development and not completely apply the manufacturing paradigm to our software development efforts. Some of the Agile techniques that TRIM employed—such as Agile planning with user stories, backlog management, sprints, and scrum—are implementations of cadence and flow in the knowledge-intensive software business.

- *Plan and manage intensively, but realistically.* One concern heard from organizations new to Agile is that the teams won't commit beyond one sprint, so the business can't plan on how much an effort will cost or when it will be done. This is a faulty implementation. As seen in Neville's project planning for TRIM (Chapter 10), planning must be done in great detail—precisely to the level at which the cost of planning begins to outweigh its benefits. Efforts must be sized for budgeting and staffing, estimated for duration, split into iterations, broken into small pieces for sprints, and managed daily for burndown. A Lean/Agile project should be much better managed and controlled than a traditional "estimate everything up front" project, and new information to fine-tune the project should be flowing in constantly to enable adjustment and refinement.

  There should be no trade-off in adopting these techniques. If it's truly possible to do all requirements accurately up front—with detailed and achievable estimates stable enough to provide the business value sought—you may have a repeatable process suitable to defined process control. If you don't have that type of effort and need empirical process control, you don't realistically have that option. You can fool yourself, as Neil repeatedly did, but consider the costs of mixing up the two models.

- *Be sure there are enough benefits to proceed with a risky project.* Project time and cost estimates are rarely too low. It modest time and cost overruns threaten the business case, your project maybe too risky and may need an adjustment.

- *Get everyone's mind into the game.* A software project is the organized application of intelligence to solve business problems. The extent to which you are able to mobilize and utilize the knowledge and skills of your team can determine your success. Team members make decisions every day; the better those decisions are, the more effective the team is. To make good decisions, team members need information and context.

Neville and Alex used many techniques in TRIM to provide this to team members. The simulation shown in Chapter 15 is one of the best techniques; it provides visual, personal learning in a powerful and fun way. The team room, A3s, daily scrums, knowledge-sharing Web sites, and monthly demonstrations are other mechanisms TRIM relied upon. CU, on the other hand, did not encourage broad learning; team members were kept in their boxes, taking specified input, doing their tasks, and laying results into an outbox for the next step. That is a faulty application of the manufacturing paradigm.

- *Success is completely dependent on quality of people, culture, and learning.* You cannot build a complex business system without building its development team simultaneously. Focus on both. Neil and Trevor in Cremins United seemed to think that they could just order up more team members from GRI whenever they needed them, as we saw in Chapter 20, and that they could drop in and be productive and then leave without hurting the effort. Consultants and contractors can certainly help a project—they were also used extensively in TRIM and in Mary's sales dimension of CU, both of which succeeded—but they need to be used as part of an overall strategy of team and knowledge creation.

- *Don't commit to doing things your team isn't ready to do.* Do what you are capable of now, develop your team while doing it, and do bigger things later.

- *Consider multiple options.* System development is about learning, and learning requires consideration of options and rigor in path selection. Toyota's engineers are known for their trade-off curves— for example, size of radiator versus heat dispersion capability. They focus on understanding and formalizing trade-offs. We should do this in our development processes as well. Consider the Sales–Production system linkage in CU. One design was specified, and it was the same for all interfaces. No trade-off matrix as to the suitability of this design was done, and no knowledge was built, until Mary and Wes did that later in the project. Compare to TRIM, in which the team sought more than one way to deliver information to the public (Chapter 21).

The Process as practiced in the CU project worked to defeat this type of learning. In it, requirements (not a range of requirements, but rather a single specification) were handed off to a designer, and a single design was done and handed "forward" to a coder. This defeats learning and commits the project to directions too early. Even if everyone gets it right, little learning is happening.

- *Partner intensively and wisely.* This recognizes that other organizations, whether in your company or outside it, know more about some things than you do. Toyota's expertise in partnering and supplier development is well known and documented. Mary recognized this in her part of the Cremins United project, partnering with CSMPro to provide a better solution than her own software could. She also respected CSMPro's experience by not trying to force her methods on the consultants, while sharing her own expertise and helping CSMPro improve its capabilities (Chapter 12).

- *Create a culture of openness in communication, problem solving, and continuous improvement.* As we saw in Chapter 3, when Mary joined Cremins United, she was like a fish out of water. This wasn't just because she was used to a different development methodology or role; it was also because she was leaving a culture that comprised many of the principles listed earlier. It was simply impossible for her to change the CU culture in any material way from where she sat. She was limited to creating, as best she could, that culture in her own subteam and avoiding friction to the extent possible. Culture is created by the sum of goals (creating Lean operational value streams) and the people, processes, and tools used to pursue them.

The use of visual management can reinforce the openness required to identify problems early and solve them. Compare the "fact-based" lists of bugs in the Cremins United project presented by staff members terrified of drawing conclusions (Chapter 20) to the one-page, visual "psychedelic chart" Neville continually shared with his manager and peers, as we saw in Chapter 19. Compare the "handoff" session of requirements to the designers in CU (Chapter 16) with the highly visual simulation in TRIM (Chapter 15).

There is no secret sauce or "magic bullet." Becoming effective at software development is achieved by many individual actions, creating organizational capability and great people who work together well. Pick the domain in which you have influence and the tools or processes that make the most sense in that domain; then, accelerate your journey to becoming lean and agile!

Index

The Author

Michael K. Levine has led a 26-year career primarily focused on how to profit through the application of information technology. He was educated in international relations and economics at Carleton College and Princeton University and began his career in international trade negotiation in Washington, D.C. He moved on to commercial lending and financial product management at First Bank System in Minneapolis. In each of his early jobs, he saw the promise of applying information technology to solve business problems; eventually, he moved his career more formally in that direction by joining Norwest Corporation as strategic technology planner and large-scale software project manager. Michael continued his immersion in technology leadership when he became chief technology officer of Moore Data/Vista Information Solutions, a leading provider of information technology solutions to the real estate field. For the last 6 years, Michael has been at Wells Fargo Home Mortgage, leading Operations and Technology Groups.

One of the constant elements in Michael's work has been the innovative, business-driven application of information technology. The accomplishments of his teams range from the first system to calculate duties on unfair trade, to cross-business line customer information systems in two large banks, to an early Internet-based real estate search engine, to an image-based, straight-through/exception-based loan processing system. His continuing search for better ways to build complex business software drew him to the operations and product development approaches coming out of Toyota ("Lean") and the Agile software development movement. Michael and his teams have used many of the Lean and Agile approaches over the last several years. This practical application experience, in addition to his extensive, successful career at the junction of business operations and software technology, gives Michael a unique, practical perspective on how business leaders can improve their results through better technology leadership.

Printed in the United States
by Baker & Taylor Publisher Services